*Southern Literary Studies*
Louis D. Rubin, Jr., Editor

# Mark Twain and Science

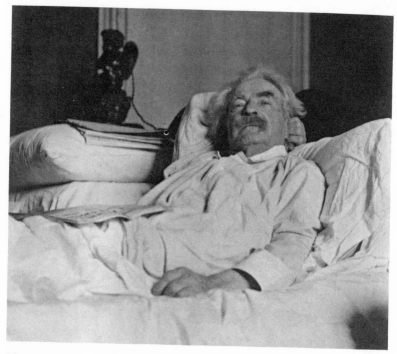

The intellectual adventurer at 70

*I ought to state that he was in bed when we arrived. He loved this loose luxury and ease, and found it conducive to thought.*

—Albert Bigelow Paine, *Mark Twain: A Biography*

SHERWOOD CUMMINGS

# Mark Twain and Science

## Adventures of a Mind

Louisiana State University Press
Baton Rouge and London

Copyright © 1988 by Louisiana State University Press
Manufactured in the United States of America

97  96  95  94  93  92  91  90  89  88     5  4  3  2  1

Designer: Laura Roubique Gleason
Typeface: Palatino
Typesetter: The Composing Room of Michigan, Inc.
Printer: Thomson-Shore, Inc.
Binder: John H. Dekker & Sons, Inc.

Library of Congress Cataloging-in-Publication Data
Cummings, Sherwood, 1916–

 Mark Twain and science : adventures of a mind / Sherwood Cummings.
  p. cm. — (Southern literary studies)
 Includes index.
 ISBN 0-8071-1441-3 (alk paper)
 1. Twain, Mark, 1835–1910—Knowledge—Science.   2. Literature and
science—United States—History—19th century.   3. Science in
literature.   I. Title.   II. Series.
PS1342.S3C86 1988
818'.409—dc19
                                                         88-11776
                                                         CIP

Frontispiece courtesy Mark Twain Papers, The Bancroft Library

The paper in this book meets the guidelines for permanence and durability of the
Committee on Production Guidelines for Book Longevity of the Council on Library
Resources.∞

*To the memory of*
*Sheryl Ann*
*Our Susy*

# Contents

# Preface

THE READER WHO ENTERS here will search in vain for discussions of balloon travel and racing with comets, of microbic civilizations and chartless cruising on a water drop. Mark Twain's science fiction is a worthy subject and has been worthily studied, but it is not the subject of this book. Nor is Mark Twain's technical knowledge the subject. It is true that as a riverman he had practical experience in the "science of piloting" and as a silver prospector in geology, that he was an inventor and industrialist of sorts, and that he could glory in technological progress; nevertheless, he spent very little time in his writing, even in *A Connecticut Yankee*, on the technical aspects of science. Persistently philosophical, he was after bigger game. He looked to science for such meanings as it could give in answering social, moral, and cosmological questions.

That quest is betokened in his reading in science, a lifelong engagement. Science titles in his library number well over a hundred. Their principal subjects—astronomy, geology, anthropology, and evolution—are such as someone seeking a world view would take up. His major intellectual problem, both as a private person and as an author, was that before acquiescing in the world view of modern science he had established indissoluble loyalties, first to a theistic world view and later to a deistic one.

The result was personally to involve him in the conflict between the cosmogony of Genesis and science's disclosures about the antiquity of the universe and the evolution of life. As a writer he was caught in subtler, but no less painful, conflicts. In his formative years as a novelist he went to school, along with William Dean Howells, to Hippolyte Taine, the French philosopher who applied science to the arts and humanities and who gave American realism its theoretical foundation. From Taine he learned something of the realist's method, and from Taine and others he learned the clinical approach to personality and society—an approach that sporadically conflicted with the mythical or heroic views of life that he had previously absorbed.

His mind was not, as Howells' was, to be settled by a science-based theory of literature. Howells' often-repeated explanations of realism made the novelist's relation to reality seem simple and noble: It was the novelist's privilege and duty to reflect the creation honestly and with detailed accuracy, for behind that reflection lay truth. To Mark Twain, however, because of his revulsion with historic tyrannies, including American slavery and its aftermath, the creation sometimes seemed absurd, even vile; and as a creator himself, he was now and then moved to tamper with it or to reject it altogether in favor of a fantasy of his own. At the opposite pole, and as a way of suppressing his revulsion, there was his growing conviction that the laws of nature, especially as they applied to behavior, were perfect and infrangible and that they directed human thought and activity so minutely as to make moral judgments beside the point.

Between these extremes Mark Twain responded to the implications of science in certain other rather wonderful ways, which are explored herein. Perhaps a value of this exploration is to suggest a basis in the history of ideas for his alternating "patterns of consciousness" (Forrest G. Robinson's phrase). As well as being a humorist and storyteller, Mark Twain was exquisitely sensitive to the intellectual currents of his time. Unfortunately for his peace of mind, he lived in an era that featured the collision of antithetical world views.

I have taken so much time in writing this book that time has run out for two people I would like to thank. Without Henry Nash Smith's help, this book would not have been written. It was he who, in 1960, arranged for my year in the Mark Twain Papers, and it was his *Mark Twain: The Development of a Writer* that opened my eyes to much I had not seen before. His generous reading of my manuscript several months before his death led to decisive improvements. Henry knew something of my gratitude, but I am afraid I never properly thanked Fred Anderson, Series Editor of the Mark Twain Papers, for his efficiencies and kindnesses. They were offered and accepted as matters of course; it is only in retrospect that they appear, in their true light, as rare virtues.

In sharing his special knowledge with me, Robert Hirst, General Editor of the Papers and of the Works of Mark Twain, has furnished me with important information and has kept me from making certain missteps. His generous interest in my project has given me sustenance.

Colleagues at California State University, Fullerton, who read all or parts of the work in progress, giving me needed advice and much needed encouragement, are Jane Hippolito, Keith Neilson, Donald Sears, George Spangler, Albert Vogeler, and Martha Vogeler. I am especially grateful to the Vogelers for their sustaining zest in scholarship.

I thank two colleagues in Cal State Fullerton's History Department for letting me pick their brains—Leland Bellot, with his special knowledge of the French and English courts, and Ronald Rietveld, with his of the Civil War and Reconstruction. Two colleagues elsewhere also have my gratitude—Alan Gribben for his encouragement and Louis Budd not only for his encouragement but also for sharing his awesome bibliographical knowledge with me.

I am beholden to Elizabeth Cummins (then Cogell) for information uncovered in her research for the master's thesis she wrote under my direction—"The Influence of Mark Twain's Reading in Science on the Ideas of *What Is Man?*" (University of South Dakota, 1962). As for the more than three hundred graduate students in my Mark Twain seminars at Cal State Fullerton, to name a few would be to slight the many. I salute them all. Each learned with me for a semester; I learned from them for twenty years.

# PART I

# Samuel Clemens and Science

# CHAPTER 1

# Around 1870

*[S]cience has given us a new reading of nature, has opened the higher
questions of life and human relations, has furnished a new method to
the mind, and is fast becoming a new power in literature.*
— *Galaxy*, XI (January, 1871)

AROUND 1870, AMERICANS WERE uneasily aware that a
new era had come into being while they had been distracted by the
Civil War and its aftermath. As a consequence, they were being
hustled into a philosophical conflict that Europeans had been en-
gaged in for some time. The new era was that of modern science.
The conflict was between the old faith in the existence of an unseen
world and the new conviction that only the apparent world was
real. An interesting manifestation of the new era was the growing
popularity of Mark Twain, whose *Innocents Abroad* set a tone of
mockery for revered old values. But since Mark Twain was a complex person as well as a manifestation, it is not surprising to find him
sharing in the conflict.

Mark Twain and science, then, were phenomena that were catch-
ing the attention of Americans simultaneously and not unrelatedly.
Their rise together is neatly exhibited in the pages of *Galaxy*, a young
and growing magazine in 1870. Its enterprising editors, in casting
about for ways to attract more subscribers, introduced two departments within months of each other. The first was Mark Twain's
"Memoranda," beginning in May, 1870. The second, making its
debut in January, 1871, was "Scientific Miscellany."

For Mark Twain the *Galaxy* contract was another step in his transformation from wild-western humorist to eastern citizen. He had
come a long way in the three years since, as an uncelebrated correspondent for the *Alta California*, he had stepped off the steamship
*San Francisco* in New York City. He had seen his first two books
published. The second one, *Innocents Abroad* (1869), proved that the
author of the regional and unremunerative *Jumping Frog* (1867) could
write a book that not only sold very well indeed but received the
attention of important reviewers. In his personal life he had tri-
umphed like the disguised prince in a fairy tale. He had won not

3

only the gentle Olivia Langdon for his bride but Jervis Langdon, the upstate New York millionaire (or close to it), for his father-in-law. It was Jervis' money that bought Sam Clemens an interest in and an editorial position on the Buffalo *Express* and a sumptuous house at 472 Delaware Avenue.

Even so, Clemens thought of himself as at best a successful humorist and newspaperman (*Innocents Abroad*, after all, was a polished version of weekly newspaper travel "letters"), and he aspired to a higher estate. *Galaxy* would not, he wrote exultantly to "Mother" Fairbanks, require him to write "a *Humorous* department, but simply *a* department." He was so pleased with moving up to magazine status that the pay (a munificent $25 per page) was immaterial: "Do you know, Madam, that I would rather write for a magazine for $2 a page than for a newspaper at $10? I *would*. One takes more pains, the 'truck' looks nicer in print, & one has a pleasanter audience."[1]

*Galaxy's* decision to produce "Scientific Miscellany," which would run nearly two hundred items a year on science, was its accommodation to the "scientific revival." Other magazines had preceded *Galaxy* in featuring science. *Atlantic Monthly* added the obligatory word to its subtitle with the October, 1865, issue, to become "A Magazine of Literature, Science, Art, and Politics." *Appleton's Journal* was started in 1867 for the purpose of "emphasizing scientific news"; and *Harper's* began its monthly "Editor's Scientific Record" in 1869, the same year that, in England, *Nature* issued its first number.[2] Meanwhile, *North American Review* had been devoting scores of pages per volume to the discussion of recently published science books. *Popular Science* would begin publication in 1872.

Although *Galaxy* was not the first journal to cater to the public's hunger for scientific information, its acknowledgment of science was as handsomely expressed as any other magazine's:

In introducing the present department into THE GALAXY at this time, its conductors are but simply yielding to that acknowledged tendency in the world of thought which is giving increasing interest and importance to scientific subjects. To rehearse the triumphs of science is superfluous; they are witnessed on every side, and civilization is full of them. To have resolved

1. Dixon Wecter (ed.), *Mark Twain to Mrs. Fairbanks* (San Marino, Calif., 1949), 127–28, 9.

2. Richard Hofstadter, *Social Darwinism in American Thought* (Philadelphia, 1945), 9, 22.

matter into its elements, to have anatomized the crust of the planet, to have arrived at the exact laws of power, to have learned the constitution of the stars, to extract pictures from sunbeams, and to be able to do business instantaneously by lightning with almost the whole world, are certainly very marvelous things; but more than all these, science has given us a new reading of nature, has opened the higher questions of life and human relations, has furnished a new method to the mind, and is fast becoming a new power in literature.[3]

Samuel Clemens surely read this tribute to science. For him it must have been still another lesson in what mattered in the society he had recently joined and in which he aimed to succeed. In eastern journals he saw the word *science* everywhere written, like the name of a god, and science itself credited with enormous powers. Science was producing machines and devices that made life easier and more exciting. It daily provided news about the immensity of the universe, the antiquity of the earth, and the ancestry of man. It offered a way of thinking that promised to carry the light of reason into the last dark corners of mystery. And in a special aside to writers—those practitioners of the mythical art of storytelling—it said: Be realistic.

Clemens' response to science was profound, pervasive, and complex; in the words of his biographer, Albert Bigelow Paine, it "amounted to a passion."[4] But before we examine that response, we need to find out what kind of science instruction Clemens and laymen like him were getting from the leading magazines around 1870.[5]

The reader of these magazines would get a clear idea of what science was, but conflicting—and often emotionally charged—instruction in how to feel about it. Science, he would gather, is a method of observing and thinking about aspects of nature for the purpose of understanding what nature is and the way it works. The method could be one of "induction from the facts of particular observations" or it could be the "originating of grand generalizations with endless patience and caution in verifying them."[6] At any rate, scien-

---

3. "Scientific Miscellany," *Galaxy*, XI (January, 1871), 135.

4. Albert Bigelow Paine, *Mark Twain: A Biography* (3 vols.; New York, 1912), I, 512.

5. The magazines discussed here are chosen not only because they were at the forefront of science journalism but because Clemens was familiar with them. See Alan Gribben, *Mark Twain's Library: A Reconstruction* (2 vols.; Boston, 1980).

6. "Peabody's Positive Philosophy," *North American Review*, CVI (1868), 286; "Science," *Atlantic Monthly*, XXX (1872), 508.

tific understanding was based on observable fact, and it aimed at cosmology. Science "collects facts eagerly, steadily. . . . Then, from these facts patiently observed, brought together, coordinated, classified, science deduces a *law*, a positive law, which is the expression of reality, of truth itself."[7]

Although writers about science expressed many doubts and fears, they did not question either the efficacy of the scientific method or the assumption that nature was worth understanding. The Newtonian tradition was still strong: One lived in an orderly universe whose workings were intelligible. As John Fiske, one of America's champions for science, put it, he had "faith in the constancy of nature, and in the adequacy of ordinary human experience as interpreted by science."[8]

But the Newtonian ideology had become complicated during the last century. In 1776, Jefferson could begin his Declaration of Independence by proclaiming that the separation of the colonies from England was authorized by "the laws of nature and of nature's God." This heady abstraction contains the grand idea not only that human events could and should be part of the cosmic scheme but that the laws of nature and the laws of God are identical. Between the deist's God and nature there was an absolutely harmonious relationship. In succeeding decades, however, nature became popularly romanticized and religion sentimentalized. At the same time, scientists were making radical explorations into an unsentimental universe. The two apprehensions, of "revealed" religion and of reason and science, were becoming aligned against each other. By 1870, the God of evangelical Christianity and the nature that science was revealing were poles apart, yet many an American cherished both his religion and his rationalism. Two ways of knowing, two avenues to Truth, were in conflict.

The conflict was fully and widely appreciated. It was the anguish of the times and was stated and restated in the magazines. "We see no common ground on which Science as Science, and Christianity as Christianity can come together," lamented A. A. Lipscomb in *Harper's*. "And by this we mean, that truth as an object of faith and truth as an object of reason are essentially distinct things in their relations to the mind."[9]

7. Charles Boysett, "Science and the Moral Order," *Galaxy*, XVII (January, 1874), 130.

8. John Fiske, "The Descent of Fire," *Atlantic Monthly*, XXVII (1871), 530.

9. A. A. Lipscomb, "Warfare of Modern Religious Thought," *Harper's*, XXXVI (1868), 371, 372.

Lipscomb was a Christian who regretted that the rage for "evidences" was causing men to "reject the character and offices of Christ." In his reaction he represented a considerable group, but the conflict was treated in a variety of ways. An opposing way was to claim that science had superseded religion, that mankind had come to the last of Auguste Comte's "famous three stages of development—the theological, the metaphysical, and the positive or scientific."[10] If one believed that science was the last and best of all religions, as did Charles Boysett, he spoke of it in worshipful tones:

They [the laws of science] form a kind of strong and manly communion, for they have nothing to do with phantoms and chimeras. In short, here is the new dogma which, dismissing phantasms, reserves all its homage for those indestructible ideas which determine the everlasting relations of things, and which are themselves the everlasting and absolute truth.

Yes, science alone can set upon a firm basis *moral order*—that *moral order* so childishly and so dangerously sought for in old methods of expression, in defunct doctrines, in superannuated and fossil dogmas, which some people undertake to exhume to-day with infinite labor.[11]

Between the defenders of Christianity and the evangels of science, there were those (very few) who spoke with contempt for scientists: "our modern prowlers into the earth's crust in search of lower and obscurer specimens." There were also those who, without relishing scientists' views, wrote respectfully about their methods: "Whatever may be thought of [Darwin's] generalizations, no one can deny the author the merit of painstaking and conscientious industry in the accumulation of facts." Then there were those who chastised scientists for being unscientific: "he goes astray to a degree hardly to be credited in a man of undoubted capacity and scientific training." There were also those who, like Henry James, recognized the conflict but preferred to remain above it: "We have not the purpose of discussing this doctrine; it opens up . . . the quarrel between the minds which cling to the supernatural and the minds which dismiss it." And there were those who, without quarreling and gently, as if to save the traumatized Christian from unnecessarily harsh blows, felt obliged to insist that hard ideas, such as Herbert Spencer's rejection of special creation, were correct: "We believe that sooner or later all disciplined minds will confirm this estimate of the 'special-creation hypothesis,' severe as it may

10. "Maudsley's Physiology and Pathology," *North American Review*, CVI (1868), 279.
11. Boysett, "Science and the Moral Order," 130.

seem."[12] Finally, there were those brave souls who tried to reconcile faith with science. Their efforts were strenuous and their confusion wonderful:

Science . . . is to-day reacting powerfully upon metaphysics and tomorrow will quite as powerfully react upon theology; but its influence is beneficial rather than destructive, and will only establish more solidly whatever real truth has been seized by its elder sisters. Development, not violent metamorphosis, is the history of man. The greatest weakness of positivism in its present condition, the mark of its immaturity, is its inaptitude for profound metaphysics, and its childish contempt for theology. We admit with perfect readiness that the metaphysics and theology now existent deserve all, if not quite all, the contempt they receive from positivism; but none the less sure is it that, as positivism becomes strong and self-contained, it will see more and more to respect, as well as worthy of study, in the history of philosophy and religion.[13]

Thus wrote one anonymous conciliator. Another's effort follows:

We accordingly mean no reproach, but a sincere homage to science, when we express our conviction that any old dame, with spectacles on nose, who devoutly patterns [her life upon] her Bible, even at the risk of swallowing its marvels as literally true, has a much better, though latent, intellectual relation to the future of thought, than even our sturdiest eaglets of science, who are yet content to find in their knowledge of what they call "the laws of nature" a full satisfaction to their spiritual aspirations, or thirst for truth.[14]

This oscillating rhetoric conveys more information about the writers' troubled minds than intrinsic meaning. The contest between science and religion is conceived as being between personified forces, neither one the putative champion, for the virtues of each are contradicted. Science in the first piece is young and powerful but careless and childish; theology is an offended and grand elder sister but temporarily deserving of contempt. In the second, piety is a saintly old dame but in danger of swallowing Bible stories whole; scientists are sturdy young eagles but without spiritual fulfillment.

12. "Mr. Hardhack on the Derivation of Man from the Monkey," *Atlantic Monthly,* XIX (1867), 301; "Darwin's Variations of Animals and Plants Under Domestication," *Atlantic Monthly,* XXII (1868), 122; "Man's Origin and Destiny," *North American Review,* CVII (1868), 369; Henry James, "Taine's English Literature," *Atlantic Monthly,* XXIX (1872), 470; F. E. Abbot, "The Principles of Biology by Herbert Spencer," *North American Review,* CVII (1868), 378–79.

13. "Maudsley's Physiology and Pathology," 279–80.

14. "Wallace's Contributions to the Theory of Natural Selection," *Atlantic Monthly,* XVI (1870), 758.

It was a dismaying conflict. There might be a winner, but small sense of victory.

Not all of science journalism was concerned with the conflict between science and religion. A flood of factual articles and items offered the reader a thorough lay knowledge of every current branch of science. Most commonly reported on were geology (for example, "Varying Density of the Earth's Crust"), astronomy ("The Approaching Solar Eclipse"), biology ("Evolution by Natural Selection"), medicine ("Detection of Brain Diseases"), archaeology ("New Discovery of Neolithic Remains"), paleontology ("Plesiosaurus in Australia"), anthropology ("Aborigines of California"), and physics ("The Spectroscope and Its Revelation"). Mixed among such items and under the rubric of science were articles that emphasized the practical, technical, or technological—for example, "Removal of Grease from Marble," "Rendering Articles Water-Proof," "Moving the Sewing Machine by Electricity," "Correction of Echo in Public Halls," and "Improved Mode of Nickel Plating." Science writers and readers were not necessarily naïve about the difference between pure science and its practical applications. Phrases such as *theoretical and applied science* and *scientific truth* as opposed to *practical utility* occasionally appeared.[15] Science was simply a fecund parent with large progeny. It embraced without embarrassment both theory and machinery.

The journalistic voice of science as technology was *Scientific American,* first published in its new series in 1859. An organ of the Munn and Company patent agency of New York, its emphasis was practical. Editorially, it aimed to be "a complete repository of useful information . . . from the Workshop, the Manufactory, the Laboratory, the Farm."[16] Actually, its purpose was to celebrate the machine. Each week its front page bore the picture and description of a new machine—reaper, cider press, cannon, typesetter, railroad car seat, sewing machine, steam plow, lathe, power loom (the forms are legion)—and inside there was a list of all the patent claims registered with the United States Patent Office during a previous week. The machines are pictured in loving detail. The eye seeks out the connections among cams and levers, bearings and braces; in imag-

15. "Summary of Scientific Progress," *Harper's,* XLIV (1872), 302; Jacob Abbott, "The Spectroscope," *Harper's,* XLI (1870), 720.
16. *Scientific American,* n.s., I (1859), 25.

ination, hands and feet work the handles and treadles. Fifty-two such machines a year are featured—from 1860 to 1880, more than a thousand.

Mark Twain's time, more significantly than ours, was the machine age. Although machines surround us in these last years of the twentieth century, they are hidden behind sleek surfaces of metal and plastic. Only their nerve endings, so to speak, are presented to us. Their impact on our imaginations is likely less, certainly of a different order, than it was a century ago, when their moving parts were visible. Then, the elegance, precision, and harmony of a machine's operation could be admired, and even appreciated as a symbol of the workings of the universe.

Although *Scientific American*'s editors avoided overt metaphysical statements, their writing radiates the assurance of men who have found their calling. In a period when the idea of the universe as a divine mechanism strongly persisted, what could be more right than to be a mechanician? By turning to machines, men had at last got in tune with the universe and were accordingly blessed. They had touched the right spring, and the multitude of machines implicit in the nature of things was being realized. Inventing and making machines and writing about them were proper forms of worship. Such grand ideas are not expressed in the pages of *Scientific American*, whose writers, like Mark Twain's Connecticut Yankee, were "practical . . . and nearly barren of sentiment"; but the sense of ultimate importance is there. That readers caught that sense is suggested in a letter from "J. G. S.," who declared, "[S]hould poverty ever compel me to sell my library, my Bible and my *Scientific American* should remain to grace the otherwise empty shelves."[17]

Thus science around 1870. Its authority was immense. It was based on the compelling idea that the creation was reasonable, whole, and orderly. What is more, it worked. The marvelous technological progress of the time proved it. Nevertheless, it appeared to deny the equally (to many) authoritative and urgent doctrine of Christianity, particularly in details of cosmogony and in the concept of a Father who personally cares.

And how was it between Samuel Clemens and science around 1870? His aim was to succeed in eastern society. If a measure for such

17. *Ibid.*, 16.

success is responsiveness to the ideas of the time, he was destined for fame. In his own person he joined those who thrilled to the revelations, accomplishments, and promises of science; and he as fervently joined those others who feared and distrusted science as the enemy of traditional values.

Illustrating his enchantment with science is his letter to Olivia Langdon of January 8, 1870, a few weeks before their marriage. The epistle, like several of his other love letters, concerned something he had read, for one of the roles he had undertaken during the courtship was that of Livy's professor of literature. He would make instructive comments about a work and, if the work were suitable, would mark its pages for Livy to study. The works in question in this particular letter were two articles reprinted in the January, 1870, issue of *Eclectic Magazine*, and their information about the enormous size and number of heavenly bodies and the vast distances between them led him into ranging imaginative and philosophical speculations.[18] There are, he wrote Livy, "stars within reach of our telescopes whose light requires 50,000 years to traverse the wastes of space & come to our earth." Then, adjusting his rhetoric to his subject, he created a sentence so long with its piled-on modifiers and so spacious in its imagery that it leaves the reader breathless:

And so, if we made a tour through space ourselves, might we not, in some remote era of the future, meet & greet the first lagging rays of stars that started on their weary visit to us a million years ago?—rays that are outcast & homeless, now, their parent stars crumbled to nothingness & swept from the firmament five hundred thousand years after these journeying rays departed—stars whose peoples lived their little lives, & laughed & wept, hoped & feared, sinned & perished, bewildering ages since these vagrant twinklings went wandering through the solemn solitudes of space?[19]

In this letter he contemplates the astronomer's cosmos with Jovian equanimity. Among the "millions & millions of worlds that hold their majestic courses above our heads," our earth is a "pigmy little world." The vision teaches him wonder; it should teach humility to those who go about "prating complacently of our speck as the Great World." As for the "new arguments to prove that the world is very old, & that the six days of creation were immensely long periods," they are all right with him.

18. "The Early History of Man," *Eclectic Magazine*, XI (January, 1870), 1–16; "Solar Wonders," *Eclectic Magazine*, XI (January, 1870), 112–14.

19. Dixon Wecter (ed.), *The Love Letters of Mark Twain* (New York, 1949), 133.

But his mood was sharply different a few months later, when he read "Our Earliest Ancestors," a review of Louis Figuier's *Primitive Man* (London, 1870), which organized the available paleontological and archaeological knowledge of prehistoric cultures. The reviewer began by declaring that Figuier "deprecates the wrath of those narrow theologians who imagine that Geology, Paleontology, and Archaeology are sworn enemies to Holy Writ. He shews that the conventional allowance of six thousand years of age to the human species arises not from any statement in the Book of Genesis, but from the erroneous interpretation of the chronologists."[20] This time Clemens found himself closer to the "narrow theologians" than to the scientists. "Our Earliest Ancestors" prompted him to write "A Brace of Brief Lectures on Science," which expressed deep suspicions about scientists' claims to understand prehistoric phenomena from present evidence. He began by invalidating the geologists' estimates of the age of the earth by showing that they were in disagreement. Then he became elaborately satirical about "paleontologists" (archaeologists, really) who claimed they could tell what primitive man ate and how he dressed, hunted, and worshiped on the basis of unearthed bones and artifacts. In his second "Lecture," for example, he pretended to be a scientist himself, but one who used the common sense lacking in his "brother paleontologists" to interpret their finds correctly: "As concerns the proud paleontological trophy, the 'flint hatchet' and its companion the 'flint knife,' I am compelled again to differ with the other scientists. I cannot think that the so-called 'flint knife' is a knife at all. I cannot disabuse my mind of the impression that it is a file. No knife ever had such a scandalous blade as that." At the end of his burlesque lectures, his tone changed, and it now incongruously appeared that he had been demonstrating that though there had been contradictory interpretations of archaeological finds, "science cannot help it. Science is full of change. Science is progressive and eternal. The scientists of twenty years ago laughed at the ignorant man who had groped in the intellectual darkness of twenty years before." This final obeisance to science does little to mitigate the satire of the rest of the "Lectures." It does show, as Hamlin Hill has remarked, that in this essay Clemens was subject to "unstable and incompatible opinions" about science.[21]

20. "Our Earliest Ancestors," *Chamber's Journal*, XLVII (1870), 521.

21. Hamlin Hill, Jr., "Mark Twain's 'Brace of Brief Lectures on Science,'" *New England Quarterly*, XXXIV (1961), 236, 237, 238–39. "Lectures" first appeared in the

His responses to science continued to be at odds with one another during the early 1870s. Three of his activities in 1871 seem to put him in the proscience camp. In April he tried to save a philologist named Ruloff from being hanged for murder on the grounds that if this "scientist" were executed, society would lose his "subtle analysis, vast knowledge in his peculiar field of research, comprehensive grasp of subject, and serene kingship over its limitless and bewildering details." He was so worked up over the case that he made an offer in the New York *Tribune* to "bring forward a man who, in the interest of learning and science, will take *Ruloff's crime upon himself, and submit to be hanged in Ruloff's place.*" His zeal was tempered by embarrassment; he signed his public letter simply "Samuel Langhorne."[22] That summer he and Joe Goodman, his Nevada crony, combined their miners' knowledge of minerals with what Paine calls their "poetic interest in geology" to collect and speculate on the age and origin of rocks gathered around Quarry Farm, near Elmira, New York.[23] Late that fall he studied the first four chapters of Darwin's *The Descent of Man.*

But all this enthusiasm for science is contradicted in his "Some Learned Fables, for Good Old Boys and Girls" (1874). This story treats satirically and at length—ten thousand words—the methods and conclusions of archaeologists, paleontologists, and geologists. Throughout, the point of view is staunchly obscurantist. Twain imagines a group of insects and small animals—for example, Professor Snail, Professor Woodlouse, Engineer Herr Spider, Professor Field-Mouse—sallying out of their woods on a scientific expedition into Man Territory, where they ludicrously misinterpret every phenomenon they observe: A railroad is a parallel of latitude, a passing locomotive is the vernal equinox, a telegraph line is a spider web, a house is a cavern whose courses of brick are geological strata, and so on. Never seeing a man, they are nevertheless willing to theorize on his physical appearance and culture. The hero of the fable is the Tumble-Bug, whose humble vocation and earthy common sense lead him closer to the truth than the scientists' speculations. When the scientists declare that a pile of dung is a Mound Builder's Monument, the Tumble-Bug replies, "So it is, indeed, to the shrewd keen

---

September and October, 1871, issues of the *American Publisher*, edited by Clemens' brother Orion.
    22. Paine, *Mark Twain: A Biography,* I, 437, III, 1628–29.
    23. *Ibid.,* I, 436.

eye of science; but to an ignorant poor devil who has never seen a college, it is not a Monument, strictly speaking, but it is a most rich and noble property." The Tumble-Bug's observation in the final sentence delivers the fable's moral: "He said that all he had learned by his travels was that science only needed a spoonful of supposition to build a mountain of demonstrated fact out of; and that for the future he meant to be content with the knowledge that nature had made free to all creatures and not go prying into the august secrets of the Deity."[24] Scientists are not only made to seem ridiculous for their absurd speculation on tenuous evidence, but they become meddlers in "the august secrets of the Deity" as well.

Clearly, Samuel Clemens was of two minds about science around 1870. Its revelations could inspire his expansive acceptance or suspicious recoil. His emotional and intellectual development so far had prepared him both to march bravely into a science-dominated future and to long for a time in the past before modern science had disturbed the simple verities.

His pattern of response to the machine was quite different from that to science. Not much concerned with the machine or technology around 1870, he would within a decade begin investing much of his mind and money in the invention and production of machinery. During his middle years he had three of his ideas patented; he invested (fruitlessly) several hundred thousand dollars in a steam generator, a steam pulley, a process for printing illustrations, and a typesetting machine; he could claim that he was the world's first user of the telephone and the fountain pen and the first novelist to use a typewriter and phonographic dictation.[25] He was, remarked Bernard DeVoto, "as awestruck by the mirage of Progress as any platform lecturer of his time."[26]

But the machine came to mean more to him than profits and progress. In his later years he had intimations of a metaphysical meaning for which the machine was a symbol. His typesetter was to him "a magnificent creature of steel . . . as elaborate and complex as that machine it ranks *next* to . . . —Man"; and the typesetter's inventor, James W. Paige, was "a poet, whose sublime creations are

24. Samuel Clemens [Mark Twain], *Sketches New and Old*, Author's National Edition: The Writings of Mark Twain (25 vols.; New York, 1907–18), XIX, 186, 189.

25. Sherwood Cummings, "Mark Twain and the Sirens of Progress," *Journal of the Central Mississippi Valley American Studies Association*, I (1960), 17–24.

26. Bernard DeVoto, *Mark Twain's America* (Boston, 1932), 296.

written in steel."[27] And in a rare moment it seemed to him that a man could invent and construct a machine only because God, "the only Originator," had "made the materials of all things; He made the laws by which and by which only, man may combine them into machines and other things which outside influences may suggest to him."[28] For all his fascination with the machine, however, his faith in technology and progress was to be undermined, as evidenced in *A Connecticut Yankee* and "The Chronicle of Young Satan."

Around 1870, Samuel Clemens was ambivalent about science and had not begun his doomed love affair with technological progress. So far, no consistent pattern has emerged, a fact that should not be surprising, considering that he was living through an era of critical change. He did have his inconsistencies, but, then, so did his age.

27. Albert Bigelow Paine (ed.), *Mark Twain's Letters* (2 vols.; New York, 1917), II, 516; Paine (ed.), *Mark Twain's Autobiography* (2 vols.; New York, 1924), I, 72.

28. Albert Bigelow Paine (ed.), *Mark Twain's Notebook* (New York, 1935), 361.

# CHAPTER 2

# Strata

*When I was a small boy, Lem Hackett was drowned—on a Sunday. . . . There was a ferocious thunderstorm that night. . . . Not a doubt entered my mind that all the angels were grouped together discussing this boy's case and observing the awful bombardment of our beggarly little village with satisfaction and approval.*

—*Life on the Mississippi*, Chapter 54

*I think the goodness, the justice, and the mercy of God are manifested in His works.*

—From a credo written around age forty-five

*The Book of Nature tells us distinctly that God cares not a rap for us— nor for any living creature.*

—From a credo written at age sixty-three

IT WAS SAMUEL CLEMENS' fate to live successively within four cultures and to become deeply involved in each culture's world view. As a result, the four cultures—Calvinistic, deistic, evangelical Christian, and post-Darwinian scientific—laid down incompatible strata in his mind. Intellectually, Clemens progressed from one level to the next, but he could not really rid himself of certain ideas once held dear. The biblical story of creation and of Adam and Eve and Eden, for example, continued to engage him even though he came to accept the scientific explanation of geological and biological development. In his old age he could think just as easily in terms of the biblical account of creation as in terms of the scientific view. For example, in "The Chronicle of Young Satan," Satan shows the boys the history of humankind as beginning in "the garden of Eden" and enduring for "five or six thousand years"; he then switches to the scientific perspective: "For a million years the race has gone on monotonously propagating itself."[1] Clemens was not unaware of his incompatible strata of belief. In middle age he observed "that the religious folly you are born in you will die in, no matter what appar-

---

1. William M. Gibson (ed.), *Mark Twain's Mysterious Stranger Manuscripts* (Berkeley, 1969), 134–38.

ently reasonabler religious folly may seem to have taken its place meanwhile and abolished and obliterated it."[2]

The religion Sam Clemens was born in told him that this world is a preparation for the next. The way one lived here had a good deal to do with whether one would go to a psalm-singing heaven or a burning hell. The rules for right conduct and proper spiritual preparation were perfectly clear, and they were advertised as efficacious; but the final decision was up to the close-hovering Deity, who was just, but awful and mysterious. Following the rules served not only as an application for heavenly bliss but as a way, reinforced through prayer, of assuring material blessings, just as ignoring them precipitated temporal warnings and punishments. The good prospered, and the wicked were laid low.

That such was young Sam's understanding of religion is indicated in both *Tom Sawyer* and *Huckleberry Finn*. It is made explicit in passages from the *Autobiography*[3] and *Life on the Mississippi*. In the latter book, Clemens told how he was frightened into contrition by a thunderstorm generated for his personal benefit the night after one of his playmates was drowned:

Things had become truly serious. I resolved to turn over a new leaf instantly; I also resolved to connect myself with the church the next day, if I survived to see its sun appear. I resolved to cease from sin in all its forms, and to lead a high and blameless life forever after. I would be punctual at church and Sunday-school; visit the sick; carry baskets of victuals to the poor . . . ; I would instruct other boys in right ways, and take the resulting trouncings meekly; I would subsist entirely on tracts; I would invade the rum shop and warn the drunkard—and finally, if I escaped the fate of those who early became too good to live, I would go for a missionary.[4]

Such was the regimen of those who wished to appease the immanent and angry God. There was no doubt about what was good and what was bad, nor any doubting of dogma and doctrine by the orthodox.

2. Henry Nash Smith and William M. Gibson (eds.), *Mark Twain–Howells Letters* (2 vols.; Cambridge, Mass., 1960), II, 461.

3. Albert Bigelow Paine (ed.), *Mark Twain's Autobiography* (2 vols.; New York, 1924), I, 133–35, II, 175–76; Bernard DeVoto (ed.), *Mark Twain in Eruption* (New York, 1940), 108.

4. Samuel Clemens [Mark Twain], *Life on the Mississippi*, Author's National Edition: The Writings of Mark Twain (25 vols.; New York, 1907–18), IX, 401.

Doctrine was based on the Bible, or on biblical exegesis, for one surmises that Clemens' Sunday school teachers and preachers emphasized Old Testament texts about Jehovah's power and wrath. The Bible, Clemens opined in 1904, was a pharmacy stocked with poisons and medicines, purges and salves, from which theologians took what filled the current religious prescription.[5] At any rate, he was made to know the Bible; he had to memorize passages, and was "compelled . . . to read an unexpurgated Bible through"[6] before he was fifteen. His early Bible reading stocked his memory with biblical characters, incidents, and precepts, which appeared again and again in his writing as allusions, analogues, and themes.[7] It also indoctrinated him in Old Testament cosmology and in the account of creation as given in Genesis and determined by Bishop James Ussher to have taken place in 4004 B.C. The Bible's imprint on his mind remained indelible under the palimpsest of later scientific knowledge.

Nevertheless he was early tempted toward skepticism. In his autobiographical dictation for August 15, 1906, Clemens told how his first schoolteacher, Elizabeth Horr, had piously averred that "whosoever prayed for a thing with earnestness and strong desire need not doubt that his prayer would be answered." Sam prayed for gingerbread and then gratefully accepted the gingerbread that a neighboring student had negligently left within reach. Succeeding prayers were never "competent to lift that gingerbread again," however; and he concluded "that if a person remains faithful to his gingerbread and keeps his eye on it, he need not trouble himself about your prayers."[8]

The gingerbread story that he dictated is humorous, and perhaps his secretary or Albert Bigelow Paine chuckled at it. At any rate, Clemens wrote privately, as if he had not got his real meaning across, a poignant testimonial of his religious disillusionment:

5. Samuel Clemens [Mark Twain], "Bible Teaching and Religious Practice," in *Europe and Elsewhere*, ed. Albert Bigelow Paine (New York, 1923), 387–93.

6. Albert Bigelow Paine, *Mark Twain: A Biography* (3 vols.; New York, 1912), III, 1280–81.

7. Allison Ensor finds that the persistent biblical themes in Twain's works are those of Adam, Eve, Eden, and the Fall; of Noah and the flood; and of the Prodigal Son. *Mark Twain and the Bible* (Lexington, Ky., 1969), 30.

8. DeVoto (ed.), *Mark Twain in Eruption*, 108–109.

Why should one laugh at my praying for gingerbread when I was a child? What *would* a child naturally pray for?—a child who had been lied to by teachers and preachers and a lying Bible-text?

My prayer failed. It was 65 years ago. I remember the shock yet. I was as astonished as if I had caught my own mother breaking a promise to me.

Was the doubt planted then, which in 50 years grew to a certainty: that the X and all other religions are lies and swindles?†[9]

Both the dictation and the private note hark back "sixty-five years"—that is, to 1841, when Sam was five or six. By this reckoning, his growing doubt about the validity of any religion became absolute when he was in his middle fifties, halfway between finishing *A Connecticut Yankee* and beginning *Pudd'nhead Wilson*.

The gingerbread story aside, he was exposed to dogma and freethinking concurrently; and he responded strongly to both. His family immersed him in a welter of confusing religious values. His mother was pious and vivacious, his father agnostic and dour. His religious sister Pamela supervised his bedtime prayers, and his Universalist (and therefore "infidel") uncle John Quarles presided benevolently over Sam's boyhood summers on the Quarles farm. His brother Orion boxed the compass of religious attitudes during his lifetime, suggesting through his conversions and defections the variety of influences that had operated on the sons of John and Jane Clemens.

Probably the most persistent force in combat with the powerful myth of his childhood religion was the sheer matter-of-factness of life. At least it prevailed in the daytime. Night was his time for anguished piety; daylight restored his cheerfulness. During the thunderstorm following Injun Joe's death, he "shrivelled and shrank together in mortal terror" at each lightning flash and lamented and prayed, as he said, "with an energy and feeling and sincerity quite foreign to my nature. But in the morning I saw that it was a false alarm and concluded to resume business at the old stand and wait for another reminder."[10] The thunderstorm following the death of his friend Lem Hackett brought on another spasm of contrition. But the next morning, "[t]he world looked so bright and safe

---

9. Mark Twain Papers, Paine #277. All previously unpublished words by Mark Twain are identified by the following symbol: †.

10. Paine (ed.), *Mark Twain's Autobiography,* II, 176.

that there did not seem to be any real occasion to turn over a new leaf."[11] His repentances, he wrote in 1898,

could not stand the daylight. They faded out and shredded away and disappeared in the glad splendor of the sun. They were creatures of fear and darkness, and they could not live out of their own place. The day gave me cheer and peace, and at night I repented again. In all my boyhood life I am not sure that I ever tried to lead a better life in the daytime—or wanted to. In my age I should never think of wishing to do such a thing. But in my age, as in my youth, night brings me many a deep remorse. I realize that from the cradle up I have been like the rest of the race—never quite sane in the night.[12]

Light and darkness early became for Clemens symbols for cheerful matter-of-factness and religious terror. Such a division might be included in his often discussed "twainness," but it was by no means peculiar. It had been shared by perhaps a majority of Americans, or at least by as many as lived in communities (beginning with Plymouth and Boston) where both religious intensity and robust practicality were honored.

What we know about Samuel Clemens' inner life from the time he left Hannibal at seventeen until he became a cub pilot at twenty-one is not much, but his experiences were undoubtedly secularizing. He was on his own in the cities of St. Louis, Philadelphia, New York, Cincinnati, and Keokuk, where he earned his keep as a printer; and though he was no scapegrace, neither was he a churchgoer, so far as the record tells us. We know that he was a serious reader and that he remembered himself as listening to certain radical arguments by a fellow roomer. Certainly his mind was venturing beyond Hannibal's provincialism. But it took a special experience to give shape and sanction to his growing skepticism. That experience was his reading, as a cub pilot, Thomas Paine's *The Age of Reason* "with fear and hesitation, but marveling at its fearlessness and wonderful power."[13]

It is nearly impossible to exaggerate the impact of *The Age of Reason* on the mind of Samuel Clemens. Of the books that shaped his philosophies, it is the one whose echoes are the most durable and substantial in his succeeding thought. He read it when he was twenty-one or twenty-two, and apparently not again until he was in

11. Clemens, *Life on the Mississippi*, 401.
12. Paine (ed.), *Mark Twain's Autobiography*, I, 134.
13. Paine, *Mark Twain: A Biography*, III, 1445.

his seventies; yet its pristine meanings—and even phraseology—were lodged in the foundations of his memory.[14] The book converted him. Paine's equating traditional religions with superstition helped Clemens submerge his dreadful Calvinism. And in its place, Paine offered an enlightened theology and cosmology based on Newtonian science. Clemens accepted the offer. Tom Paine's "deist's bible" provided Clemens with a creed for his young manhood and middle years.

The first clear sign of Clemens' conversion to deism is his joining the Polar Star Masonic Lodge of St. Louis, on February 18, 1861.[15] Masonry, endorsed by Paine himself, was the nearest thing to what might be called a church of deism.[16] More dramatic proof of Paine's radical influence is Clemens' two private declarations of faith, the first recorded about 1870, the second a decade or so later. Both are paraphrases of parts of *The Age of Reason*, written, it may be, from unconscious memory.

The first, a sixteen-page manuscript, is based on the second half of Paine's "Chapter XIII." Paine begins by telling how at the age of seven or eight he "revolted at the recollection" of a sermon on God's redemption through Christ and "thought to myself that it was making God Almighty act like a passionate man that killed his son." "How different," he continues, "is the pure and simple profession of Deism! The true Deist has but one Deity; and his religion consists in contemplating the power, wisdom, and benignity of the Deity in his works, and in endeavoring to imitate him in everything moral, scientific, and mechanical." Clemens begins by declaring, "The difference between the God of the Bible & the God of the present day, cannot be described, it can only be vaguely & inadequately figured to the mind." He rejects the God of the Bible as "an irascible, vindictive, fierce and ever fickle & changeful master" and cleaves to the "true God . . . whose beneficent, exact, & changeless ordering of the machinery of his colossal universe is proof that he is at least steadfast in his purposes; whose unwritten laws . . . show that he is just and fair."[17]

14. *Ibid.*

15. Alexander E. Jones, "Mark Twain and Freemasonry," *American Literature,* XXVI (1954), 366–73.

16. Paine wrote an essay on Masonry to show that "its doctrines and his had always been fundamentally the same." Harry Hayden Clark (ed.), *Thomas Paine: Representative Selections* (New York, 1944), xxxi.

17. Paine, *Mark Twain: A Biography,* I, 412.

Paine proceeds by contrasting the foolish biblical notion of a geo-centric universe with the modern "belief of a plurality of worlds." He has come to appreciate the "infinity of space" through the "use of the globes and of the orrery," and he declares that our earth "is infinitely less in proportion than the smallest grain of sand is to the size of the world." Clemens concurs: The "modern" universe "consists of countless worlds of so stupendous dimensions that in comparison ours is grotesquely insignificant; they swing in spaces so vast that in comparison the spaces of the Biblical universe are but as those of an orrery." Conceive, writes Clemens, of the biblical universe as "a grain of sand on the shore & then draw the proportions of the modern Deity upon the boundless expanse of the waters."†

Concerning our own planet, Paine writes, "[W]e find every part of it—the earth, the waters, and the air that surrounds it—filled and, as it were, crowded with life down from the largest animals that we know of to the smallest insects the naked eye can behold, and from thence to others smaller and totally invisible without the assistance of a microscope." Clemens notes the same biological marvel: "The God of the Bible did not know that the mountains & the everlasting rocks are built on the bones of his dead creatures. . . . He did not know that every drop of water & every grain of matter is populous with living forms. The very microscope has created a world compared with which the entire universe of the Bible is meagre, unmarvelous, & inconsequent."†[18]

Clemens' second deistic credo is an even more elaborate echo of *The Age of Reason*. Its format is strikingly like that of Paine's "profession of faith": Both men present a series of statements beginning "I believe" and "I do not believe," though for his ideas Clemens depends on other parts of *The Age of Reason* as well. Paine begins: "I believe in one God, and no more"; Clemens' first declaration is "I believe in God the Almighty." Paine declares, "I totally disbelieve that the Almighty ever did communicate anything to man by any mode of speech, in any language, or by any kind of vision or appearance"; and Clemens agrees: "I do not believe He has ever sent a message to man by anybody, or delivered one to him by word of mouth, or made Himself visible to mortal eyes at any time in any place." Paine reviews the claims of Jews, Christians, and "Turks" to the effect that their respective religions are based on *revelation or the word of God* and concludes, "Each of those churches accuse

18. Clark (ed.), *Thomas Paine: Representative Selections*, 275–78; Mark Twain Papers, Paine #60.

the other of unbelief; and, for my part, I disbelieve them all." Clemens puts the same idea this way: "I believe that the Old and New Testaments were imagined and written by man, and that no line in them was authorized by God, much less inspired by him." Paine's declaration that God's universe "manifests his goodness and beneficence" becomes Clemens' "I think the goodness, the justice, and the mercy of God are manifested in His works." Paine's tenet that "the system of laws established by the Creator . . . governs and regulates the whole" is also Clemens': "I believe that the universe is governed by strict and immutable laws." Paine's "I trouble not myself about the manner of future existence" is in the same tone as Clemens' "[T]here may be a hereafter and there may not be. I am wholly indifferent about it."[19]

Both Paine and Clemens found the doctrine of the Trinity incomprehensible; both regarded Old Testament stories of sex and violence as "obscene"; both identified the church as the enemy of science; and both regarded Jesus as a great and emulable person but not as the son of God.[20] And so, with Paine as his prophet, Clemens for some thirty years—from around 1860 to around 1890—took heart in the idea that the laws of the universe imposed a certain order and meaning upon the world of men.

Samuel Clemens' conversion to evangelical Christianity presents a problem. Instead of marking, as it should, a break with a former period, it fits without apparent trouble into his deistic years. The dates of his zealous quest for grace and his living as a Christian are 1868 to 1870. Was his conversion genuine? Some have doubted it. Let us look at the record.

When Clemens visited the Langdons late in the summer of 1868, it was ostensibly to join Charlie Langdon, his *Quaker City* shipboard friend; but once inside the door, he paid less attention to Charlie than to his sister Olivia. He wooed her for fourteen days, proposed

19. Clark (ed.), *Thomas Paine: Representative Selections*, 325, 324, 327, 292, 332, 293; Samuel Clemens [Mark Twain], "[Three Statements of the Eighties]," *What Is Man? and Other Philosophical Writings*, ed. Paul Baender (Berkeley, 1973), 56–57, Vol. XIX of the Works of Mark Twain.

20. Clark (ed.), *Thomas Paine: Representative Selections*, 330, 247, 299–300, 284, 239; Robert Pack Browning, Michael B. Frank, and Lin Salamo (eds.), *Mark Twain's Notebooks and Journals* (3 vols. completed; Berkeley, 1979), III, 489; Paine, *Mark Twain: A Biography*, III, 1280–81, 1354, 1535; Albert Bigelow Paine (ed.), *Mark Twain's Notebook* (New York, 1935), 394; Albert Bigelow Paine (ed.), *Mark Twain's Letters* (2 vols.; New York, 1917), I, 323.

to her on the fifteenth, was refused, and left. It required two more visits and Sam's most ardent persuasion to make Olivia say yes late in November. Livy's parents refused to vote with her, however. They put Sam on probation and laid down conditions that he described to his sister this way: 'When I am permanently *settled*—& when I am a Christian—& when I have *demonstrated* that I have a good, steady, reliable character, her parents will withdraw their objections, & she *may* marry me."[21]

Even before conversion to Christianity was made one of the requirements for Sam's election into the Langdon family, Livy was working a sea change in her lover's religion. She was sincerely, if conventionally, devout and must have admonished him (to his delight, since everything she did delighted him) to pray, seek grace, and accept the Savior. Sam had heard something like this before, of course, but Livy's genteel Congregationalism had a different ring from his Hannibal religion. Hers was sweet and devotional and was founded on the promises of the New Testament; Hannibal's was absolute and awesome and depended for authority upon the threats of the Old Testament God. Livy was an effective evangelist. On September 21, two weeks after Sam's first proposal, the wavering skeptic wrote to Livy: "You say to me: 'I shall pray for you daily.' Not any words that ever were spoken to me have touched me like these. . . . I *will* 'pray with you,' as you ask: and with such faith & such encouragement withal, as are in me, though feeble & of little worth I feel they must be" (21). Two months later he could write: "I have no fears—none. I believe in you, even as I believe in the Savior in whose hands our destinies are" (25).

During that same fall, Samuel Clemens acquired another religious mentor—Joseph Twichell, pastor of Hartford's Asylum Hill Congregational Church. In October, Clemens visited Hartford to confer with his publisher, Elisha Bliss, Jr. There he met Twichell, whom he immediately "made a friend," and "went with him to the alms house & helped him preach and sing to the inmates (I helped in the singing, anyhow)" (22–23). Twichell was exactly the right person to lead Clemens into the mysteries of devotional religion. Athletic, extroverted, even bawdy in masculine company, he practiced an active, liberal Christianity at the same time that he preached the necessity of prayer, the doctrine of salvation, and the promise of immortality. If Clemens had any notion that there was something

---

21. Dixon Wecter (ed.), *The Love Letters of Mark Twain* (New York, 1949), 28. Further references to *The Love Letters* are indicated by parenthetical page numbers in the text.

womanish about Livy's religion, he could be reassured in seeing that the virile Twichell was as devout as she. If Twichell prayed, prayer was manly; and a few weeks after Clemens met his pastor, they were praying together for Livy and he was writing thus to Twichell about the joy of his love: "I am full of gratitude to God this day, and my prayers will be sincere" (34).

A striking testimonial to the growing literalness of Clemens' faith is his Christmas Eve (1868) letter to Mary Mason Fairbanks, another of his *Quaker City* shipmates and friends. To Mrs. Fairbanks he made confidences, and from her he sought advice. They corresponded until 1895, and his attitude toward her was consistently affectionate and respectful. All this, in addition to the fact that Mrs. Fairbanks was a pious woman, makes it extremely unlikely that the following was meant as irony:

About this time, (past midnight, and so, Christmas is here) eighteen hundred and sixty nine years ago, the stars were shedding a purer lustre above the barren hills of Bethlehem—and possibly flowers were being charmed to life in the dismal plain where the Shepherds watched their flocks—and the hovering angels were singing Peace on earth, good-will to men. For the Saviour was come. . . . [D]on't you realize again, as in other years, that Jesus *was* born there, and that the angels *did* sing in the still air above, and that the wondering shepherds *did* hold their breath and listen as the mysterious music floated by? *I* do.[22]

The pilgrim made remarkable progress in 1869. On January 6 he wrote Livy: "I see the Savior dimly at times, and at intervals, *very near*—would that the intervals were not so sad a length apart! Sometimes it is a *pleasure* to me to pray, night and morning, in cars and everywhere, twenty times a day" (45). Later that month he wrote a confessional letter to Livy, admitting that the life he had lived "would be hateful in your eyes" but adding, "I am striving and shall strive to reach the highest altitude of worth, the highest Christian excellence" (60). He felt confident enough of his conversion to write Livy's mother on February 13, "I now claim that I am a Christian" (65); and thereafter he often acted like one. He read "a Testament lesson" and prayed each night before retiring, and in November he assessed the past ten months as providing him a "new, strange, beautiful life . . . , a broadening and aspiring life" marked by "an unaccustomed stirring within me of religious impulses" (122).

His Christian zeal seems to have waned shortly before his mar-

22. Dixon Wecter (ed.), *Mark Twain to Mrs. Fairbanks* (San Marino, Calif., 1949), 59.

riage to Livy, on February 2, 1870. Indeed, the reading in astronomy that inspired his letter to Livy of January 8 perhaps caused his deism to reemerge and perhaps even led him to write the first of his credos in emulation of Tom Paine. At any rate, although as a newlywed he attended church and read the Bible with Livy, he soon gave up such pieties. Bible reading, he told Livy, "is making me a hypocrite. I don't believe in the Bible. It contradicts my reason. I can't sit here and listen to it, letting you believe that I regard it, as you do, in the light of gospel, the word of God." He felt obliged to make a confession of unbelief to his pastor, whose church he ceased attending, but Joseph Twichell remained his dear friend and in 1910 prayed at Clemens' funeral.[23]

What are we to make of this brief but intense flood of religious expression? Was it merely a "lover's gambit" (9), as Dixon Wecter suggested—a move Clemens had to make to capture the white queen? I think not. Such a judgment would make Clemens out to be devilishly tricky with the woman he adored. Clemens was not devious. He was complicated but candid. If we accept his Christian devotion as heartfelt, it will point up the tension between his religious need and the difficulties that evidences put in the way of fulfilling that need. More than most men, he was preoccupied with religion. He was the person who, around 1874, would write to his sister that in the matter of Christianity he was "an entire and absolute unbeliever," but he was also the person who would for the rest of his life now and then love to sing hymns and spirituals; and he was the person who in middle age hoped that his nephew Samuel Moffett would become a minister, because there should be a minister in every family.[24] He was the person who, in his older age and bereft of faith in any religion, described his heroine Joan of Arc as one "who had spoken face to face with the princes of heaven, the familiars of God, and seen their retinue of angels stretching back into the remoteness of the sky, myriads upon myriads, like a measureless fan of light, a glory like the glory of the sun streaming from each of those innumerable heads, the massed radiance filling the deeps of space with a blinding splendor."[25]

23. Paine, *Mark Twain: A Biography*, I, 411, II, 631.

24. Samuel C. Webster (ed.), *Mark Twain, Business Man* (Boston, 1946), 131, 13.

25. Samuel Clemens [Mark Twain], *Personal Recollections of Joan of Arc*, Author's National Edition: The Writings of Mark Twain (25 vols.; New York, 1907–18), XVII, 161.

A likely consequence of Clemens' Christian zeal in 1868 and 1869 was an intensification of the conflict between his loyalty to science and reason on the one hand and his loyalty to the "august secrets of the Deity" on the other. It is true that he never countered science with specifically Christian doctrine. Nevertheless, the basis for his suspicion of certain sciences was certainly theological. And if that theology was mainly deistic, it was in some ways also supported by lessons he had learned from his Christian teachers.

The sciences he *really* believed in were those of the eighteenth century, as interpreted by Tom Paine. Principally, they were astronomy and such branches of biology as discovered and named the myriad forms of life that inhabited the planet. They were sciences that let you *see* things and sort them out. They let you know that there was a vast and regular cosmos out there and that on earth there was an orderly arrangement of life into its biological classifications. Clemens hated to give up the majestic verities of those sciences, partly because they were so demonstrably true and partly because they gave plan and purpose to the universe. They obviously pointed to a Creator who had brought all these wonders into being and kept them going with his benevolent laws. Clemens' deism, however radically in conflict with his boyhood theology in general, reinforced his belief in the basic Christian idea that God *did* create the world and that man was the climax of that creation. Paine himself would not categorically deny that Adam was the first man.

The newer sciences—archaeology, paleontology, anthropology, and Darwinian biology—were not to be trusted. They posited theories based on "evidence" so flimsy and arcane as to insult common sense. Worse, if by any chance there was truth in them, they opened up a pre-Adamic vista so pointless in its savage vitality and stretching so far back into the mists of chaos that they threatened one's faith in a particular and reasonable Creation. Geology was a borderline case. Clemens had been a practical geologist as silver prospector in Nevada, and thereafter he now and then indulged himself in amateur musings on geology—remarking a layer of oyster shells in rock far above sea level, speculating on the age of strata in a gorge, or meditating on the antiquity of a fossil in a marble bench. Still, there was something about the inconceivable stretches of geological time that repelled his imagination. His mind accepted the "facts" of geology—and eventually those of the newer sciences as well—but his heart was not in them.

The degree of his acceptance of the various sciences can be measured by the way they stirred his imagination. In response to astronomy and microscopy—those deistic sciences—he wrote engaging fantasies: "A Curious Pleasure Excursion" and *Captain Stormfield's Visit to Heaven,* "The Great Dark" and *3,000 Years Among the Microbes.* Paleontologists and their modern ilk earned only burlesque treatment, as in the Riffelberg expedition chapters in *A Tramp Abroad.* Geology—that "borderline" science—intrigued him; and once he projected "a love-story of the Quartenary [sic] Epoch which would begin, 'On a soft October afternoon 2,000,000 years ago,' " but nothing came of it.[26]

It is my purpose in this chapter to limn the stages of Samuel Clemens' beliefs, with particular reference to the way science affected them. (Here the concern is with Samuel Clemens the citizen. The knottier problem of Mark Twain's response to science will take up the rest of the book.) The picture looks like this: Samuel Clemens' indoctrination in the old-time religion was first challenged by practical skepticism and then overlaid with a rational, deistic faith that, except for a Christian episode, endured for three decades and then expired under the evidences of modern science. The picture is, I believe, accurate in outline; but in its very accuracy it is misleading, for it makes no room for human complexities and anomalies, of which Samuel Clemens had his share.

The persistence in his thinking of the Genesis account of creation has already been noted. Other early beliefs cropped up in his older age: For all his professed indifference about life after death, he could not get heaven or hell out of his thinking. In his later years he confessed that he was "strongly inclined to expect" an afterlife even though there was "not the slightest evidence" for it; and as for hell, he said: "I don't believe in it, but I am afraid of it. It makes me afraid to die."[27]

A different kind of anomaly is his dabbling throughout his deistic period and beyond in various secular mysticisms. Although his center and norm as a satirist was common sense, he was vulnerable to his own brand of satire in his recurrent fascination with the occult. He loved to have his fortune told, whether by palmistry, clairvoyance, or horoscope; and he more than half believed in the

26. Paine, *Mark Twain: A Biography,* III, 1162.

27. *Ibid.,* 1431; Grace King, *Memoirs of a Southern Woman of Letters* (New York, 1932), 214.

prophecies of the seers he visited.[28] He dabbled in spiritualism, experimented privately in communication with the dead, and entertained mediums and a hypnotist in his Hartford house.[29] His interest in extrasensory perception is documented in two essays on "mental telegraphy." He would never forget the lore of omens and charms that he learned from slaves and whites in Hannibal; and when he was nearly sixty years old, he confessed that he was "very superstitious."[30]

Beginning in 1891, a flood of ideas about the animality of man, the amorality of nature, and the disconnection between existence and cosmic purpose poured from Samuel Clemens' mind. For twenty years and more, Clemens had been resisting the notion of a pre-Adamic world laboriously evolved through countless ages. But in 1891, the same year, according to his own calculation, that he came to believe that all religions are "lies and swindles," he gave up the struggle and for the first time publicly and casually treated the prehistoric eras and the slow evolution of man as matters of fact. In a slight piece called "The Cradle of Liberty," he referred to the time "before primeval man himself, just emerged from his four-footed estate, stepped out upon this plain, first sample of his race, a thousand centuries ago . . . and before the big saurians wallowed here, still some eons earlier."[31]

His view of God and nature was transformed. In the early 1880s, he could write as part of his second credo, "I think the goodness, the justice, and the mercy of God are manifested in His works; I perceive that they are manifested toward me in this life; the logical conclusion is that they will be manifested toward me in the life to come, if there should be one."[32] But after 1891, there is no trace of the teleology implied in that earlier statement—no trace left of a faith that the creation expresses God's benevolence. Clemens' third credo—written in 1898 and covering four pages of his notebook—

28. Paine, *Mark Twain: A Biography,* I, 157–59, III, 1410; Paine (ed.), *Mark Twain's Notebook,* 374, 380; Paine (ed.), *Mark Twain's Letters,* II, 706–707.

29. Mary Lawton, *A Lifetime with Mark Twain* (New York, 1925), 204, 210.

30. Paine (ed.), *Mark Twain's Letters,* II, 621. Mark Twain's interest in the occult has been definitively treated in Alan Gribben, " 'When Other Amusements Fail': Mark Twain and the Occult," in Howard Kerr, John W. Crowley, and Charles L. Crow (eds.), *The Haunted Dusk* (Athens, Ga., 1983), 171–89.

31. Samuel Clemens [Mark Twain], *What Is Man? and Other Essays,* ed. Albert Bigelow Paine (New York, 1917), 202.

32. Clemens, *What Is Man? and Other Philosophical Writings,* 56.

demonstrates the change. Deistic in some of its overtones (it invokes a vision of God's "great suns, swimming in the measureless ocean of space"), its subject is man's alienation from God:

The Bible of Nature tells us no word about any future life, but only about this present one. It does not promise a future life; it does not even vaguely indicate one. It is not intended as a message to us, any more than the scientist intends a message to surviving microbes when he boils the life out of a billion of them in a thimble. The microbes discover a message in it; this is certain—if they have a pulpit.

The Book of Nature tells us distinctly that God cares not a rap for us—nor for any living creature. It tells us that His laws inflict pain and suffering and sorrow, but it does not say that this is done in order that He may get pleasure out of this misery. We do not know what the object is, for the Book is not able to tell us. It may be mere indifference. Without a doubt He had an object, but we have no way of discovering what it was. The scientist has an object, but it is not the joy of inflicting pain upon the microbe.[33]

Clemens' new view of nature led him to make classic statements of social Darwinism—the notion that men are basically animalic and competitive, living by barely disguised jungle laws in their personal and economic struggles with one another, and that nations in waging war and conquest obey the law of survival of the fittest. His first expressions of social Darwinism appear in *The American Claimant*, a book he was writing in 1891. Although it goes much against his grain, Berkeley, a reserved Englishman living in an American boardinghouse, finds he has to use his fists against the house bully. When another boarder, a young tinner, is made an outcast because he has lost his job and his ability to support himself, the explanation Berkeley is given is: "Don't you know that the wounded deer is always attacked by its companions and friends? . . . I say that's human nature; that occurs everywhere; this boarding house is merely the world in little; it's the case all over—they're all alike."[34]

Clemens used his newly formulated social Darwinism to explain the phenomena of war and imperialism. As much as he was sickened by the atrocities of conquest that he observed or heard about in his round-the-world lecture tour (1895–1896), his judgment on the whole pattern of empire was that the conquering of a weaker people by a stronger was "the law of custom": "The signs of the times show

33. Paine (ed.), *Mark Twain's Notebook*, 361–62.
34. Samuel Clemens [Mark Twain], *The American Claimant and Other Stories and Sketches*, Author's National Edition: The Writings of Mark Twain (25 vols.; New York, 1907–18), XXI, 103–104.

plainly enough what is going to happen. All the savage lands in the world are going to be brought under subjection to the Christian governments of Europe. I am not sorry, but glad."[35] He was, perhaps, ironic in identifying the aggressor nations as Christian, but not in his concession to the inevitability of conquest.

The spirit of patriotism, he recorded in his notebook at about the same time, "is the spirit of the dog and the wolf. . . . The spirit of patriotism being in its nature jealous and selfish, is just in man's line, it comes natural to him—he can live up to all its requirements to the letter; but the spirit of Christianity is not in its entirety possible to him." Another entry, this in 1904, declares: "Man has not a single right which is the product of anything but might. Not a single right is indestructible: a new might can at any time abolish it, hence, man possesses not a single permanent right."[36] There is, in short, no law except the one animals follow, and consequently nothing that can be called by the name of morality: "There is no such thing as morality; it is not immoral for the tiger to eat the wolf, or the wolf the cat, or the cat the birds, and so on down. . . . It is not immoral for one nation to seize another nation by the force of arms, or for one man to seize another man's property or life if he is strong enough and wants to take it."[37]

A corollary idea, that nature is full of blind antagonisms, seems to have been triggered by his hearing a story about a carnivorous New Zealand parrot that "drives his beak into the sheep's side & digs out the kidney fat."†[38] That was his notebook entry of November 2, 1895. Five days later he was ready to philosophize about nature's treacheries: "Idiots argue that Nature is kind and fair to us," he began, "if we are loyal and obey her laws." The idiocy of the idea is abundantly apparent: Cholera strikes even people who practice sanitation; unsuspecting caterpillars are lignified by an infesting fungus; dogs and men become undeservingly "loaded up" with tapeworms. "Nature's attitude toward all life," he concluded, "is profoundly vicious, treacherous and malignant." Man is equally the

35. Samuel Clemens [Mark Twain], *Following the Equator,* Author's National Edition: The Writings of Mark Twain (25 vols.; New York, 1907–18), VI, 322–24.

36. Paine (ed.), *Mark Twain's Notebook,* 322–23, 394.

37. Paine, *Mark Twain: A Biography,* III, 1335. Although Clemens continued to be a theoretical social Darwinist throughout his last decade, he began, in 1900, to carry out with Howells a courageous campaign, in periodicals, against Western imperialism in the Philippines, China, and the Belgian Congo.

38. Mark Twain Papers, Mark Twain's unpublished notebook #44, 26 TS.

victim of inanimate nature, he declared a few months later. For his habitation, man has only two-fifths of the planet's surface. "On one-fifth of it he can raise snow, icicles, sand, rocks, and nothing else; and on the other fifth he can raise enough food to keep his race alive, but it takes hard grubbing to do it, and then the weather that he must fight—the drought, the flood, the hail, the hurricane."[39]

The distance Samuel Clemens had come since around 1870, when he resented the new scientists' meddling with the august secrets of the Deity, can be measured by his marginalia in Alexander Winchell's *Sketches of Creation*. Clemens bought the book in 1908, hoping to find in it the last word on geology. To his disappointment, he discovered that the book was a 1903 reprint of the original 1870 edition. Deistic in tone, the book would have pleased him mightily if he had read it when it was first published. Now, in his old age, he observed that the book's copyright date showed that it was "written in the carboniferous period,—a time where grown-up children were still trying to mix facts and fiction: geology and theology."† On page 160, where Winchell writes, "The far-seeing Planner of the universe stored the carboniferous fuel in the repositories where it could never perish, and where it could await the uses of the coming race of man," Clemens responded, "And man was on earth 200,000 years before God remembered whom it was He built the coal for."† And where Winchell describes the world as an Eden whose pro-prietor "has left here the evidences of his thoughtfulness and expec-tation of a wearied visitor," the disenchanted old reader countered, "To make the similitude complete, conceal a death-trap here & there; a cobra or two; a tiger; a hidden well to break your neck in; & a multitude of cunningly-devised diseases & undeserved miseries."† [40]

Samuel Clemens appears to have embraced the implications of the new science with a vengeance; but curiously, the more he gave in to those implications, the more he returned in his musings and story-telling to the subject of Eden and Adam and Eve. He is not generally thought of as troubled by the popular debate about the origin of man, perhaps because he did not publicly join in it and because, as an iconoclast and an admirer of Robert Ingersoll, he would be ex-pected to be on the side of evolution. But evidence can be assembled to indicate that at *one* level of his thinking, at any rate, he was

39. Paine (ed.), *Mark Twain's Notebook*, 255–56, 288.
40. Clemens' copy of Winchell's book is in the Mark Twain Papers.

classically troubled, even in his old age, over the choice between Genesis and Darwin.

Clemens' introduction to Darwin came through *The Descent of Man*, a book he said "startled the world." He read it very shortly after its publication in 1871.[41] In his copy, as in all of the books he responded to, there are many underlinings and marginalia. Clemens' marginal conversations with his authors are always fun to read; they are personal and often polemic or sarcastic. Curiously, he approached Darwin, whose ideas were to trouble him for decades, as a respectful and diligent scholar. For example, in Chapter 1, "The Evidence of the Descent of Man from Some Lower Form," he underlined thirty-nine technical words and wrote their definitions in the margin. The words range in difficulty from *arboreal*, which Clemens defined as "forest," to *supra-condyloid foramen*, alongside which he wrote, "soft end of a bone 2 perforation." Almost all the other marginalia are substantiating illustrations for the points Darwin made. Where, for example, Darwin discussed the intellectual faculties of animals, Clemens wrote: "War horses learn the bugle notes. Fire horses rush at the fire alarm. That is educated excitement and interest, and imagination, and memory."† And he responded to Darwin's section on the sociability of animals with, "Sheep eat with their heads all turned the same way on the hillside—cows, mostly, too."†[42] That latter observation, interestingly, was to stick in his mind and reappear in both *Huckleberry Finn* and *What Is Man?*.

The deferential tone of these marginalia is in keeping with Clemens' several subsequent expressions of admiration for Darwin as man and scientist; for example, Darwin was "that great mind laboring for the whole human race."[43] Nevertheless, Clemens found it hard to digest Darwinian ideas, and his reactions to them over the next four decades ranged from flippancy through sober uneasiness to resigned acceptance.

Whatever he had learned from reading *Descent of Man* is hardly evident in his allusion to "Darwinians" made shortly thereafter in *Roughing It*; nor does the respectful tone of the marginalia reemerge:

41. Paine (ed.), *Mark Twain's Autobiography*, I, 146. Paine says *The Descent of Man* was part of Clemens' "earlier reading." *Mark Twain: A Biography*, III, 1540. Evidence from a notation in the book puts the date as late November or early December, 1871.

42. Clemens' copy of the two-volume edition of Charles Darwin, *The Descent of Man in Relation to Sex* (New York, 1871), is in the Mark Twain Papers. Clemens' markings appear only in the first four chapters.

43. Albert Bigelow Paine (ed.), *Mark Twain's Speeches* (New York, 1923), 337–38.

"The Bushmen and our Goshoots are manifestly descended from the self-same gorilla, or kangaroo, or Norway rat, whichever animal-Adam the Darwinians trace them to."[44] And in a London speech in 1872, he used the man-from-monkey controversy as a way of getting a laugh: "I visit the mortuary effigies of noble old Henry VIII, and Judge Jeffreys, and the preserved gorilla, and try to make up my mind which of my ancestors I admire the most."[45] In 1875 he repeated his distrust of "those ponderous scientific people" who "prove" what happened in the remote past on the basis of recent records: Given certain statistics of the Mississippi's diminishing in length, "[g]eology never had such a chance, nor such exact data to argue from: Nor 'development of species,' either! Glacial epochs are great things, but they are vague—vague."[46] In 1881 he could confide to his notebook: "Geology. Paleontology. destroyed Genesis."[47] But two years later he had a dazzling idea for saving Adam from extinction: "Turn Statue of Liberty Enlightening the World into Adam."[48]

Clemens' writing about two projects, one real and one imagined, for erecting a monument to Adam provides the richest evidence of his anguished involvement in the conflict between Genesis and evolution. The first is "A Monument to Adam," which he wrote in 1905 about an 1879 enterprise. It tells how leading citizens of Elmira, New York, planned, with Clemens' dubious help, to raise a monument to Adam. His ambivalence about the project, even twenty-six years later, can only be described as symmetrical: He was genuinely attracted to the idea of preserving Adam's memory, since "Mr. Darwin had left Adam out altogether"; he was also on the side of those enlightened citizens who would see the monument as a joke. He claimed that he was "jesting" when he proposed the idea to Thomas K. Beecher and that the monument would be an "insane oddity." But his objection to the monument was that Adam's name "would outlast the hills and the rocks without any such help." Nevertheless, he himself framed the "petition to Congress begging the government to build the monument, as a testimony of the Great Republic's

44. Samuel Clemens [Mark Twain], *Roughing It*, ed. Franklin R. Rogers and Paul Baender (Berkeley, 1972), 145, Vol. II of the Works of Mark Twain.

45. Paine (ed.), *Mark Twain's Speeches*, 38.

46. Clemens, *Life on the Mississippi*, 151.

47. Frederick Anderson, Lin Salamo, and Bernard L. Stein (eds.), *Mark Twain's Notebooks and Journals* (3 vols. completed; Berkeley, 1975), II, 417.

48. Browning, Frank, and Salamo (eds.), *Mark Twain's Notebooks and Journals*, III, 13.

gratitude to the Father of the Human Race and as a token of her loyalty to him in this dark day of his humiliation when his older children were doubting him and deserting him"; and it did seem to him "that this petition ought to be presented," even though in 1905 "it would be widely and feelingly abused and ridiculed and cursed." But in spite of that abuse, "[w]e ought to have carried out our monument scheme; we could have managed it without any great difficulty, and Elmira would now be the most celebrated town in the universe."[49]

In that same year of 1905 he began a novel, "The Refuge of the Derelicts," around the idea of a monument to Adam; but although he completed 181 typescript pages, he neither stuck to the subject nor finished the novel. The story concerns George, a poet and portrait painter, age twenty-six, who goes to Anchor Watch, home of Admiral Stormfield, now eighty and retired, to sell Stormfield on the idea of supporting the monument project. Thereafter, the narrative rambles, and the monument is only occasionally referred to. One of the references, however, in the words of Stormfield, is as clear a statement as any in existence of Clemens' nostalgia for the Adam myth in the face of the destructive scientific evidence that he could not deny:

Well, I have thought these things all over, and my sympathies are with Adam. Adam was like *us,* and so he seems near to us, and dear. He is kin, blood kin, and my heart goes out to him in affection. But I don't feel that way about that [primal] germ. The germ is too far away—and not only that, but such a wilderness of reptiles between. You can't skip the reptiles and set your love on the germ; no, if they are ancestors, it is your duty to include them and love them. Well, you can't do that. You would come up against the dinosaur and your affections would cool off. You couldn't love a dinosaur the way you would another relative. There would always be a gap. Nothing could ever bridge it. Why, it gives a person the dry gripes just to look at him!

Very well, then, where do we arrive? Where do we arrive with our respect, our homage, our filial affection? At Adam! At Adam, every time. We can't build a monument to a germ, but we can build one to Adam, who is in the way to turn into myth in fifty years and be entirely forgotten in two hundred.[50]

49. Samuel Clemens [Mark Twain], *The $30,000 Bequest and Other Stories,* Author's National Edition: The Writings of Mark Twain (25 vols.; New York, 1907–18), XXIV, 234–36.

50. John S. Tuckey (ed.), *Mark Twain's Fables of Man* (Berkeley, 1972), 221.

Stormfield's peroration on Adam is preceded by a burlesque on the process of evolution: The primal germ develops into fleas, flies, bugs, and fish; the "whole lot" is crossed to produce a reptile, which proliferates into lizards, spiders, toads, alligators, and congressmen; man is finally generated through the union of the Missing Link and a mermaid.[51]

Through burlesque, Clemens could fend off claims against Adam's existence. He understood Darwinism and worked its corollaries into the fabric of his best books; nevertheless, from first to last, he needed to think in terms of the first man. Two of the earliest things he wrote, when he was sixteen and seventeen, "Blabbing Government Secrets" and "Oh, She Has a Red Head," referred to Adam; the latter was signed "A Son of Adam." Much of his major work concerns the confrontation of an innocent with the soiled world. In his greatest book he caused Huckleberry Finn to be reborn in the Eden of Jackson's Island, where he was lonesome until he was provided with a partner, where the wild animals were tame, and where a snake brought the first trouble. In Clemens' old age, when his quarrel with God reached its strident peak and when his contempt for believers in the old faith was most bitingly expressed, he paradoxically returned more and more often to Genesis for his themes, as in "That Day in Eden," "Eve Speaks," "Adam's Soliloquy," "Eve's Diary," and "Adam's Diary."

In these late fantasies there is a playful attempt to reconcile the apprehensions of science and myth. In "Eve's Diary," for example, Eve is the first scientist; she feels "exactly like an experiment," understands her new world through empirical reasoning, discovers fire, and has a brontosaurus for a pet. But generally science and the Genesis myth ran on separate tracks in his mind, the latter mostly underground and therefore unperceived. What has been shown to the world of his last years is the face of a curmudgeonly agnostic who was rather well satisfied to have put his religious superstition behind him. His biographer's record of Clemens' musings on A. D. White's *A History of the Warfare of Science with Theology* is a beautiful example of Clemens' cultivated pose:

That is an amusing book of White's. When you read it you see how those old theologians never reasoned at all. White tells of an old bishop who figured out that God created the world in an instant on a certain day in October exactly so many years before Christ, and proved it. And I knew a preacher

51. *Ibid.*, 220–21.

myself once who declared that the fossils in the rocks proved nothing as to the age of the world. He said that God could create the rocks with those fossils in them for ornaments if He wanted to. Why, it takes twenty years to build a little island in the Mississippi River, and that man actually believed that God created the world and all that's in it in six days.[52]

Those words were uttered during the last year of his life, but they were not his last on the "warfare of science with theology." Published a few weeks before his death was his "Turning Point of My Life," in which he declared that "the scene of the real turning point of my life (and yours) was the Garden of Eden."[53]

52. Paine, *Mark Twain: A Biography*, III, 1506–1507.
53. Clemens, *What Is Man? and Other Philosophical Writings*, 463.

# PART II

# Mark Twain: Becoming Modern

# CHAPTER 3

# A Bewilderment of Beginnings

*[The narrator of* Roughing It] *is systematically and progressively initiated into a world of unreliable illusions.*
—Forrest G. Robinson, "Seeing the Elephant"

*The most outrageous lies that can be invented will find believers if a man only tells them with all his might.*
—Mark Twain on showmanship at age thirty-one

WHAT MIGHT BE CALLED the Darwinian master idea changed the course and character of American literature. That master idea was derived from the sciences that prepared the way for Darwin, from Darwin's method of assembling information and his consequent vision of nature's processes, and from the words of those who explained Darwin's theories and extended them to every realm of human thought and action. It said that nature (of which man is part) is all, that one comes to understand the world through the patient observation of nature's restless details, and that myths, ideals, and traditional assumptions are shortcuts to error. It said that the visible world is neither the imprint of an Ideal nor the finished creation of a divine personality. Darwin's achievement was to unfix nature, to disconnect it from absolutes and ideals, and to turn public attention from nature's so-called laws to its processes.

In response to the master idea, writers took everyday reality as their subject and, in so doing, created a literature fundamentally different from the old one. Overarching the pre-Darwinian literary landscape in America from, say, 1836, the date of Emerson's "Nature," to around 1870 is a supernatural presence, perceived, for example, by Emerson as the Oversoul, by Poe as Supernal Beauty, by Melville as the "clear spirit" of the corposants, and by Whitman as "thou transcendent." Thereafter that presence is gone. Relieved of supernaturalism, writers of the period 1870 to 1910, of whom Howells, James, Crane, and Dreiser were leading lights, turned to "realism" and "naturalism." Like scientists, they recorded their characters' environments, activities, and inner lives objectively and in detail. They presented those characters as biological and social organisms living in and responsive to authentic milieus. Their characters' life histories could display endless and interesting variations, but always within the strictly held limits of natural possibility. All this they did in awareness of their new role as writers in the scientific dispensation.

Not every writer, of course, reacted in precisely the same way to the Darwinian view of reality. Those, like Howells, who grew up in the old time, would, though dedicated to realism, be nostalgic for the old idealisms. Those born after the Civil War, and consequently raised in a spiritually arid time, tended by reaction to become, in Edwin Cady's phrase, neo-idealistic.[1] Norris, Dreiser, and London would seek in inchoate ways to renew the cosmic connection and to discover in the evolutionary process a new teleology. Only Crane appeared resigned to living in a soulless universe. Nevertheless, all of them have been studied for the self-conscious way they adapted manner and matter to the demands of the master idea.

Of the major writers of his period, Mark Twain is least represented as having taken instruction from the new scientific philosophy. Not only has his interest in science been given scant treatment, but doubts about his ability to formulate a literary philosophy have been expressed. "He must not," wrote Bernard DeVoto in an early study, "be required to base his fiction on a system of philosophy"; and Robert Wiggins echoed him some thirty years later: "Twain could not see the logical relation between the technique of realism and a body of philosophical principles."[2]

These two scholars have a point, if not a commanding one. Mark Twain was anything but doctrinaire in the area of literary theory. Nowadays often lumped with the realists, he never called himself a realist or even used the term *realism*. His excursions into literary theory are incidental and modest. He gave good tips on how to tell a story, but he was all diffidence in explaining his own process of writing. He was simply an "amanuensis" to his muse; he could write only when his "tank" was full; he often started a story with little sense of how it would come out, hoping somehow to find the "right form" for it; he took little credit for his novelistic ideas, since they were the result of "unconscious cerebration."[3]

1. Edwin Cady, *The Light of Common Day* (Bloomington, Ind., 1971), 45.
2. Bernard DeVoto, *Mark Twain's America* (Boston, 1932), 296; Robert Wiggins, *Mark Twain: Jackleg Novelist* (Seattle, 1964), 84.
3. Bernard DeVoto (ed.), *Mark Twain in Eruption* (New York, 1940), 196–99.

But Mark Twain cannot be called unphilosophical. "He is as much of a Philosopher as anything, I think," wrote his daughter Susan when she was fourteen; and Howells, in remembering his friend, declared, "It is in vain that I try to give a notion of the intensity with which he pierced to the heart of life, and the breadth of vision with which he compassed the whole world, and tried for the reason of things, and then left trying."[4] When one thinks of his numerous excursions into the moral and cosmological mysteries, he appears, along with Melville, as one of our most questing novelists.

Nor can Mark Twain be called unsophisticated. In spite of his cultivating the pose of the American innocent, he was in actuality a cosmopolite. He was familiar with distinguished people on two continents and entertained many of them in his well-staffed and sumptuously appointed Hartford house. He crossed the Atlantic twenty-five times, vacationed in Bermuda, and lived in Europe for more than a decade. He read in three languages.

We have only begun to appreciate the range and rigor of his reading since the publication, in 1980, of Alan Gribben's heroic work, *Mark Twain's Library: A Reconstruction*. Evidence therein—the description of the thousands of books and other items that Mark Twain read, his haunting of libraries, his continual acquisition of new books and his subscription to numerous magazines, his constant references to his latest reading—proves that he required the daily nourishment of the printed word. Nor was his reading "light" as a rule, or crankily limited to a few favorite subjects. It was catholic enough in both subject and period to make him well acquainted not only with the tradition of literature, which he would magnify, but with the universe of ideas. Of the books and articles he read, 160 are on science.

He was, moreover, open to new ideas in science, no matter how disturbing. From youth, when he read astronomies, to old age, when, for example, he meditated on the meaning of the Curies' discovery of radium, he sought out and absorbed what was new and important. (Concerning radium, the first known of the elements producing energy through atomic fission, he wrote an ominous fable in which he speculated that if atomic power were unleashed, "the world would vanish away in a flash of flame and a puff of

4. Edith Colgate Salsbury (ed.), *Susy and Mark Twain* (New York, 1965), 222; William Dean Howells, *My Mark Twain* (New York, 1910), 100.

smoke, and the remnants of the extinguished moon would sift down through space a mere snow-shower of gray ashes!")[5]

Mark Twain did not lack for ideas. What he lacked was training in handling them. Almost without formal education, he was never taught the academic strategies of using abstract terminology, of citing sources, or of being consistent. In dealing with matters however abstruse, he was personal, colloquial, and concrete. His "vernacular style," to use Henry Nash Smith's phrase, "limited the power of Mark Twain . . . to deal with abstract thought" (however much it contributed to the power of *Huckleberry Finn*) and gave a primitive cast to his thinking.[6] The blithe way he had of ignoring the possible source of the ideas he wrestled with (he confessed to being an unconscious plagiarist) makes it sound, as Howells remarked, "as if he were the first man who was ever up against the proposition in hand."[7]

One reason, then, that little attention has been paid to Mark Twain's response as a writer to the new era of science is that his ideas on the subject are not on scholarly display. He did not abstract and organize them for us. He left them as they dropped from his pen— as musings, metaphors, and parables, sometimes, even, as cries of indignation or pain.

Indeed, he often hid their development from view—his own, perhaps, as well as ours. A scholar who wishes to trace the line of Mark Twain's thought from first to last can be disconcerted by the sudden emergence in that line of new attitudes. Such attitudes appear to have precipitated out of what one takes to be long foregrounds of private or perhaps unconscious rumination. Mark Twain could receive ideas that did not fit into his current thinking, silently store them up for years or decades, and suddenly—when he was ready for them or when to his surprise they surfaced—express them in a heartfelt and cogent way. A precipitated attitude might thereafter dominate his thinking, but not necessarily. What mattered was that once he had been pushed to express a new (and, more often than not, disenchanted) attitude, it was not so difficult for him to express it again.

5. Samuel Clemens [Mark Twain], "Sold to Satan," in *Europe and Elsewhere*, ed. Albert Bigelow Paine (New York, 1923), 333.

6. Samuel Clemens [Mark Twain], *Adventures of Huckleberry Finn*, ed. Henry Nash Smith (Boston, 1958), xxviii.

7. Howells, "Mark Twain: An Enquiry," *My Mark Twain*, 178.

A major precipitation of attitude, upon his losing, in 1891, the last shred of his deistic faith and admitting the inanity of nature, was discussed in Chapter 2. The master precipitation (and the culmination of a series of lesser ones) was his writing the first draft of *What Is Man?* in 1898. The main ideas for it came from three books he had read between 1869 and 1874—Holmes's *Autocrat of the Breakfast Table*, Darwin's *Descent of Man*, and Lecky's *History of European Morals*—when determinism was foreign to his thinking. He harbored the ideas for some twenty-five years; then they surfaced in his philosophical essay, some of them in their original phraseology.[8]

This and other of his precipitations of attitude will be discussed in later chapters; but as a kind of index to the stages of his intellectual pilgrimage, I will mention the important ones here:

1865 "Story of the Bad Little Boy." A vengeful destruction of the myth that Providence punishes the wicked.

1875 The paragraph in Chapter 9 of *Life on the Mississippi* beginning "It turned out to be true." A stunning descent from a mythical and deistic view of nature to a Darwinian view.

1879 "Legend of the 'Spectacular Ruin,'" in Chapter 17 of *A Tramp Abroad*. A rejection of the legendary past and a dedication to the values of modern science, technology, and business enterprise.

1883 The Bricksville-Boggs-Sherburn episode, Chapters 21 and 22 of *Huckleberry Finn*. An unprecedented expression of disgust with the bestiality, cruelty, and cowardice in human nature.

1883 Buck's query "Why, where was you raised?" in Chapter 18 of *Huckleberry Finn* and the soliloquy in Chapter 34, where Huck expresses his bewilderment that Tom, who is "respectable and well brung up," could stoop to stealing Jim out of slavery. His first statements, though veiled, of the pessimistic side of the idea that training is everything.

1887 The paragraph in Chapter 18 of *A Connecticut Yankee* beginning "Oh, it was no use to waste sense on her. Training—training is everything; training is all there is *to* a person." His first explicit statement of what will become the text for *What Is Man?*.

Another reason that Mark Twain's response as a writer to modern science has not been extensively studied is that it is mixed up with so many other responses, several of which preceded his response to

8. Sherwood Cummings, "*What Is Man?*: The Scientific Sources," *Essays on Determinism in American Literature*, Kent Studies in English, I (Kent, Ohio, 1964), 108–16.

science. There is his indoctrination in the old-time religion. Its consequences in his writing—his moralism, his being dogged by conscience, his using biblical rhythms in his prose and biblical themes and concepts in his stories—have been noted by scholars. Then his indoctrination into deism through Paine's *Age of Reason* imbued him with the idea of system. Evidences of cosmic system could inspire him to write exalted prose. The apparent breakdown of system induced his satire. His belief in system was the foundation of his determinism; and his craving for system, once he became convinced that God's plan excluded concern for mankind, led him in his old age to create fantastic universes of his own.

Two other responses complicated his later response to science. They did so not only because they were early but because they were antithetical to realism—that is, to writing objectively about the customary world. The first of them was his satirical response to the absurdity of his Nevada experience.

As a young man, Samuel Clemens was remarkably old-fashioned. By the time he was twenty-two (and had read *Age of Reason*) in 1858 he had progressed philosophically about as far as Benjamin Franklin had at the same age in 1728. Both he and Franklin had been raised in Christian orthodoxy, both read the Bible and *Pilgrim's Progress* as boys, and both rebelliously embraced deism as young men. They were similar too in their practical philosophies. Both improved on their limited schooling through learning the literate trade of printing and by setting up programs of self-education. Although Sam did not try, as Ben Franklin did, to perfect himself in the practice of thirteen virtues, he was a moral and conscientious young man. Before leaving home at seventeen, he promised his mother not to "throw a card or drink a drop of liquor," and later he asked his sister to "[t]ell Ma that my promises are faithfully kept."[9]

As an apprentice pilot on the Mississippi at age twenty-one, Clemens took up a career less specifically like Franklin's but still in the tradition of personal enterprise and rigorous self-discipline. Learning the river was "an incredible labor . . . compared with which the efforts needed to acquire the degree of Doctor of Philosophy at a University are as light as a summer course of modern novels."[10] His apprenticeship completed, he was for two years

9. Albert Bigelow Paine (ed.), *Mark Twain's Letters* (2 vols.; New York, 1917), I, 22.
10. Samuel E. Moffett, "Mark Twain: A Biographical Sketch," in Samuel Clemens [Mark Twain], *Literary Essays*, Author's National Edition: The Writings of Mark Twain (25 vols.; New York, 1907–18), XXII, 319.

(1859–1861) a pilot—one of the kings of the river. His known behavior during that period is what one would expect from a young man properly reared and well circumstanced. He enjoyed the affluence and prestige of his profession, was regardful of his mother and sister, was a beau to belles but seducer of none, was a reader of books and abstainer from serious vices. The best evidence of his philosophy then (besides the fact that he became a Mason early in 1861) is a worn clipping entitled "How to Take Life" preserved in the pages of his current notebook. "Take it," the clipping reads, "as it is—an earnest, vital, and important affair." And it concludes, "The miracle, or the power that elevates the few, is to be found in their industry, application, and perseverance under the promptings of a brave, determined spirit."[11]

In Clemens' philosophy, as in Franklin's, there were promises. Indoctrinated in the Puritan ethic and later in the deistic gospel of an orderly cosmos, Clemens would expect to be rewarded for his virtue and industry. And rewarded he was! Having realized his fondest boyhood dream in becoming a pilot—having been paid off so handsomely for his hard work—he must have been sure that he lived in a moral universe.

What happened to him next must surely have shaken that faith. The Civil War not only ended his piloting career but found him unprepared to respond to it. Healthy, single, and twenty-five, he would be under some pressure to take a combatant role. But not much concerned with the political issues of the war and essentially uncommitted to either side, he was briefly a volunteer in the Confederate militia and then a deserter. What could he do after skedaddling? Like Huck Finn, who also found himself at odds with "civilization," he lit out for the Territory, specifically the Nevada Territory, where for a year he prospected for silver and for two more worked as reporter on the Virginia City *Territorial Enterprise*. Uprooted from a verdant valley, deprived of a prestigious profession earned through discipline and expertise, a runaway from military duty, he found himself a member of an unshapely community newly populated by silver-feverish prospectors, miners, promoters, and hell raisers. In migrating from the Mississippi Valley to Nevada, he had moved from homeland to a natural and moral wilderness, from an environment that had nurtured him in a classic American philosophy to one that moved him to mockery.

11. Albert Bigelow Paine, *Mark Twain: A Biography* (3 vols.; New York, 1912), I, 154–55.

We might expect that as reporter for the *Enterprise*, Mark Twain would write in the classical vein. His current religion was deism, based on Newtonian science. That science had regulated the language, tone, and philosophy of eighteenth-century English literature; had made elegance, order, and clarity the standards of expression; had, in short, given English writers their Age of Reason. It can be argued that Twain's newly minted style *was* more classical than modern. Certainly, his impeccable grammar and syntax and his rich and precisely managed vocabulary were as different as possible from the calculated illiteracies of an Artemus Ward or Josh Billings. He was, moreover, fond of using rhetorical devices more in evidence in the eighteenth century than in his own—parallelism, antithesis, and numerous qualifiers. In an early letter to the *Enterprise*, for example, concerning an unintelligible court order, he delivered himself of these balanced periods: "If it is a charge, I do not make it; if it is an insinuation, I do not endorse it; if its expressionless exterior conceals a slur, I do not father it." A year later, he splendidly listed the characteristics of schoolboy composition as

the cutting to the bone of the subject with the very first gash, without any preliminary foolishness in the way of a gorgeous introductory; the inevitable and persevering tautology; the brief, monosyllabic sentences (beginning, as a very general thing, with the pronoun "I"); the penchant for presenting rigid, uncompromising facts for the consideration of the hearer, rather than ornamental fancies; the dependency for the success of the composition upon its general merits, without tacking artificial aids to the end of it, in the shape of deductions or conclusions.

This formal command of language, this balanced rhetoric, is classical and surely reflects Mark Twain's responsiveness to the deistic ideal of order and regularity, but the subject and tone of much of his Nevada writing are quite the opposite. His droll exaggerations and understatements, his burlesques and hoaxes, his hating to have "to do with figures, measurements and solid facts"[12] when such had been the essence of his previous profession, his adversarial stances and his penchant for destroying personalities, whether of friends or foes, are not only unclassical; they smack of derangement. His most straightforward reporting for the *Enterprise* was likely to be fractious, and his hoaxes were outrageous. Readers were either amused or incensed by his drolleries. They were taken in by his fictitious report about a settler who cut off his wife's right hand, split her head

12. Henry Nash Smith, *Mark Twain of the Enterprise* (Berkeley, 1957), 35, 136, 17.

open, killed six of his offspring, and slashed his own throat; but they would hardly see it, as we may now—through the author's symbolic mutilations of the organs of writing, thinking, and speech—as symptomatic of his repressed anxiety and anger.[13] Nor would they be likely to notice passages such as "unnatural and diabolical scrawl, devoid of form, regularity or meaning" and "At this point order and regularity cease—the dancers get excited—the musicians become insane—turmoil and confusion ensue—chaos comes again,"[14] in which his phraseology epitomizes the tension between the deistic order he hoped for and the chaos that seemed to prevail. His character changed: "[D]eprived of home influences," he confessed that his conduct could not recommend him "to the respectful regard of a high eastern civilization."[15] He took up serious drinking; and more seriously, he apparently abandoned his earlier program of study and reading.

His resentment over the broken promises of his philosophy became explicit in 1865: After three unprosperous years in Nevada and during an even worse period in and around San Francisco (toward the end of which he came close to blowing out his brains), he wrote a bitter fable for the *Californian*, with the ironic title "The Christmas Fireside."[16] Now known as "Story of the Bad Little Boy," it mocks the myth that heaven punishes the unrighteous. No matter how bad Jim in the fable was, "everything turned out differently with him from the way it does to bad Jameses in the books."[17] Wicked as hell, he prospered lavishly; and even though he brained his family with an axe, he thereafter became a respected member of the legislature. Thus, at the nadir of his career and seeking revenge on a mendacious creed, Mark Twain experienced a major precipitation of attitude.

Twain's western experience led him to write in a mocking way and to think nihilistic thoughts. His years in Nevada and California had, as Forrest G. Robinson has observed, amounted to "an innocence shattering practical joke from which [he] never recovered."[18]

---

13. Ivan Benson, *Mark Twain's Western Years* (Stanford, 1938), 176–77.

14. Smith, *Mark Twain of the Enterprise*, 37, 40.

15. Dixon Wecter (ed.), *The Love Letters of Mark Twain* (New York, 1949), 37.

16. Justin Kaplan, *Mr. Clemens and Mark Twain* (New York, 1966), 15.

17. Samuel Clemens [Mark Twain], *Sketches New and Old*, Author's National Edition: The Writings of Mark Twain (25 vols.; New York, 1907–18), XIX, 55.

18. Forrest G. Robinson, " 'Seeing the Elephant': Some Perspectives on Mark Twain's *Roughing It*," *American Studies*, XXI (Fall, 1980), 53.

It is true that his bitter mood did not outlast the circumstances that inspired it and that his deism reasserted itself. When, in the spring of 1866, he was given a job that delighted him—correspondent to the Sacramento *Union* from the Sandwich Islands—he regained his cheerfulness and matter-of-factness. His letters from the islands are full of health and high spirits and of facts, statistics, and detailed descriptions. Upon returning briefly to Missouri, in 1867, he asked to be reinstated in his Masonic lodge in St. Louis. Nevertheless, he would in later years be liable now and then to the nihilistic impulse he first experienced in the West. In the grip of that impulse, he could mock (as in the destructive ending of *A Connecticut Yankee*) what in his writing he himself had bravely built.

The other of Mark Twain's early responses that complicated his response to science was his fascination with the way a showman can create something out of nothing. It arose out of his own experiences on the lecture platform and his witnessing the way that spellbinding performers could transform their audiences.

As New York correspondent for the *Alta California*, in 1867, Mark Twain reported on a stage extravaganza called "The Black Crook," a P. T. Barnum spectacle, the Imperial Japanese Jugglers, Italian actress Adelaide Ristori, a speech by feminist Anna Dickinson, and the preaching of Henry Ward Beecher and Edwin Hubble Chapin. He studied what it was about a performance that captivated an audience.

Substance, he concluded, was of little account. "The scenery and the legs are everything," was his judgment on "The Black Crook"; and he opined that Ristori's New York stage triumphs, all the more astounding since she spoke only in Italian, were wholly attributable to newspaper publicity. As to the worthiness of Anna Dickinson's argument that women be permitted to "earn their bread elsewhere than in kitchens and factories," he had nothing to say. He had eyes and ears only for her seductive delivery: "Her prose poetry charms, her eloquence thrills, her pathos often moves to tears." Neither her subject nor her logic mattered: "Her vim, her energy, her determined look, her tremendous earnestness, would compel the respect and the attention of an audience, even if she spoke in Chinese—would convince a third of them, too, even though she used arguments that would not stand analysis." In his enraptured treatment of Beecher's sermon, he dwelt on Beecher's "rich, resonant voice" and "distinct enunciation," on his "felicitous similes and metaphors," on his "rockets of poetry" and "mines of eloquence," but failed to mention the text.[19]

He was driving toward a philosophy of showmanship and arrived at it while pondering the galvanic preaching of Edwin Hubble Chapin. Chapin could "just seize a congregation"; it was as if there were "an invisible wire leading from every auditor's soul straight to a battery hidden away somewhere in that preacher's head." What was it about Chapin's delivery, Mark Twain mused, that "chained" his listeners? He concluded: "[I]t must be Mr. Chapin's strong, deep, unmistakable earnestness. There is nothing like that to convince people. Nobody can have confidence in cold, monotonous, inanimate utterances, though they were teeming with truth and wisdom. Manner is everything in these cases—matter is nothing. The most outrageous lies that can be invented will find believers if a man only tells them with all his might."[20]

*Manner is everything; matter is nothing.* As risky as that idea is, both philosophically and artistically, Mark Twain was to put it into literary practice more than a few times. It was a principle germinated by his reaction to the absurdity of his western years and abetted by his experience in show business. From his first lecture appearance, in San Francisco in 1866, to his last, in Capetown thirty years later, his motive for stepping onto the platform was not to deliver a truth but to attract paying customers, and to that end he put on a performance. He read and recited, told funny stories and scary ones, all with skill and deliberation. His lecturing was a calculated art: "[T]he same old practising on audiences still goes on," he wrote Livy while on tour in 1871, "the same old feeling of pulses & altering manner & matter to suit the symptoms."[21] Or again, "The other night in Meriden I struck upon an entirely new manner of telling a favorite anecdote of mine—and now, without altering a single word it becomes so absurd that I have to laugh myself."[22] In 1885 he praised one of Howells' stage readings for its "simplicity, sincerity, & absence of artificiality." "Sincerity *is* a great & valuable thing in front of an audience," he continued, and wondered how Howells had

19. Franklin Walker and G. Ezra Dane (eds.), *Mark Twain's Travels with Mr. Brown* (New York, 1940), 85, 173–74, 104–106, 93–94.

20. *Ibid.*, 174–75.

21. Wecter (ed.), *The Love Letters of Mark Twain*, 162.

22. Clara Clemens, *My Father, Mark Twain* (New York, 1931), 46.

learned to project it. "Observation & thought I guess. And practice at the Tavern Club?—yes; & that was the best teaching of all."[23] "Sincerity" here—something that can be improved through practice, and a valuable thing before an audience—is drawn from the performer's lexicon. Its meaning has little to do with purity of feeling and much to do with technique and effect.

Because he was a showman as well as a writer, and also because he was gifted with a powerful imagination, Mark Twain was led deeply into the problem of which is more real—things as they are or things as they are invented and projected. On stage he could use a set of techniques to create in his audience emotions that, however ephemeral, were vivid and real. As novelist he could use his imagination and a different set of techniques to create a world that used to be or might have been or never was. His powers of enchantment complicated his view of reality.

His imagination was beyond compare when it worked with things as they were or might have been; but when the spellbinding urge struck him, when he exalted manner, when he gave his story over to characters whose devotion to "style" exempted them from sympathy and common sense—such as Tom Sawyer in the last chapters of *Huckleberry Finn* or the Connecticut Yankee who was supposed to train King Arthur's people in nineteenth-century rationality but who instead cowed them with fireworks and mumbo jumbo—his meanings were subject to confusion. A daydream he entertained in his old age makes explicit a hankering he may well have felt many times before—the hankering to be rid of the need to reflect reality in his writing, the need to write about a world that had already been created. He makes Satan in "The Chronicle of Young Satan" to be the perfect creator. Satan is not in the least constrained by the way things are. His mind, he explains, simply "creates. Do you get the force of that? Creates anything it desires—and in a moment. Creates without materials; creates fluids, solids, colors—anything, everything—out of the airy nothing which is called Thought."[24] Such is the wistful climax of the pondering begun when, as a young journalist, Mark Twain speculated that in the spellbinder's art "matter is nothing."

23. Henry Nash Smith and William M. Gibson (eds.), *Mark Twain–Howells Letters* (2 vols.; Cambridge, Mass., 1960), II, 527.

24. William M. Gibson (ed.), *Mark Twain's Mysterious Stranger Manuscripts* (Berkeley, 1969), 114.

Although I have pointed to places in a few novels that are, it seems to me, marred by Twain's impulses to mock and destroy or to create out of nothing, I do not wish to be mistaken as saying that the more realistic a work is, the better it is. The tensions among Mark Twain's amazingly strong and numerous impulses give his writings not only a unique flavor and interest but the right to be taken as major documents of their time. The point I am making is that those contrary impulses do exist and that they will complicate our attempt to single out his writer's response to science.

# CHAPTER 4

# The Science of Piloting

*Whosoever has done me the courtesy to read my chapters which have preceded this may possibly wonder that I deal so minutely with piloting as a science.*

—*Life on the Mississippi*, Chapter 10

THERE IS SOMETHING QUAINT and touching about cub pilot Clemens' shock at discovering *The Age of Reason* at the very moment when Darwin's *Origin of Species* was being prepared for publication. When other readers were being served their first course of Darwin, Clemens would be trying to digest Newton via Paine. Laggard that he was, he would need to be more than ordinarily hustled to make the crossing of the great philosophical divide.

Mark Twain was drawn into the Darwinian view because as a deist he was taught to respect science. His progress from 1867, when he migrated to the East Coast, to 1875 was gradual and not self-conscious—that is, he seems not to have formalized a debate in his mind between the older views of reality and the new. Nevertheless, that progress came to a startling climax in 1875. Three books that he read certainly hastened the transition, though there must have been subtler influences as well.

As touchstones for testing Mark Twain's philosophy early in this 1867-to-1875 period, two passages from his work will be offered here. The first is his remarkable meditation on the wonders of navigation, composed in January, 1867, toward the end of his voyage from California to New York:

The ship has beautiful charts, compiled by Lieut. Maury, which are crammed with shoals, currents, lights, buoys, soundings, and winds, and calms and storms—black figures for soundings, and bright spots for beacons, and so on, and an interminable tangle, like a spider's web, of red lines denoting the tracks of hundreds of ships whose logs were sent to Maury—everything mapped out so accurately that a man might know what water he had, what current, what beacon he was near, what style of wind he might expect, and from which direction, on any particular day of the year, at any given point on the world's broad surface. "They that go down to the sea in ships see the wonders of the great deep"—but this modern navigation out-wonders any wonder the scriptural writers dreampt of. To see a man stand in the night, when everything looks alike—far out in the midst of a boundless sea—and measure from one star to another and tell to a dot right where the ship is—tell the very spot the little insignificant speck occupies on a vast expanse of land and sea twenty-five thousand miles in circumference! Verily, with his imperial intellect and his deep-searching wisdom, man is almost a God.[1]

The apprehension here, rising out of a listing of a multitude of details and climaxing in an exaltation, is that of a religious experience. Mixed in it are elements of his old-time religion, his deism, and an optimistic humanism. The tone and structure of his meditation are psalmlike; and for added measure, a verse from Psalm 107 is quoted, and another from Psalm 8—"For thou hast made man but little lower than God"—is paraphrased. The thrust of his meditation, however, is to belittle what is ancient and scriptural and to take confidence in what is modern, scientific, and human. Specifically deistic is the reference to measuring "from one star to another" to find one's bearings. God's constellations are dependable. Also deistic is the idea that nature yields meaning to the inquiring intellect. At the heart of deism is the contract between the intelligence of man and the intelligibility of the physical world. Nature follows laws; therefore it can be understood. Mark Twain's faith in those laws and in man's reason is complete. In his moment of deistic beatitude it seems to him that ocean weather can be as reliably predicted as the tides and that man in his ability to read the creation is endowed with an "imperial intellect." In that last sentiment he echoes Tom Paine's declaration that the "choicest gift of God to man [is] the GIFT OF REASON."[2]

The second passage, composed in 1868, is from *The Innocents Abroad*. Visiting the catacombs, with its festoons of bones and skulls, Mark Twain is shocked at a monk's casually illustrating a love story by fingering the bones of the deceased lover. He protests:

There are nerves and muscles in our frames whose functions and whose methods of working it seems a sort of sacrilege to describe by cold physiological names and surgical technicalities, and the monk's talk suggested to me something of this kind. Fancy a surgeon, with his nippers lifting ten-

1. Franklin Walker and G. Ezra Dane (eds.), *Mark Twain's Travels with Mr. Brown* (New York, 1940), 77–78.
2. Harry Hayden Clark (ed.), *Thomas Paine: Representative Selections* (New York, 1944), 256.

dons, muscles, and such things into view, out of the complex machinery of a corpse, and observing, "Now this little nerve quivers—the vibration is imparted to this muscle—from here it is passed to this fibrous substance; here its ingredients are separated by the chemical action of the blood—one part goes to the heart and thrills it with what is popularly termed emotion, another part follows this nerve to the brain and communicates intelligence of a startling character—the third part glides along this passage and touches the spring connected with the fluid receptacles that lie in the rear of the eye. Thus, by this simple and beautiful process, the party is informed that his mother is dead, and he weeps." Horrible![3]

Stated here is a revulsion against cold scientific analysis. Implied is a belief that life to be meaningful must be lived on the warm, familiar, human level.

A declared opponent of anatomizing, Mark Twain was about to begin a transformation that would take half a lifetime. The change would be completed some thirty years later when as the author of *What Is Man?* he would relentlessly analyze the springs of behavior of the "machine" ordinarily called man. Aptly enough, it was a book by a professor of anatomy that began the transformation.

Oliver Wendell Holmes's *The Autocrat of the Breakfast Table* (1858) is not, of course, a textbook on anatomy. Mark Twain chose it in the spring of 1869 as a "courting book,"[4] something first to be read and marked by him and then to be read by Livy, probably because of its lively wit and noble sentiments. But intermixed with the fanciful analogies and romantic rhetoric are ample evidences of Dr. Holmes's professional interest: "The nerves that make us alive to [music] spread out . . . in the most sensitive region of the marrow, just where it is widening to run upwards into the hemispheres."[5] "The hydraulic arrangements for supplying the brain with blood are only second in importance to its own organization" (7). A minister on Sunday "uses up more phosphorous out of his brain than on ordinary days" (156).

3. Samuel Clemens [Mark Twain], *The Innocents Abroad*, Author's National Edition: The Writings of Mark Twain (25 vols.; New York, 1907–18), II, 12.

4. Bradford A. Booth, "Mark Twain's Comments on Holmes's *Autocrat*," *American Literature*, XXI (1950), 456–63.

5. Oliver Wendell Holmes, *The Autocrat of the Breakfast Table* (Boston, 1892), 132, Vol. I of Holmes, *The Works of Oliver Wendell Holmes*, 13 vols. Further references to *The Autocrat* are indicated by parenthetical page numbers in the text.

It would be difficult to invent an influence more seductive than Holmes's book. An enthusiast, a deist, and a scientist, Holmes could be enraptured with the marvels of anatomy and with the elegance of the universal scheme at the same time that he regarded man as a mechanism with little or no will of his own. Mark Twain the deist would surely respond to Holmes's declarations that "[t]he more we study the body and the mind, the more we find both to be governed, not *by*, but *according to* laws, such as we observe in the larger universe" (71), and that from a pebble "an archangel could infer the entire inorganic universe as the simplest of corollaries! A throne of the all-pervading Deity, who has guided its every atom since the rosary of heaven was strung with beaded stars!" (84).

But what do the laws of "the larger universe" amount to when applied to human behavior? They control man just as they control the universe; and just as the cosmos is a kind of machine, so is man. "Physiologists and metaphysicians have had their attention turned a good deal of late to the automatic and involuntary actions of the mind" (134), wrote Holmes; and "the more we observe and study, the wider we find the range of the automatic and instinctive principles in body, mind, and morals, and the narrower the limits of the self-determining conscious movement" (85).

Holmes's analogies for the processes of mind and body are therefore almost always mechanical: "Laughter and tears are meant to turn the wheels of the same machinery of sensibility; one is of wind-power, and the other water-power; that is all" (90). A "hint" coming to the senses can stir "the automatic machinery of association" (78). The mind is an "intellectual mechanism" (130), "mental machinery" (135), or "the wheels of thought" (185); and the "human body is a furnace" (150).

Mark Twain—deist, humanist, foe of analysis, and believer in man's imperial intellect—seems not to have been immediately persuaded by Holmes's anatomizing. But Holmes's mechanistic philosophy was lodged in the recesses of Twain's mind. That philosophy would surface from time to time and finally emerge full panoplied in *What Is Man?*.

Similarly with Charles Darwin's *The Descent of Man:* Large stretches of *What Is Man?* ("Man's Sole Impulse—The Securing of His Own Approval," "The Thinking Process," and "Instinct and Thought") are minutely indebted to Chapters 2 and 3 of Darwin's book, and yet there is little evidence of Darwinism in Twain's thought for some years following his reading of *The Descent of Man* in 1871. But since it is clear that he received Darwin's ideas,[6] and since one of those ideas became a part of his understanding and portrayal of human behavior from *The Prince and the Pauper* on, we might briefly examine it.

It concerns the development and function of conscience. In the Darwinian view conscience is a fact, but moral values are neither absolute nor transcendent. They are evolved out of the interaction between individual impulses and the demands of society. Three factors in human nature make it possible for man to entertain moral values. The first is the sense of satisfaction or dissatisfaction, pleasure or pain, that follows the carrying out of an impulse. The second is man's social instinct; he is capable of feeling dissatisfaction when an otherwise pleasant act displeases other individuals. The third is reflection; a man can remember that a former act met with public disapproval. "Man will then feel dissatisfied with himself, and will resolve with more or less force to act differently for the future. This is conscience; for conscience looks backwards and judges past actions; inducing that kind of dissatisfaction, which if weak we call regret, and if severe remorse."[7]

Conscience thus developed will not lead to a universal sense of right and wrong but will be sharply adapted to the demands of the particular society. A man is "greatly influenced by the wishes, approbation, and blame of his fellow-men" (82). If the values of a particular society are what would generally be called evil, then the members of that society would be conscientious in their wickedness. If men were raised "under precisely the same conditions as hive-bees," unmarried females would regard it "a sacred duty to kill their brothers, and mothers would strive to kill their fertile daughters" (70). Although this is an extreme and hypothetical example, Darwin points out that among primitive tribes, lying and treachery are virtues when practiced on strangers (91), and he notes that "an Indian Thug conscientiously regretted that he had not

6. Besides the numerous parallels between Darwin's statements and passages in *What Is Man?* there is Albert Bigelow Paine's statement that the influence of *The Descent of Man* "was always present" in Mark Twain's thought. *Mark Twain: A Biography* (3 vols.; New York, 1912), III, 1540.

7. Charles Darwin, *The Descent of Man in Relation to Sex* (2 vols.; New York, 1871), I, 87. Further references to *The Descent of Man*, I, are indicated by parenthetical page numbers in the text.

strangled and robbed as many travellers as did his father before him" (90).

All of this objective analysis of human behavior and the resulting moral relativism must have been hard for thirty-six-year-old Clemens to digest. He had had his knocks and had seen his share of human meanness; nevertheless, the moral absolutes of his boyhood religion were not forgotten. He had lately declared himself a Christian and later still had written his first deistic credo. But in three decades he would be pleased to corroborate Darwin. In *What Is Man?* he wrote: "I knew a kind-hearted Kentuckian whose self-approval was lacking—whose conscience was troubling him, to phrase it with exactness—*because he had neglected to kill a certain man*—a man whom he had never seen. The stranger had killed this man's friend in a fight, this man's Kentucky training made it his duty to kill the stranger for it."[8] In the meantime, he had in *Huckleberry Finn* written about the Grangerfords, whose code of honor made them eager to kill Shepherdsons. But in 1871 the idea that man was simply a kind of process obedient to the laws of his nature and to the pressures of his social environment must have been a shock.

W. E. H. Lecky's *History of European Morals* (1869), which Mark Twain read probably in the summer of 1874,[9] need not have shocked him, for it offered him a choice. In Lecky's view, there are two rival moral philosophies: the "intuitive" and the "utilitarian." Members of the intuitive school believe that men have a "natural power" or an innate intuition that tells them the difference between right and wrong and that obliges them to act morally. Members of the utilitarian school believe that man acquires his morals through observation and experience and on the principle that happiness is the highest good. Intuitionists are men of faith and confirm the traditional moral and spiritual values. Utilitarians are men of intellect who question and analyze conventional beliefs.

Lecky was himself an intuitionist; and although he explained the utilitarian position in detail, he made it clear that he disagreed with it. When Twain first read Lecky, he was inclined to be on Lecky's side; but as his "discussion" with Lecky continued for the next thirty years he migrated to the contrary position. The process of his

---

8. Samuel Clemens [Mark Twain], *What Is Man? and Other Philosophical Writings*, ed. Paul Baender (Berkeley, 1973), 141, Vol. XIX of the Works of Mark Twain. Further references to *What Is Man?* are indicated by parenthetical page numbers in the text.

9. Paine, *Mark Twain: A Biography*, I, 510–11.

thought as he wrestled with Lecky's alternatives is, as three scholars have shown, abundantly reflected in his work.[10]

The debate was subliminal to begin with; but by the time he wrote *What Is Man?*, and when it was too late to recapture the idealism of youth, he realized where he had come out. Young William Lecky (he was Clemens' junior by three years, and thirty-one when he published his prodigious *History*) was back there with young Sam Clemens. Both were naïve and wrong. Old Mark Twain was experienced and right, but it gave him little satisfaction. Young Lecky had, in effect, warned him against the dangers of analysis and speculation: "We owe more to our illusions than to our knowledge. The imagination, which is altogether constructive, probably contributes more to our happiness than the reason, which in the sphere of speculation is mainly critical and destructive."[11] Mark Twain allowed his Young Man in the *What Is Man?* dialogue to express the same idea. Why, asks the Young Man, should anyone be told that his motives are selfish? "[I]sn't it best to leave him in ignorance, as long as he *thinks* he is doing good for others' sake" (171)? The Old Man's defense is that in his scheme of things there are "no concealments, no deceptions" (170). Old Mark Twain allows the Young Man to criticize the Old Man's philosophy bitterly: "[I]t is a desolating doctrine; it is not inspiring, enthusing, uplifting. It takes the glory out of man" (208). Although the Old Man counters this criticism, and has the last word, Mark Twain admitted the cost of his anatomizing: "I only know that ciphering [my ideas] out," he wrote to Sir John Adams, "and (apparently) establishing them has much diminished the vanity I used to feel in being a member of the human race."[12] And a few months later he confessed to Howells, "Since I wrote my Bible (last year) . . . Man is not to me the respect-worthy person he was before."[13]

10. Walter Blair, *Mark Twain and Huck Finn* (Berkeley, 1960), 135–44; Harold Aspiz, "Lecky's Influence on Mark Twain," *Science and Society* (New York), XXVI (1962), 15–25; Howard G. Baetzhold, *Mark Twain and John Bull* (Bloomington, Ind., 1970), 54–65, 134–43, 218–28, and *passim*.

11. W. E. H. Lecky, *History of European Morals from Augustus to Charlemagne* (London, 1910), 51.

12. Lawrence Clark Powell, "An Unpublished Mark Twain Letter," *American Literature*, XIII (1942), 407.

13. Henry Nash Smith and William M. Gibson (eds.), *Mark Twain–Howells Letters* (2 vols.; Cambridge, Mass., 1960), II, 689.

In a deistic universe, science should bring man more and more meaning as it reveals the wonderful secrets of things; but Mark Twain's probing with a scientist's curiosity into the workings of human behavior only saddened him. That particular probing was climaxed in *What Is Man?*; but much earlier, in 1875, and perhaps as a more immediate response to his reading of the three books, he was similarly saddened when he considered how the beauty of the river that he knew so well as a young man had been destroyed by another kind of scientific understanding.

In recalling and writing about his learning the river in "Old Times on the Mississippi," he wrote not simply about piloting but about the *science* of piloting, and because to begin with he was excited by what he was rediscovering, "the marvelous science," the "wonderful science," "this great science," the "noble science of piloting."[14] He used the word *science* appropriately. The way a pilot learns the river is exactly like the Darwinian method of understanding nature. Relentlessly objective, indefatigably thorough, the pilot, like the scientist, comes to understand his subject only after months and years of assimilating and organizing data.

The first step in learning the river, Clemens' mentor, pilot Horace Bixby, explains to him, is to "get a little memorandum-book, and every time I tell you a thing, put it down right away." In due time cub Clemens "had a note-book that fairly bristled with the names of towns, 'points,' bars, islands, bends, reaches, etc."; but since the information was only in the book and not in his head, his next task was to get the names of things "by heart." Once memorized, the data remained a "curiously inanimate mass of lumber." To know the name of a bend is of little help to a pilot. He must know the *shape* of the bend and, finally, "the shape of the river perfectly." Clemens set to work mentally "photographing" the shapes of parts of the river, only to find that the shapes were always changing. They changed geologically—"The banks are caving and the shape of the shores changing like everything"—and they changed with perspective:

I would fasten my eyes upon a sharp, wooded point that projected far into the river some miles ahead of me, and go to laboriously photographing its shape upon my brain; and just as I was beginning to succeed to my satisfaction, we would draw up toward it and the exasperating thing would begin

14. Samuel Clemens [Mark Twain], *Life on the Mississippi,* Author's National Edition: The Writings of Mark Twain (25 vols.; New York, 1907–18), IX, 42, 86, 140.

to melt away and fold into the bank! If there had been a conspicuous dead tree standing upon the very point of the cape, I would find that tree inconspicuously merged into the general forest, and occupying the middle of a straight shore, when I got abreast of it! No prominent hill would stick to its shape long enough for me to make up my mind what its form really was, but it was as dissolving and changeful as if it had been a mountain of butter in the hottest corner of the tropics.

"It was plain," Clemens concluded, "that I had got to learn the shape of the river in all the different ways that could be thought of,—upside down, wrong end first, inside out, fore-and-aft, and 'thort-ships.'" But Bixby's advice, already given, is "No! you only learn *the* shape of the river; and you learn it with such absolute certainty that you can always steer by the shape that's *in your head*, and never mind the one that's before your eyes."[15]

More than an amusing reminiscence, Mark Twain's formulation of the science of piloting, propitiously accomplished in the flood tide of his genius, is a philosophical statement of considerable power and striking modernity. The river, like Darwin's planet, has been presented as a *process*. The vision that arises out of *Origin of Species* is of a global crust that for eons has risen, cracked, fallen, folded, never repeating a shape, and of generational streams of organisms, forming ever new varieties and species while old ones die, disappear, or are luckily fossilized. Darwin achieved this vision only by moving beyond taxonomy, the comfortable science of naming things, just as cub Clemens later found that learning the names of things was only a beginning to understanding the shape of the ever-changing river.

Mark Twain was sure that he had discovered something new and important in the science of piloting. "I wish to show," he wrote, "in the most patient and painstaking way, what a wonderful science it is."

Ship channels are buoyed and lighted, and therefore it is a comparatively easy undertaking to learn to run them; clear water rivers, with gravel bottoms, change their channels very gradually, and therefore one needs to learn them but once; but piloting becomes another matter when you apply it to vast streams like the Mississippi and the Missouri, whose alluvial banks cave and change constantly, whose snags are always hunting up new quarters, whose sandbars are never at rest, whose channels are forever dodging and shirking, and whose obstructions must be confronted in all nights and all weathers without the aid of a single lighthouse or a single buoy. . . . I feel

15. *Ibid.*, 59, 60, 70–71, 72, 75, 76, 72.

justified in enlarging upon this great science for the reason that I feel sure no one has ever yet written a paragraph about it who had piloted a steamboat himself, and so had a practical knowledge of the subject.[16]

When he wrote this, Mark Twain could hardly have had the Darwinian revolution in mind. Nevertheless, his contrast between the ease of navigating marked or unchanging channels and the difficulty of coping with the Mississippi is neatly analogous to the contrast between the manageable view of nature held when "fixity of species" was the byword and the Darwinian realization of nature as ever changing and ever requiring new adaptations.

In formulating this new science, Mark Twain moved beyond deism and its inherent Platonism. At first glance, Twain's learning to steer by *the* shape of the river, the one in his head rather than the one before his eyes, may seem Platonic. But *the* shape of the river in terms of the pilot's responsibility cannot possibly signify some unchanging channel beneath the shifting surface of the water. Instead, *the* shape must be determined anew at every bend and stretch. Safe water is not necessarily where it was last season or even last week, though the river's apparent shape may not have changed. Not only shapes but countless signs and myriad memories point to the channel of the moment. *The* shape of the river is its three-dimensional reality, and the pilot by virtue of his superbly trained nervous system can, as it were, see to the bottom everywhere, can see where to run in easy water and where to avoid snags. Nor do the river's plumbed secrets yield any news of the cosmic connection between nature and man. The river is obedient to the laws of physics but is indifferent to human weal.

Did Mark Twain realize that he had moved beyond deism? The answer is dramatically evident in a single amazing paragraph. Having explained the process of learning the river and having capped his exposition with a couple of delightful anecdotes, he exultantly begins his summation and evaluation: "The face of the water, in time, became a wonderful book—a book that was a dead language to the uneducated passenger, but which told its mind to me without reserve, delivering its most cherished secrets as clearly as if it uttered them with a voice." The metaphors here are rich and mythic. The river communicates; it has a mind and, as it were, a voice. The river's message verges on the metaphysical. One is reminded of Tom Paine's declaring that "[t]he creation speaketh a universal lan-

16. *Ibid.*, 86–87.

guage. . . . It is an ever existing original which every man can read."[17]

Twain continues in this exuberant vein for a sentence or two: "There never was so wonderful a book written by man; never one whose interest was so absorbing, so unflagging, so sparklingly renewed with every re-perusal." Then he was surprised and swamped by a surge of contradiction. The face of the water is *not* a wonderful book. It does *not* yield "cherished secrets." It simply tells the pilot of hidden perils. A "faint dimple" on the water's surface marking a submerged wreck or rock is "hideous to a pilot's eye." The river's face is not attractive "but the grimmest and most dead-earnest of reading matter."[18] A paragraph begun in a deistic exaltation ends in horror.

From this storm of ambivalence, Mark Twain sought the harbor of antithesis: "Now when I had mastered the language of this water . . . , I had made a valuable acquisition. But I had lost something, too." His acquisition was "the amount of usefulness it could furnish toward compassing the safe piloting of a steamboat." His loss was that "all the grace, the beauty, the poetry, had gone out of the majestic river!"[19]

To express his dismay over the disenchantment that accompanies professional knowledge, he chose again an analogy from medical practice. This time he did not look with revulsion over the shoulder of the surgeon lifting muscles and tendons with his nippers. He had through the sympathy of experience become like the doctor: "Since those days, I have pitied doctors from my heart. What does the lovely flush in a beauty's cheek mean to a doctor but a 'break' that ripples above some deadly disease? Are not all her visible charms sown thick with what are to him the signs and symbols of hidden decay? Does he ever see her beauty at all, or doesn't he simply view her professionally, and comment upon her unwholesome condition all to himself? And doesn't he sometimes wonder whether he has gained most or lost most by learning his trade?"[20]

And so, in the course of writing a few hundred words, Mark Twain lived through a wrenching philosophical crisis, from its pouncing advent through its domestication under the whip of rhetoric. Like other such precipitations of attitude, it signaled the end of

17. *Ibid.*, 82; Clark (ed.), *Thomas Paine: Representative Selections*, 258.

18. Clemens, *Life on the Mississippi*, 83.

19. *Ibid.*, 83–85.

20. *Ibid.*, 85.

rumination and the beginning of a new train of thought, however sporadically it might thereafter surface.

His new realization was that there is not, as deism had promised, a meaning inherent in nature. To the practiced eye and the trained mind, nature simply is. It has neither grace nor beauty nor poetry. In the flood of this understanding, his mind cast up images of disease and death, for in the moment of seeing the world as without magic, one's mortality becomes oppressive.

A consequence of Mark Twain's existential moment is discernible in a passage from the closing chapters of *Tom Sawyer*, the work Twain returned to after completing "Old Times." In Chapter 33, after he had Tom and Becky rescued from the cave and had disclosed the fate of Injun Joe, the villain, all that remained for him to do was to reward Tom and Huck with the money. But he paused at this point to write a gratuitous meditation on the lack of cosmic meaning. Injun Joe is discovered to have starved to death in the sealed cave, his only food in his last days being candle stubs and stray bats and his water a drop falling every three minutes from a stalactite. It is a pathetic picture, and Mark Twain envelops it within the broadest of historical frames in search for a meaning to Joe's life of villainy and death of agony. From the beginning to the end of the range of human time, the inane, metronomic beat of the waterdrop, obedient to the laws of nature, is heard:

It is falling now; it will still be falling when all these things shall have sunk down the afternoon of history, and the twilight of tradition, and been swallowed up in the thick night of oblivion. Has everything a purpose and a mission? Did this drop fall patiently during five thousand years to be ready for this flitting human insect's need? And has it another important object to accomplish ten thousand years to come? No matter.

A beneficial consequence of his rehearsing the science of piloting may be evident in the fact that when he returned to his *Tom Sawyer* manuscript, he finished it within two months. For four years he had been working with it off and on, unable to bring it to a conclusion. Could he have been wrestling by analogy in "Old Times" with the science of novel writing, and could his insights have led him to see the shape of his novel?

Such may well have been the case. To begin with, he was a novice at novel writing. By 1875, he had still not written a whole novel. True, there was *The Gilded Age*, but half of it was written by Charles

Dudley Warner; and their method of assigning each other alternate chapters and chapter clusters led to unsolved problems of tone and organization. Mark Twain's training in the narrative had been in the shorter forms of the tale and the sketch; and in the longer forms that he had undertaken—his travel books—novelistic cohesion and shape were not required. He had not been much of a novel reader, either, certainly not, so far as we can tell, with the purpose of analyzing technique and structure.

Now in the midst of *Tom Sawyer* and looking for a way out, he may well have realized that in "Old Times" he was writing not simply about learning the river but about how the mind puts things together; and when he broke the process down into steps—noting, remembering, assimilating, and shaping—he had made a helpful, if general, statement of the novelist's method.

There are further hints that the science of piloting (which he knew by heart) is a metaphor for the science of writing a novel (which he was trying to learn). In several places in "Old Times," Mark Twain likened the river to a book. Moreover, the chapter in "Old Times" called "A Pilot's Needs" might well be titled "A Novelist's Needs," for in it he ruminates on the marvels of memory, on the operation of the unconscious mind, on the temptation of slipping from one memory to another, irresponsibly, through association, and on the need for sound judgment. A good part of the chapter is, in fact, about storytelling rather than piloting, and illustrates how meaningless a narrative becomes when the author exercises no control over the shaping of it.

Mark Twain understood that the way one gained control over either the shape of the river or the shape of a novel was partly a mystery, for the process of receiving and making meaning out of information is often unconscious. "And how easily and comfortably the pilot's memory does its work; . . . how *unconsciously* it lays up its vast stores, hour by hour, day by day,"[21] he wrote; and about himself as novelist he wrote nearly the same thing many years later. In his autobiography he recalled that he had laid aside the *Tom Sawyer* manuscript when his "tank ran dry": "It was then that I made the great discovery that when the tank runs dry you've only to leave it alone and it will fill up again in time, while you are asleep—also while you are at work at other things and are quite unaware that this unconscious and profitable cerebration is going on."[22]

21. *Ibid.*, 110.
22. Bernard DeVoto (ed.), *Mark Twain in Eruption* (New York, 1940), 197.

Perhaps the most intriguing hint that Mark Twain did make an analogy between learning the shape of the river and learning the shape of a novel appears in *Huckleberry Finn*. He finished *Tom Sawyer* in a burst of creative energy in the summer of 1875. The next summer, still exuberant, he began *Huckleberry Finn*. After a surge of writing that brought him near the end of what is now Chapter 16, he lost his inspiration. In his frustration at his blocked imagination, he has Huck say, "You can't tell the shape of the river, and you can't see no distance."

CHAPTER 5

# Twain, Taine, and Howells

*Exact knowledge of all those appearances by which man manifests himself; and exact divination of the inner workings of the mind and heart—it is by these two means that the reliable foresight and sure touch required to manage all things pertaining to humanity are to be attained.*

—Hippolyte Taine, *Notes on England*

THE FRENCH INTELLECTUAL Hippolyte Taine (1828–1893) was, through his writings, a major shaper of Mark Twain's ideas. Variously called "one of the most original thinkers of the nineteenth century," a philosopher who held "two generations of writers and scholars in Europe and America . . . more or less under his spell," and "the intellectual leader of the second half of the nineteenth century," Taine became famous for his brilliant attempt to apply the laws and methods of the physical sciences to the humanities and social sciences.[1]

To Taine, all aspects of existence—whether things or events, individual acts or historical epochs, natural objects or works of art, measurable phenomena or private thought—are related. They are all parts of a rational, pantheistic universe and are joined by chains of cause and effect. Every fact is at the same time the effect of its cause and the cause of a new but predictable effect. If people had enough information and wisdom, they might look ahead along the chain of cause and effect to see future developments. They can now use the scientific method to work backward along the causal chain to discover the origin of existing facts, for "a cause is a fact which, once known, enables us to deduce from its nature, relationships and changes of the other dependent facts." Science's ultimate mission is to discover the primal cause, "the cause of causes which is that of the universe." To Taine all things could be "deduced from a supreme and single law."[2]

1. Leo Weinstein, *Hippolyte Taine* (New York, 1972), 34; Sholom J. Kahn, *Science and Aesthetic Judgement: A Study in Taine's Critical Method* (New York, 1953), ix; Edward Hyams (ed.), *Taine's Notes on England* (London, 1957), xxiii.

2. Weinstein, *Hippolyte Taine*, 32, 43.

Taine's philosophy is a marvel of eclecticism. Although it scandalized conservative members of the church and state, it had something in it for the most diverse of philosophical sensibilities. Its pantheism, derived from Spinoza, corresponded with certain romantic convictions. Its seeing the workings of the world as obedient to universal law would please deists. Transcendentalists could respond to its organicism and idealism. But its widest appeal would be to modern thinkers who were impressed with the prestige of science and the efficacy of the scientific method. For Taine insisted on using the inductive method in approaching the study of any subject, whether psychology, social history, literature, or art. One first assembles a mass of data, precisely observed. One will find those data falling into natural groupings, for behind particular facts is the "general fact." General facts themselves coalesce into significant abstractions. Out of an intensive study of the countless activities and artifacts of a nation, for example, will emerge the "soul" or "central character" of that nation.[3] Only when one has painstakingly arrived at such an abstraction may he make deductions from it.

Taine's philosophy is easily translated into a rationale and method for realistic writing. In order to show the "soul" of their people, novelists would carefully detail aspects of their characters' formative environments and of their characters' speech, movements, and thoughts as the people interacted with their environments.

Taine's name is, of course, associated with the realistic movement, and curiously his influence was more seminal in the United States than in his own country. By the time he came into prominence in France in the late 1850s, French realism had been under way for two or three decades. But the movement of American realism was only incipient when Taine's doctrine and reputation crossed the Atlantic around 1870. Shapers of the new movement, especially Howells, took the opportunity of basing their realism on a full-blown philosophy.

The publication in New York in 1871 of a translation of Taine's *History of English Literature*, complete with his introduction, did much to stimulate American interest in Taine's ideas. Responding to that interest, the *Atlantic Monthly* under William Dean Howells' editorship gave the book and its ideas no fewer than four notices during the following year and a half. Howells himself reviewed the

3. *Ibid.*, 34, 36.

book in the February, 1872, issue; he called Taine's method "admirably brilliant and effective" but had some reservations about Taine's theory. Henry James reviewed it again two months later, expressing some distaste for Taine's ideas. In the April, 1873, number there was a notice of an abridged edition of the *History* called *The Class-Room Taine* (suggesting how quickly and broadly Taine's ideas were being disseminated) and a penetrating review of George Eliot's *Middlemarch*, in which the author, A. G. Sedgwick, after quoting from Taine's *History of English Literature*, showed how the novel's excellence derived from Eliot's application of Taine's philosophy to fiction. It was Sedgwick's essay that completed Howells' conversion to "Taine's theory of realistic literature as the laboratory of mankind."[4] Thereafter, the *Atlantic's* references to Taine, along with discussions of Taine's theory, of the appropriateness of applying the scientific method to literature, and of realism in general, appeared as matters of course.

Did Mark Twain know of Taine's *History of English Literature* during those first years after its American publication? He could not have avoided it. As a writer who aspired to *Atlantic* authorship and who was the special friend and protégé of its editor, he would be particularly sensitive to that magazine's contents and currents. The fact that he made no immediate allusion to this work of Taine hardly signifies. Through his *Atlantic* reading, probably through Howells' comments, possibly through an early reading of Taine's *History* and its introduction, he undoubtedly ingested Taine's radical ideas in the early 1870s.[5] Those ideas would go through the usual period of incubation.

A major idea in Taine's introduction, that a people's development is controlled by "race, surroundings, and epoch," had, according to Henry James, "already been reiterated to satiety" by 1872.[6] Race, Taine explained, was the internal influence—"the innate and hereditary dispositions which man brings with him into the world."[7] Surroundings and epoch are the external influences. Surroundings are "all external powers which mould human matter." In the large

4. Everett Carter, *Howells and the Age of Realism* (Philadelphia and New York, 1950), 97.

5. For evidence of Clemens' reading Taine's *History of English Literature*, see Alan Gribben, *Mark Twain's Library: A Reconstruction* (2 vols.; Boston, 1980), II, 684.

6. Henry James, "Taine's English Literature," *Atlantic Monthly*, XXIX (1872), 470.

7. Hippolyte Taine, *History of English Literature*, trans. H. Van Laun (New York, 1880), 23.

picture, surroundings are nature and society and, in the fine, such things as climate, landscape, state policy, social conditions, and regnant values. Epoch is cultural momentum, the current and direction of history of a particular time or place. These three influences act with such geometric precision in shaping the soul of man or men—in transforming "the operations and processes of the human machine"—that they may be regarded as laws.[8] In their light, the moral, religious, political, and social developments of the past and present may be explained and their future direction predicated.

The second book of Taine's that came to Mark Twain's attention was *Notes on England*. There is no doubt that Twain knew it well, that he was expected to admire it, and that he probably did. Evidence for that slightly queer series of statements comes from Chapter 36 of his *Gilded Age*, a chapter he wrote as a private message to Howells and without caring that it failed to advance the plot or enhance the theme of his novel in progress.

The chapter was a response to a very pretty compliment Howells had sent him via the same medium. The third installment of Howells' *A Chance Acquaintance*, appearing in the March, 1873, *Atlantic Monthly*, revealed that the favorite reading of Colonel Ellison, cousin of the heroine, was Shakespeare's plays, *Don Quixote*, and *The Innocents Abroad*. Think of that! Howells was putting Mark Twain in company with the Olympians. Twain reciprocated with a complimentary triad of his own: Taine's *Notes on England*, Holmes's *Autocrat of the Breakfast Table*, and Howells' *Venetian Life*. Although this left Howells in company a trifle less lustrous, the choices were appropriate and the tribute sincere.

Mark Twain's message-carrying chapter—called "The Book-Store Clerk"—is almost embarrassingly revealing about his current relationship with Howells and his position vis-à-vis "culture." In it a little drama is played out between the clerk, an eager, amiable lad with appalling taste in literature, and Laura Hawkins, a beautiful, witty woman and the avatar of culture. She asks first for Taine's *Notes on England*, "a volume that is making a deal of talk just now"; the clerk guesses that it is a book of hymns. She asks next for *The Autocrat of the Breakfast Table*; the clerk thinks it must be a cookbook. Then, while she is absorbed in a copy of *Venetian Life*, "running over a familiar passage here and there," the clerk tries to interest her in

8. *Ibid.*, 25, 22.

books he has read and enjoyed—*The Pirate's Doom, Gonderil the Vampire,* and *The Jokist's Own Treasury.* The jokebook he describes as the "funniest thing!—I've read it four times, ma'm, and I can laugh at the very sight of it yet." In three pages of virtuoso writing, Mark Twain then has Laura chat with the clerk about his choices in a way that lets the reader know that she abominates them but that leaves the clerk feeling flattered.[9] In linking Howells' book with those of two esteemed writers and in contrasting all three with the rib-tickling jokebook and the sensational romances, Mark Twain signaled to Howells not only his appreciation of Howells' achievement but his reassurance that Howells could trust him to know the difference between good books and trash.

Taine's just-published *Notes on England* would be read with professional interest by both Howells and Twain, who were themselves travel writers. In this book, moreover, Taine was demonstrating his famous scientific method of arriving at the essence of a national character:

A country is its people: since I arrived here I have been collecting types. . . . After some experimenting I have decided that the best method is still that used by painters and naturalists: first, note the most salient features or expressions, study them in all their variations and shades, graduations and mixtures; check that they are to be found in sufficiently numerous individuals; by this means, isolate the principal characteristic traits, then compare, interpret and classify them. This is what painters and novelists do by instinct when, through the medium of a few characters, they give us a resumé of their times and environment.[10]

Do not, he continued, become discouraged if at first these countless impressions seem to be a jumble: "[M]emory keeps them present to the mind although the intelligence cannot yet understand them clearly. . . . [W]eek by week they become clearer, more complete, provoke questions and suggest answers, are associated one with another, become interconnected, until at last a whole, an *ensemble,* emerges" (39). Thus he wrote near the beginning of his book. The middle is filled with observations on English "types," customs, morals, education, government, and economics. Toward the end he is ready to describe the English mind. Admirable to him is the English

9. Samuel Clemens [Mark Twain] and Charles Dudley Warner, *The Gilded Age,* Author's National Edition: The Writings of Mark Twain (25 vols.; New York, 1907–18), XI, 56–61.

10. Hyams (ed.), *Taine's Notes on England,* 39.

respect for facts, a respect that is evident in contemporary English novels, which

are parcels crammed tight with small physical and moral facts, the latter in very great abundance and those, for the most part, precious jewels of observation. Never has any other literature succeeded as theirs does in revealing and following those feelings, that subterranean working, by which a character is formed.

Exact knowledge of all those appearances by which man manifests himself; and exact divination of the inner workings of the mind and heart—it is by these two means that the reliable foresight and sure touch required to manage all things pertaining to humanity are to be attained. (252–53)

Mark Twain and Howells, both of them young writers, both of them known for their travel books, both of them turning to novel writing but still tyros in the craft, could find here firm philosophical principles on which to establish their careers as novelists.

It is time to pay attention to a nudging question: What exactly was William Dean Howells' contribution to Mark Twain's theory of fiction? During the early years of the two men's friendship—from, say, 1871 to 1874—two important things were happening: As Everett Carter has shown, Howells was going from a first grappling with Taine's ideas to a complete acceptance of them as a basis for realistic literature. And Mark Twain was looking to Howells for guidance in becoming a man of letters. Would Howells not have discussed his Tainean theory with his friend and protégé? The record for this period is exasperatingly incomplete. The two men certainly exchanged ideas—in 1873, Howells reported that he and his friend "had some 'very pretty conversation' "—but what Twain might have recorded in his notebook is not available, since his notebooks from 1868 to 1877 (except for one dictated in England during June and July, 1873) are missing. Unavailable too is most of what the two men wrote to each other through 1873, "due to the accidental disappearance of a number of letters."[11]

Most or all of their letters to each other in 1874 are open to our perusal, and we search expectantly among them for glimpses of Howells' theory of realism. Howells did give editorial advice: Twain's "A True Story" in manuscript needed "a little more circum-

---

11. Henry Nash Smith and William M. Gibson (eds.), *Mark Twain–Howells Letters* (2 vols.; Cambridge, Mass., 1960), I, 8, 12.

stantiation." The night watchman's story in "Old Times on the Mississippi" "doesn't seem so natural and probable as the rest of the sketch—seems made-up, on your part." Concerning the writing of "Old Times" in general, he advised, "[S]tick to actual fact and character in the thing, and give things in *detail*."[12] Good tips, certainly, and true to Tainean principle. But they are in themselves quite untheoretical.

There can be no question that both writers self-consciously used the Tainean technique of describing "those appearances by which man manifests himself,"[13] although Mark Twain was less consistent in his application than was Howells. The most signal example of Twain's use of the technique is his "House Beautiful" chapter of *Life on the Mississippi*, in which he lists and describes scores upon scores of the objects in the interior of the "finest dwelling" in a typical southern town—furniture, pictures, books, bric-a-brac, mementos—by way of exposing the tastes and values of the absent family. It is a perfectly executed exercise, a tour de force of the Tainean technique. He would use the same technique in some of his best writing, but more organically and less obtrusively. And in some works—for example, in "The Man That Corrupted Hadleyburg," where his aim is moralism rather than realism—there is no attempt at all to reveal character through typical environment.

Howells did give Mark Twain pointers leading to the Tainean technique, but what he had to do with teaching him the philosophy behind it is problematical. The lack of record is one problem. Another is that although both men were profoundly instructed in Taine's ideas during the 1870s, they emerged with interpretations or emphases that were quite dissimilar, though equally authentic. It was a difference which, because it was imperfectly realized, they may never have argued about. Besides, insofar as they realized differences, they respected them in each other. In a nutshell, the difference is that to Howells environment revealed; to Twain it formed. To Howells it was a sign; to Twain a force.

Howells was haunted, as Twain was not, with Emerson's transcendentalism; and for all his devotion to "realism," he could not be content with the apparent meaning of things. He needed to be assured of a deeper "truth." Taine would give him that assurance in writing of the "soul" of a people and in declaring that the "visible

12. *Ibid.*, 24, 43, 46.
13. Hyams (ed.), *Taine's Notes on England*, 253.

man" should lead to an understanding of the "man invisible": "All these externals are but avenues converging towards a centre, . . . and that centre is the genuine man."[14] Using Taine as his authority, Howells counseled writers to pay particular attention to details, to "picture" life, to "portray" it, to present its surface with photographic fidelity, so as to reveal the underlying truth.[15]

Mark Twain's deism would lead him to look for laws, systems, and mechanisms in Taine; and he found them there. Through the law of cause and effect, "surroundings" had an inexorable and predictable influence on the "human machine." With Taine as his inspiration, Mark Twain reasoned that if environment formed character, it could be used to re-form character; and thus he sent his prince into a pauper's world to learn compassion. Later it occurred to him that since training *is* everything, man is totally caught in history, even beyond a novelist's meddling.

The result of the two casts of mind was that in spite of their great friendship—in which each was as open and considerate and supportive as humans can be—Twain and Howells had their involuntary privacies. They made poignant efforts to keep in touch at a deep level, even using on occasion each other's cherished metaphors. In praising Howells' *The Lady of the Aroostook*, Twain selected such phrases from Howells' lexicon as would best please him: "It is all such truth—truth to the life; everywhere your pen falls it leaves a photograph."[16] And once, when Howells was asked by an interviewer how he went about writing a novel, he replied, "I work like a pilot on a Mississippi river steamboat, with certain landmarks to shape my course by."[17] But even in the early 1870s, Mark Twain was learning to disbelieve in what Howells saw in Taine—that is, evidence of a sustaining abstraction beneath the appearance of things. By the time Howells published his realists' manifesto, *Criticism and Fiction*, in 1891, Mark Twain was far beyond being instructed in the transcendental convictions that undergirded Howells' philosophy of literature. Howells' declaration that "no author is an authority except in those moments when he held his ear close to Nature's lips and caught her very accent" could only have mystified Mark Twain.

14. Taine, *History of English Literature*, 19.

15. Howells used such phrases countless times. See, for example, Ulrich Halfmann (ed.), "Interviews with William Dean Howells," *American Literary Realism*, VI (1973), 277–399.

16. Smith and Gibson (eds.), *Mark Twain–Howells Letters*, I, 245.

17. Halfmann (ed.), "Interviews with William Dean Howells," 284.

And his further declaration that the novelist, like the scientist, cannot ignore any fact of life—for the various reasons that "nothing that God made is contemptible," that the writer "feels in every nerve the equality of things and the unity of men," and that "his soul is exalted, not by vain shows and shadows and ideals, but by realities, in which alone the truth lives"[18]—could not have elicited from Mark Twain more than a polite nod for friendship's sake.

The book of Taine's that made the deepest impression on Mark Twain was *The Ancient Regime* (1876). It is, indeed, the sixth and last of the books which fundamentally influenced the evolution of his philosophy. Taken as a whole the six books ended by giving him more trouble than comfort, for they contained fundamental contradictions. *The Ancient Regime* was not radically different from the three modern books he had recently read—*The Autocrat of the Breakfast Table*, *The Descent of Man*, and *History of European Morals*—but they were hardly in accord with either *The Age of Reason* or the Bible, which, in turn, conflicted with each other.

In *The Ancient Regime*, Taine wrote a kind of social history of France under the last three Louis before the Revolution. It is a history that pays little attention to signal events or the personalities of political leaders. Instead, it analyzes the cultural, intellectual, and moral levels of each class of France's people; it presents statistics and instances concerning life as it was lived by beggars and courtiers and those in between; and it surveys the ideas and ideals of eighteenth-century France as they were expressed by her poets, playwrights, philosophers, and scientists. Taine's aim was to expose the cultural dynamics that drove France toward revolution, and in the process he gave himself ample room to explain his philosophy and method and to comment on human nature.

Mark Twain purchased *The Ancient Regime* in 1876, the year of its American publication, and read it by the summer of 1877. He must have reread it—indeed, become engrossed in it—for he not only referred to it during the next decade in his notebooks and correspondence but borrowed liberally from it for material and incidents in both *The Prince and The Pauper* and *A Connecticut Yankee*.[19]

Both novels, moreover, are informed by Tainean concepts and attitudes, though not the same ones. Since Taine, like Walt Whit-

18. William Dean Howells, *Criticism and Fiction and Other Essays*, ed. Clara Marburg Kirk and Rudolf Kirk (New York, 1959), 14–15.

19. Gribben, *Mark Twain's Library*, II, 683.

man, is large and contains multitudes, it is quite possible to come away from his book either exhilarated by his mastery of the subject and by his confidence in his method or dismayed by his materialism and determinism. *The Prince and the Pauper* is based on certain of Taine's positive and constructive concepts. *A Connecticut Yankee* is confused by Twain's sporadic concession to Taine's astringent observations on human nature and on man's insignificant role in the larger scheme of things. As with the three other influential modern books that Twain read, Taine's *Ancient Regime* stocked his mind with ideas, many of which he simply stored away until they corresponded with and supported his darkening view of the world. Although my purpose in this chapter is to trace the development of Twain's science-based theory of literature up to around 1880, to provide an understanding of the whole impact of *The Ancient Regime* on Twain's mind, I must jump ahead for a bit and consider the pessimistic ideas of Taine's that are reflected in *A Connecticut Yankee* and in other later works.

One of these ideas is that science reveals a cosmos in which man is insignificant:

Amid this vast and overwhelming space and in these boundless solar archipelagoes, how small is our own sphere, and the earth, what a grain of sand! . . . What is life, what is organic substance in this monstrous universe but an indifferent mass, a passing accident, the corruption of a few epidermic particles? And if this be life, what is that humanity which is so small a fragment of it? Such is man in nature, an atom, an ephemeral particle; let this not be lost sight of in our theories concerning his origin, his importance, and his destiny. A mite that should consider itself the centre of all things would be grotesque.[20]

Although Mark Twain had been fond of contemplating the cosmic vastnesses—as in his letter on astronomy to Livy in 1870—he would not be prepared on first reading *The Ancient Regime* to echo this passage's disparagement of life and belittlement of man; but an image in his later work is of man as an overweening insect.

In the largest of historical views, Taine sees that there is, if not positive progress, at least a development that is made possible by the constant transactions between the individual and his environment and by the ability of humans to adapt or react to changing

20. Hippolyte Taine, *The Ancient Regime*, trans. John Durand (Gloucester, Mass., 1962), 175. Further references to *The Ancient Regime* are indicated by parenthetical page numbers in the text.

circumstances. There has been a "natural history of the soul." And through careful observation and study, we may follow, "step by step, the development by which the infant, the savage, the unculti- vated primitive man, is converted into the rational and cultivated man" (181). That sounds hopeful enough (and may, indeed, have had something to do with Twain's fictional project of transforming the uncultivated primitives in King Arthur's Britain into rational moderns), but it is undermined by two other observations that Taine was fond of making. One is that man, though adaptable, is neither good nor reasonable. He is "an animal among other animals" (176). "Hence there is in him a steady substratum of brutality and ferocity, and of violent and destructive instincts" (241). Moreover, "[w]hat we call reason in man is not an innate endowment, primitive and enduring, but a tardy acquisition and a fragile composition. . . . Properly speaking man is imbecile" (238, 239). Indicative of Taine's opinion of human nature are his frequent comparisons of men to animals; when men are docile and stupid, they are sheep; when rapacious, wolves.

Another of Taine's disconcerting observations is the deterministic one. If men do make progress toward rationality and cultivation, it is not to their credit, for human history "is a thing of natural growth . . . which is not tending to any prescribed end but devel- oping a result" (179). The development comes about because men are inevitably responsive to "the inward forces" of their needs and desires and to the multitude of environmental factors such as cli- mate, soil, economics, politics, religion, and traditions. "All these causes, each added to the other, or each limited by the other, contrib- ute together to form a total result, namely society. . . . They are conditions from which we cannot abstract ourselves" (180–81). With these uncheerful ideas of Taine—that man is insignificant in the cosmic perspective, that he displays much stupidity and cruelty, that he is animalic, and that he is the pawn of deterministic forces— Mark Twain was, in his later years, quite in accord.

I return now to 1877, when Mark Twain was receptive instead to Taine's affirmative ideas. What was available to Twain in *The Ancient Regime,* and what he demonstrably accepted, was further instruc- tion in Taine's method, abundantly analyzed and illustrated and supported with a humane philosophy.

"A historian," Taine declared in his preface, "may be allowed the privilege of a naturalist; I have regarded my subject the same as the metamorphosis of an insect" (viii). As a naturalist historian, Taine sought to know France through the accumulation and assessment of countless data. "What time, what study, what observations correcting each other, what researches into the past and present, in all the domains of thought and action, what manifold, secular efforts are necessary for acquiring a full and precise idea of a great people" (vii). Fortunately for the historian, eighteenth-century Frenchmen had left behind numerous artifacts and records. "Many of their dwellings, with the furniture, still remain intact. Their pictures and engravings enable us to take part in their domestic life, see how they dress, observe their attitudes and follow their movements. Through their literature, philosophy, scientific pursuits, gazettes, and correspondence, we can reproduce their feeling and thought, and even enjoy their familiar conversation" (viii–ix). Evidence from the past had, of course, been used by previous historians; but what Taine would examine, and what they had neglected, was whatever "was commonplace and well-known to contemporaries, whatever seemed technical, tedious and vulgar, whatever related to the provinces, to the bourgeoisie, to the peasant, to the laboring man, to the government, and to the household" (ix).

Taine's Book III, "The Spirit and the Doctrine," would be especially instructive for Twain, for in it Taine discusses the failure of eighteenth-century literature to convey the texture of life and shows how a modern scientific approach can give literature authenticity and vitality. The literature of the preceding century was part and parcel of the prevailing philosophy, which was a poisonous mixture of Newtonian science and classicism. Science in itself is salutary, but the philosophers, writers, and political leaders of eighteenth-century France used it to seal themselves off from the real world. Enamored with the Newtonian vision of universal order and elegance, they abstracted themselves from the messy particularity of life. Propriety forbade the examination of vulgar details; in speaking and writing, one never used words that were technical, provincial, familiar, and frank. Consequently, the literature of the century produced generalized characters, and its language became "attenuated and colorless" (188). Striving for precision and elegance of expression, writers omitted "the characteristic detail, the animating fact, the specific circumstance, the significant, convincing and complete example" (202). The literature therefore was "powerless to fully portray or to record the infinite and varied details of experience" (191).

It was a vitiating tradition. Worst of all, it cut the author off from that "sympathetic imagination by which a writer enters into the mind of another, and reproduces in himself a system of habits and feelings opposed to his own" (199).

Science was expected to be either epigrammatic or oratorical; crude or technical details would have been objectionable to a public composed of people of society; correctness of style drove out or falsified the little significant facts which give a peculiar sense and their original relief to antiquated characters. Even if writers had dared to note them, their sense and bearing would not have been understood. The sympathetic imagination did not exist; people were incapable of going out of themselves, of betaking themselves to distant points of view." (212)

It was, indeed, the denial of the sympathetic imagination by France's ruling class that precipitated the Revolution. Instead of examining the true character of the human condition, the aristocracy was content to operate from "hereditary prejudice" bolstered with "a blind form of reason" (211). The misunderstood and oppressed masses had no recourse except violent revolt.

The scientific method that Taine offered writers was more than a way of using homely evidences for reassembling the aspects of reality. Those same evidences were the means of induction by which the writer, and later the reader, could be led to experience someone else's subjectivity. Appreciating the facts and details of someone else's life stimulates and instructs the sympathetic imagination. Through exercising that imagination, one can reproduce "in himself a system of habits and feelings opposed to his own."

Reading *The Ancient Regime* helped Mark Twain define his true subject. That subject first gripped him in 1874, when in responding to it, he wrote "A True Story," about a former slave, Rachel Cord, then sixty and a servant at Quarry Farm, where the Clemenses usually spent their summers. The subject would become his central preoccupation. He would not be freed of it until he wrote about Roxana, another slave, in *Pudd'nhead Wilson* (1894). The subject was the cruel and irrational custom of imposing inferior status on certain human beings because of caste, race, or slavery and the kind of revolution needed to destroy the custom.

In writing the first several chapters of *Huckleberry Finn*, in the summer of 1876, Mark Twain had made a magnificent return to his subject. But after losing "the shape of the river" that August, and tossing the manuscript aside, he wrote aimlessly and with trivial results—"The Canvasser's Tale"; the play *Ah Sin*, with Bret Harte; and a disastrous play of his own, *Cap'n Simon Wheeler: The Amateur Detective*. By the summer of 1877, he was working away on "Some Rambling Notes of an Idle Excursion," more or less about a recent cruise to Bermuda. In late August he was happily led to interrupt his "notes" to describe in a letter to Howells a kind of revolution he had witnessed, in which the hearts of a family of rich white landowners had been opened toward their lowly Negro farmhand.

The scene is the same as in "A True Story"—the Cranes' Quarry Farm outside Elmira, New York: a comfortable farmhouse atop a hill, with a wide porch, a driveway leading to a porte-cochere, and an expanse of lawn sloping to the road. The characters are Theodore Crane and his wife Susie, foster sister of Livy Clemens, Livy, Livy's mother, Livy's husband Sam Clemens and their young daughters Susan and Clara, Livy's sister-in-law Ida Langdon with her two small children, and visitors Aunt Marsh and Cousin May Marsh. These luxuriating people are served by an almost equal number of retainers. There is Rosa, the nurse for the Clemens children; Nora, the nurse for Ida's children; Timothy, the coachman; the Cranes' "trio of colored servants"—Josie, the housemaid; "Aunt" Rachel Cord, the cook; and Charlotte, the laundress. There are, besides, three other blacks: John T. Lewis, the Cranes' farmhand, and his wife and daughter.

In the melodrama that ensues, the hero is the unlikeliest of candidates—John T. Lewis, black, middle-aged, poverty-ridden, and introduced as a comical figure, dressed in rags and hunched on the seat of a wagon loaded with manure. In his seven years of working for the Cranes, he has been unmercifully exploited; unable to support his family on what they have paid him, he now owes them seven hundred dollars. But in spite of the resentment and despair he might feel, and in spite of his grotesque and laughable appearance, there is in his body great strength, in his mind keen intelligence, and in his heart a selfless courage. When "Ida the young and comely," with her daughter and Nora, drive away from the farmhouse in a carriage and, in full view of the people around the house, find themselves hurtling downhill behind a runaway horse, it is Lewis who saves them.

You see, Lewis—the prodigious, humped upon his front seat, had been toiling up, on his load of manure; he saw the frantic horse plunging down the hill toward him, on a full gallop, throwing his heels as high as a man's head at every jump. So Lewis turned his team diagonally across the road just at the "turn," thus making a V with the fence—the running horse could not escape that but must enter it. Then Lewis sprang to the ground and stood in this V. He gathered his vast strength, and with a perfect Creedmoor aim he seized the gray horse's bit as he plunged by and fetched him up standing![21]

The result of his heroism is that Lewis undergoes a kind of apotheosis in the eyes of the lordly whites. When he rides up to the hilltop house after the event, "humped up on his manure wagon and as grotesquely picturesque as usual, everybody wanted to go and see how he looked—They came back and said he was beautiful. It was *so*, too—and yet he would have *photographed* exactly as he would have done any day these past 7 years that he has occupied this farm." Through this intensely dramatic event, the usually laborious Tainean process by which one works from appearance to inner reality was accomplished in an instant. Whether the sympathetic imaginations of the Cranes and Langdons were sufficiently stimulated to allow them to enter into Lewis' "system of habits and feelings" is beyond telling; at least their sense of noblesse oblige was acutely touched. The Cranes absolved Lewis of his indebtedness, the Langdons presented him with an inscribed gold watch, and from all who were grateful came "greenbacks of dignified denomination." In addition, Sam Clemens, in his summing up, listed details attesting to the true dignity and depth of Lewis' character.[22]

The account that Twain sent Howells runs well over two thousand words; it was carefully worked up. Howells was delighted with it: "As you tell it, I think it's one of the most impressive things I've ever read." Mark Twain immediately responded by explaining, uncharacteristically, the theoretical basis for his narrative. The theory is patently Tainean: "I don't really see how the story of the runaway horse could read well with the little details of names and places and things left out. *They* are the true life of all narrative."[23]

Beyond the agreement between Twain and Taine that homely details "are the true life of all narrative," there is a striking correspondence between the class structure of the ancient regime and that of Quarry

---

21. Smith and Gibson (eds.), *Mark Twain–Howells Letters*, I, 196.
22. *Ibid.*, 198.
23. *Ibid.*, 202–203.

Farm. In both, there is a privileged ruling class and an exploited lower class. In both, the ruling class is oblivious to the authentic humanity of the lower class. In both, the barrier to understanding is lack of the sympathetic imagination. In other words, both men perceived that the privileged and the powerless were separated by a void across which human feeling could hardly travel.

I do not mean that in this matter Mark Twain was simply influenced by Taine. Twain's perception was surely rooted in his experience of Hannibal, where society, whichever way you looked at it, was stratified into those in authority and those subject to authority: white householders and black slaves, respectable people and disreputable ones, adults and children. In developing his subject, however, he would range far from his Hannibal and Quarry Farm experiences. In the summer of 1876 he began (with one interruption) a four-and-a-half-year program of reading in the history of the ancient regime, the French Revolution, the Tudor court, and related topics, at first as a way of exploring his "subject" and then as research for writing *The Prince and the Pauper*. Although that novel is not about France, it is informed, it seems to me, by Taine's corroborative vision. The enormous gulf between the life of royal privilege and that of beggarly poverty is the central display of the novel. The crisscrossing of that gulf by pauper Tom Canty and Prince Edward, who are forced to lead each other's lives, activates the plot of the novel. And the prince's becoming a better ruler through the awakening of his sympathetic imagination is the moral of the book.

CHAPTER 6

# A Screeching Halt

*I haven't done a stroke of work since the Atlantic dinner; have only moped around.*
— Twain to Howells, December, 1877

WHEN MARK TWAIN BEGAN writing *The Prince and the Pauper,* in the fall of 1877, he was uniquely blessed with a sense of purpose and plan. His other novels tended to be explorations rather than constructions, but in this one he built exactly on the plot outline set down in his notebook in November, 1877. Taine had, moreover, offered him a scientific technique for recovering the past and a theory of society's being shaped by "race, surroundings, and epoch." Impressed with the Tainean idea that circumstances form character and pleased with his own notion that *different* circumstances could re-form it, he was ready to invent a bit of English history to prove his point. In his enlightened modernity, he became rather patronizing about the past.

But his feelings about the past were more complex than he thought, and his recent accession to a modern way of writing and thinking gave him less security than he supposed. His ideas in both areas were about to be thrown into confusion. He was to suffer a dark night of the soul that would last for more than a year. Only after a long struggle would he return to his former confidence in the Tainean method and his sense of mastery over the past.

What precipitated the confusion was the humiliation and remorse he felt after his burlesque speech at the Whittier birthday dinner in Boston on December 17, 1877. Sponsored by the publishers of the *Atlantic Monthly,* presided over by Howells, and attended by Whittier, Longfellow, Emerson, Holmes, and some fifty other distinguished guests, the dinner was a celebration not simply of Whittier's seventieth birthday but of the literary tradition he represented. Fittingly, the food and wine were sumptuous; the introductions, tributes, and speeches were numerous and, except for Mark Twain's, congratulatory.

When it came his turn to speak, Mark Twain told a story about a

California miner who was visited in his cabin by three rough and drunken men claiming to be the "famous littery people" Emerson, Holmes, and Longfellow. They are nothing like the persons they pretend to be: "Mr. Emerson was a seedy little bit of a chap, red-headed. Mr. Holmes was as fat as a balloon. . . . Mr. Longfellow was built like a prize fighter." The trio spout elevated poetry in a mocking response to ordinary situations. "Holmes," for example, after eyeing the miner's humble premises, intones, "Build thee more stately mansions, / O my soul!" "Emerson," protesting the beans and bacon that his host is preparing, quotes from "Mithridates": "Give me agates for my meat; / Give me cantharids to eat." After an all-night session of drinking, poker playing, and poetry, the unwanted guests leave, "Longfellow" having appropriated the miner's boots so as in departing to "leave behind us / Footprints on the sands of Time."

The nub of the story comes just after Mark Twain knocks on the miner's door the next day and introduces himself under his nom de plume. Hearing the miner's story, he reassures the miner that his previous visitors were imposters. The miner replies: "Ah! imposters, were they? are you?"[1]

By mocking his own claim of being a "littery" person, Mark Twain probably expected to arouse a relieved chuckle from his audience. But the damage as he perceived it had already been done. He was sure he had outrageously insulted his audience. His recollection was that as he proceeded with his story, his listeners " 'seemed turned to stone with horror' at the affront to the revered poets who were seated at the head table."[2] Howells found himself exquisitely caught between his loyalty to his western protégé and his reverence for his eastern literary forebears. He ended by joining Twain in an agony of embarrassment. He confided later to Charles Eliot Norton that Clemens' "performance was like an effect of demoniacal possession." Mark Twain was ready to agree. "I must have been insane," he confessed to Howells, "when I wrote that speech & saw no harm in it, no disrespect toward those men whom I reverenced so much."[3]

Henry Nash Smith, in his masterful analysis of the Whittier birthday episode, shows that what Mark Twain felt, intensely and un-

1. Paul Fatout (ed.), *Mark Twain Speaking* (Iowa City, Iowa, 1976), 111–14.

2. Henry Nash Smith, *Mark Twain: The Development of a Writer* (New York, 1967), 97.

3. Henry Nash Smith and William M. Gibson (eds.), *Mark Twain–Howells Letters* (2 vols.; Cambridge, Mass., 1960), I, 214, 212.

consciously, was not reverence but hostility. His speech "is clearly an act of aggression against the three poets as representatives of the sacerdotal cult of the man of letters." Without having worked it out consciously, Mark Twain understood that the New England writers and their "cult of ideality" (Smith's phrase) were passé and that somewhere in the "debris" of current popular literature were the "germs of a new system of values and a new literature."[4] Single-handedly—and not even that, since his conscious self abhorred the deed—he had invaded a stronghold of the venerated writers of the past generation and challenged the living value of their work. Embarrassed and bewildered by his audacity, he slunk away like an imposter who had been found out.

Mark Twain's "hideous mistake" blocked his creativity. A week or two after the event he confessed to Howells, "I haven't done a stroke of work since the Atlantic dinner; have only moped around."[5] There is some evidence that he returned to the writing of *The Prince and the Pauper* early in 1878; but if so, he abandoned it shortly. He was, he complained to his mother in February, the victim of "a badgered, harassed feeling." Business worries, "annoyances," and "other things" "consume my time and defeat my projects. Well, the consequence is, I cannot write a book at home." His solution was to flee with his family "to some little corner of Europe and budge no more until I shall have completed one of the half dozen books that lie begun, up stairs."[6] Once abroad, however, he lost interest in working on any of his unfinished books and decided instead to begin still another one—a travel book based on his current European visit. But he could do no effective writing on it until December, 1878, by which time his period of unproductivity had spread to a year.

It was not only his writing that was blocked by the Whittier dinner fiasco. His progress toward modernity also came to a screeching halt. For the past ten years or so—through his reading in Holmes, Darwin, Lecky, and Taine, through rehearsing the science of piloting, and through his tutelage under Howells—he had been working his way out of the eighteenth century and into his own time. For several months after the Whittier dinner, his thinking,

4. Smith, *Mark Twain: The Development of a Writer*, 97, 107.

5. Smith and Gibson (eds.), *Mark Twain–Howells Letters*, I, 214, 215.

6. Albert Bigelow Paine (ed.), *Mark Twain's Letters* (2 vols.; New York, 1917), I, 319–20.

which had been so progressive, became timid and morose. He practically quit reading; at least he made virtually no reference to books in his 1878 correspondence and notebooks—a circumstance quite at variance with his usual custom. His notebook for the winter of 1877–1878 contains few references of any kind, let alone to his reading; and in the second quarter of the year, when the entries become more numerous, they record, for the most part, memories and mundane observations. Those entries that could be called creative generally concern undertakers, coffins, corpses, and going to heaven.

His death wish in the spring of 1878 was specific and potent; and as unhealthy as that may sound, it was a necessary preliminary to his amazing psychic recovery. Always his own psychiatrist, and a rather good one considering how hypersensitive and complex his patient was, he was about to take himself through a four-phase, yearlong program that would restore his creativity as well as his confidence in his lately acquired scientific theory and method of writing fiction.

The first phase in the program was his spiritual death, rebirth, and rejuvenation. As the time neared for his Atlantic crossing, he was ready for some kind of translation. He was "so jaded and worn" that at a dinner for Bayard Taylor, who as minister to Germany was to board the *Holsatia* on April 11 along with the Clemens family, he could not remember the speech he had prepared. "I am very nearly tired to death," he wrote his mother in explaining his lapse.[7] And to celebrate the moment of boarding, he wrote in his notebook a little funeral service for himself: "To go abroad has something of the same sense that death brings—I am no longer of ye—what ye say of me is now of no consequence—but of how much consequence when I am with ye & of ye! I know you will refrain from saying harsh things *because* they can't hurt me, since I am out of reach & cannot hear them. This is why we say no harsh things of the dead."[8] The "harsh things" said of him, and to which he hoped to become mercifully remote, must surely be the reactions to his Whittier dinner speech.

For a while it looked as if he had been pointed the wrong way when he "died." At sea he suffered an "afternoon hell in this ship, daily." Modes of torture were the sounds of shrieking children and the "pounding of the screw, with an occasional avalanche of crash-

---

7. *Ibid.*, 327.
8. Frederick Anderson, Lin Salamo, and Bernard L. Stein (eds.), *Mark Twain's Notebooks and Journals* (3 vols. completed; Berkeley, 1975), II, 64.

ing crockery, as the ship lurches. . . . But the piano is the *special* hell—how it hurts one's head!"[9]

Fortunately, his shipboard suffering turned out to be only a kind of purgatory. By May 4, he could write triumphantly to Howells from Frankfurt that in spite of two "devilish weeks at sea" he had safely arrived on the other side. "Ah, I have such a deep, grateful, unutterable sense of being 'out of it all.' I think I foretaste some of the advantage of being dead. Some of the joy of it. . . . What a paradise this land is!" Appropriately for an awed new arrival in heaven, he reported himself as going about "day by day, in a smileless state of solemn admiration." Weeks later, in Heidelberg, his euphoria persisted, and his situation was specifically celestial. The Clemenses were "divinely located" in the Schloss Hotel, perched on a mountainside. From glass-enclosed balconies they could "look down upon Heidelberg Castle, & upon the swift Neckar, & the town, & out over the wide green level of the Rhine valley— a marvelous prospect." The hotel was so far above the busy world that the only sounds one heard were the "happy clamor of the birds" and the "muffled music" of the river below. "It must have been a noble genius who devised this hotel," Mark Twain concluded. "Lord, how blessed is the repose, the tranquility of this place!"[10]

The effect of his crossing over was to refresh and rejuvenate him. During the summer, he was delighted by the novelties and adventures of foreign travel. He was joined on August 1 by his friend Joseph Twichell (who becomes Harris in *A Tramp Abroad)*, and the two of them set off for Switzerland. Mark Twain could write to Livy, who stayed in Heidelberg, that in spite of hiking through mud and rain for six hours, "I was as chipper and fresh as a lark all the way."[11] And alongside an alpine stream, where he raced with a piece of floating wood, the forty-two-year-old author changed into a Tom Sawyer. As Twichell described the event, "Mark was running downstream after it as hard as he could go, throwing up his hands and shouting in the wildest ecstasy, and when a piece went over a fall and emerged to view in the foam below he would jump up and down and yell."[12]

9. *Ibid.*, 67.
10. Smith and Gibson (eds.), *Mark Twain–Howells Letters,* 227, 229–30.
11. Paine (ed.), *Mark Twain's Letters,* I, 335–36.
12. Albert Bigelow Paine, *Mark Twain: A Biography* (3 vols.; New York, 1912), II, 629.

The second phase in Mark Twain's program of recovery, somewhat overlapping the first, was a return to and reaffirmation of his most sustaining and enduring religion—his deism. If his delight in new scenes had made him as a child again, fit to enter the kingdom of heaven, his shipboard meditation on the marvels of navigation brought him back to that period of his youth when he saw God's benevolent hand in nature. What he wrote in his notebook in 1878 is substantially a repetition of the pre-Darwinian hymn to the navigator's "imperial intellect" that he composed in 1867:

It is a marvel that never loses its surprise by repetition, this aiming a ship at a mark 3000 miles away & hitting the bull's-eye in a fog—as we did. When the fog fell on us the Capt. said we ought to be at such & such a spot (it had been 18 hours since an observation was had) with the Scilly islands bearing so-&-so & about so many miles away. Hove the lead & got 48 fathoms—looked on the chart & sure enough this depth of water showed that we were right where Capt. said we were.

Another idea. For ages man probably did not know why God carpeted the ocean-bottom with sand in one place, shells in another, & so on.—But we see, now; the kind of bottom the lead brings up shows where a ship is when soundings don't—& also it *confirms* the soundings.[13]

Absent from his language here is any hint of irony or skepticism. He says simply enough that God carpeted the sea floor in various textures as an aid to human navigation.

His next deistic moment was of a quite different order. Touring the high Alps early in September and witnessing with Twichell the glory of snowy peaks against awesome patterns of cloud and light, he had a religious experience. Several times in his notebook he tried to paint the inspiring spectacle with words—"white shreds & ribbons of ethereal clouds," "vast spreading fan-shaped shadows," "long, slanting, cleanly-cut dark ray," and, in a later insertion in different-colored ink, "[i]dyllic," "odic."[14] The experience was not a recapitulation of a previous one but a going beyond. From what the record can reveal of such ineffable matters, it was his supreme moment of beatitude. Four months later, in a letter to Twichell, who had returned to the States, he was able to express in a measure the ecstasy he had felt:

---

13. Anderson, Salamo, and Stein (eds.), *Mark Twain's Notebooks and Journals*, II, 68–69.
14. *Ibid.*, 172–75.

Those mountains had a soul; they thought; they spoke,—one couldn't hear it with the ears of the body, but what a voice it was!—and how real. Deep down in my memory it is sounding yet. Alp calleth unto Alp!—that stately old Scriptural wording is the right one for God's Alps and God's ocean. How puny we were in that awful presence—and how painless it was to be so; how fitting and right it seemed, and how stingless was the sense of our unspeakable insignificance. And Lord how pervading were the repose and peace and blessedness that poured out of the heart of the invisible Great Spirit of the Mountains.[15]

Reborn, rejuvenated, and afforded a religious experience of a high order, Mark Twain should, one supposes, have been ready to take up the pen again. But not so. Although his flight to Europe had been the right medicine for his wilted spirit, it only complicated the problem of his authorial identity, of his role and function as a modern American writer, of his proper attitude toward the past. What was he doing in Europe anyway? Hadn't he set himself against those old *Atlantic Monthly* poets who kept looking back to Europe for models? And what business did he have writing *another* travel book on Europe? Hadn't he in *Innocents Abroad* made enough fun of Europe as a museum of the dead past, at the same time establishing for himself an international reputation as a delightfully bumptious American living vividly in the present? Or had the Whittier dinner so changed his mind about his duty to the past that instead of a sequel to *Innocents Abroad* he would write a recantation?

He had not begun to answer such questions by the end of summer, 1878; nor had he made any progress on his projected book. What he had written, he confessed to his publisher, was "in disconnected form" (and destined to be discarded), though he cheerfully added, "I have been gathering a lot of excellent matter here." With Twichell's arrival, he conceived of a "new and better plan for the book": He would announce on page 1 that the book would describe a walking tour of Europe; and then, patently unconscious of the irony, he and Harris would avoid walking as much as possible.[16] Such a trivial plan! And like the diffident title itself—*A Tramp Abroad* (which may not have been conceived yet)—it was an evasion of hard questions about his authorial role and his position vis-à-vis Europe.

15. Paine (ed.), *Mark Twain's Letters*, I, 351.
16. Hamlin Hill (ed.), *Mark Twain's Letters to His Publishers* (Berkeley, 1967), 108, 109–10.

The plan did nothing to unblock his muse. Probably much more effective in the long run was his fortunate association, in Italy, with Augustus P. Chamberlaine and his wife. The Chamberlaines were Americans who, like the Clemenses, were taking a fall tour of Venice, Florence, and Rome. The two couples struck up a congenial relationship, visiting museums together and afterwards dining and chatting. Livy regarded the Chamberlaines as "wonderfully delightful people."[17] They happened also to be friends of Ralph Waldo Emerson; and from personal knowledge, they could assure Mark Twain that Emerson was *not* affronted by the Whittier birthday speech. They wholeheartedly sided with Twain in the affair. "I perceived with joy," Twain wrote later, "that the C.'s were indignant about the way that my performance had been received in Boston. They poured out their opinions most freely and frankly about the frosty attitude of the people who were present at that performance, and about the Boston newspapers for the position they had taken in regard to the matter."[18]

The Chamberlaines' sympathetic support, plus the circumstance of Mark Twain's finding himself for the second time surrounded by the paintings of Italy's "Old Masters," undoubtedly catalyzed the third phase in his psychic recovery. Eleven years before, as an innocent abroad, he had quite frankly announced himself as incompetent to appreciate or judge the paintings. On the whole, he liked the copies better than the originals, because their colors were brighter. Had he in the meantime made any progress as an art critic? Or had the Whittier dinner experience chastened him into expressing an unparticular admiration for venerated art? His first notebook reactions to the Old Masters point toward the latter alternative. In Venice he judged that "[t]he loveliest picture is Paul Veronese showing his sketches to Titian"; and arriving in Florence, he wrote delightedly, "It is wonderful how many celebrated men this little town of Florence has produced," and he named, among others, da Vinci, Michelangelo, Cellini, and Giotto.[19] But as he continued to observe the paintings, it seemed to occur to him that since his *Innocents Abroad* days he had, after all, studied under Taine and Howells and that he was thus equipped with a modern and scientific criterion for judging art: It was good if it was true to life.

17. Anderson, Salamo, and Stein (eds.), *Mark Twain's Notebooks and Journals*, II, 220.

18. Albert Bigelow Paine (ed.), *Mark Twain's Speeches* (New York, 1923), 69.

19. Anderson, Salamo, and Stein (eds.), *Mark Twain's Notebooks and Journals*, II, 223, 227–28.

He proceeded exuberantly to apply his touchstone. Titian's *Portrait of a Man* earned a paragraph of praise in his notebook, because its details were so authentic—"black robe, a trifle of lace at neck & wrists, short brown hair, thin, handsome manly features, full of character & firmness. . . . This person is so *human*—you recognize in him at once the very highest type of man." Bronzino's *Portrait of Prince Don Garzie* presented "very much the best baby I have seen in these acres of pictures. This is a *real* child, with fat face without having an apple in each cheek, has a most silly, winning, chuckleheaded childlike gleeful smile, 2 little teeth just showing in lower jaw—oh he is perfect!"[20]

Stylized and idealized representations, however, inspired his sarcasm. Most of the "saints & angels & Holy Families" in Florence's Pitti Palace he judged to be "sappy & gushy & chuckleheaded & theatrical." The boy in Raphael's *Transfiguration* in the Vatican

has monstrous arms, packed full of great muscles, as if they were stuffed with kidneys. That boy ought to be able to throw a bull over his shoulder. The woman near him is similarly muscled, & could toss/pitch the bull back.

The people in the ugly & exasperating cartoons of Raphael are similarly muscled. A begging cripple there is a Hercules.

Michelangelo has built his people in the Sistine Chapel in the same way.

To such grandiloquent portraiture he preferred a modern painting hanging in the Vatican Palace, because its artist "makes men & drapery, complexions, forms & things absolutely as they *are*. They are flesh colored people, of mere ordinary strength." He ironically concluded:

I understand good art to be, that way of representing a thing on canvass which shall be farthest from resembling anything in heaven or on earth or in the waters under the earth.

In good art, a correct complexion is the color of a lobster, or of a bleached tripe or of a chimney sweep—there are no intermediates or modifications.[21]

And so, during the year following his humiliation at the Whittier dinner, Mark Twain had gone through three phases of recovery: his death, rebirth, and rejuvenation; his reaffirmation of deistic belief; and his recollection of the realistic point of view.

20. *Ibid.*, 231, 235.
21. *Ibid.*, 231, 239, 241.

CHAPTER 7

# Penwork and Dreamwork

> But this tramp only asked,—"Were any of these heroes men of science?" This raised a laugh, of course, for science was despised in those days. But the tramp was not in the least ruffled. He said he might be a little in advance of his age, but no matter,—science would come to be honored, some time or other.
>
> —A Tramp Abroad, Chapter 17

THERE REMAINED ONE MORE phase in Mark Twain's program of recovery—a repossession of the Tainean literary theory and method. Concerning that last phase, two assertions may be made. First, Twain had to reembrace his Tainean convictions before he could finish his stalled novels. His momentum toward modernity had been thrown into reverse at the Whittier dinner because, though he hardly realized it, he had engineered a collision between the past and the future of American literature and the past won, or so it seemed to him then. His confidence in his modern scientific theories had been shattered. Yet, in his year in limbo, he had thought of no better theory and, specifically, of no better way to write *The Prince and the Pauper* than according to his Tainean plan. The second assertion is that he accomplished his last phase in the process of writing *A Tramp Abroad*, especially its first twenty chapters.

Consider, in support of these assertions, the nuclear position of *A Tramp Abroad* with reference to the composition of *The Prince and the Pauper* and *Huckleberry Finn*. Along the dimension of time, its composition lies at the center of the two novels. The *Tramp* (1878–1880) nests within *The Prince and the Pauper* (1877–1881), which nests within *Huckleberry Finn* (1876–1883). Within days of finishing *A Tramp Abroad*, Twain was back at work on *The Prince and the Pauper*, writing with "jubilant delight."[1]

Consider also the rehearsal of Tainean tenets in Twain's letter to Howells of January 21, 1879, by which time his pen had "got the old

---

1. Henry Nash Smith and William M. Gibson (eds.), *Mark Twain–Howells Letters* (2 vols.; Cambridge, Mass., 1960), I, 290.

swing again"[2] and he had written perhaps a dozen chapters of *A Tramp Abroad*. The passage is in response to his reading in Howells' *The Lady of the Aroostook*:

If your literature has not struck perfection now we are not able to see what is lacking.—It is all such truth—truth to the life; everywhere your pen falls it leaves a photograph. I *did* imagine that everything had been said about life at sea that could be said,—but no matter, it was all a failure and lies, nothing but lies with a thin varnish of fact,—only *you* have stated it as it absolutely *is*. And only you see people & their ways & their insides & outsides as they *are*, & make them talk as they *do* talk. I think you are the very greatest artist in these tremendous mysteries that ever lived. There doesn't seem to be anything that can be concealed from your awful all-seeing eye.[3]

This is sincere praise of Howells' genius, certainly; but in its explicit echoes of Taine's recommending that the novelist acquire the "[e]xact knowledge of all those appearances by which man manifests himself; and exact divination of the inner workings of the mind and heart," it is also something else. It is the recital of catechism by a writer who, through penwork and dreamwork, in *A Tramp Abroad* was reimmersing himself in the mysteries he had recently shared with his master.

The penwork is most obvious in Chapters 5 to 7, where Twain wrote a detailed, objective, and uncomfortably graphic description of saber dueling between Heidelberg students. His intention was clearly to record such observations as would first allow his reader to imagine the scenes of flashing sabers, gashed faces, and surgeons' needlework and then to understand the meanings and emotions behind the ceremony of the student duel. He was to be an American Taine, impartially and accurately displaying those appearances by which one may gain knowledge of the character of a foreign people. He was quite conscious of his method. The chapters, he wrote to Mrs. Fairbanks, are "a perfectly serious description of 5 very bloody student-duels which I witnessed in Heidelberg one day—a description which simply *describes* the terrific spectacle with no jests interlarded & no comments added."[4]

2. Albert Bigelow Paine (ed.), *Mark Twain's Letters* (2 vols.; New York, 1917), I, 349.
3. Smith and Gibson (eds.), *Mark Twain–Howells Letters*, I, 245.
4. Dixon Wecter (ed.), *Mark Twain to Mrs. Fairbanks* (San Marino, Calif., 1949), 227.

He was so intent on being scientific that his first paragraph comes close to being a parody of the scientific style, at the same time uncannily foreshadowing Hemingway's rhythms and phrasing:

One day in the interest of science my agent obtained permission to bring me to the students' dueling place. We crossed the river and drove up the bank a few hundred yards, then turned to the left, entered a narrow alley, followed it a hundred yards and arrived at a two-story public house; we were acquainted with its outside aspect, for it was visible from the hotel. We went up the stairs and passed into a large whitewashed apartment which was perhaps fifty feet long by thirty feet wide and twenty or twenty-five high. It was a well-lighted place. There was no carpet. Across one end and down both sides of the room extended a row of tables, and at these tables some fifty or seventy-five students were sitting.[5]

The measurements and numbers do help to make things clear, but directions on how to drive from the university to the public house seem a touch unnecessary. Perhaps, in assembling his resources for his scientific project, he had recalled the science of piloting, which in turn obliged him to make a note of the points, landmarks, directions, and distances on his little journey.

The dueling chapters amount to Mark Twain's saying that he *could* write in the scientific mode if he felt like it. In their length— over five thousand words—and their sustained realism and singleness of purpose they are unlike anything he had written before. But having shown what he could do, he did not feel required to continue the performance in *A Tramp Abroad*. In fact, his next chapter—an outrageous burlesque of French dueling—is a deliberate turnabout. The contrast between his serious treatment of German student dueling and his mockery of French dueling, he explained to Mrs. Fairbanks, "will be the silent but eloquent comment."[6] Thereafter in his travel book only Chapters 21 and 22, preoccupied as they are with the question of national character, could be called Tainean. The last two-thirds of the book is a mixture of touristy descriptions, spoofs, and recollections of things past. He would reserve the Tainean technique for *The Prince and the Pauper*.

---

5. Samuel Clemens [Mark Twain], *A Tramp Abroad*, Author's National Edition: The Writings of Mark Twain (25 vols.; New York, 1907–18), III, 41. Further references to *A Tramp Abroad* are indicated by parenthetical page numbers in the text.

6. Wecter (ed.), *Mark Twain to Mrs. Fairbanks*, 227.

The first twenty chapters of *A Tramp Abroad* are in large measure Mark Twain's unconscious working out of his attitudes as a modern American writer toward Europe's legendary past. He produced those chapters during the period December, 1878, through February, 1879, when he was working with some enthusiasm. "[T]he mood is everything, not the material," he wrote Twichell in January, "and I already seem to see 300 pages rising before me on that trip."[7] But he was writing without a firm sense of direction. "I have destroyed such lots of MS written for this book," he confessed to Howells four days later. "And I suppose there are such lots left which ought to be destroyed."[8]

His plan, he explained to Howells in the same letter, was, besides organizing the book around the fake pedestrian tour, to pretend that he was in Europe for the two purposes of learning the German language and of studying art and learning to paint. The plan was, of course, no plan at all, but another evasion of the question of his role as an American writer in Europe. Unconscious of the evasion but deeply uneasy, he compensated by aggrandizing his "plan." He felt it necessary to swear Howells to secrecy about it. "Mind, whatever I say about the book is a *secret*;—my publisher shall know little or nothing about the book till he gets the MS, for I can't trust his tongue—I am trusting *nobody* but you & Twichell. I like mighty well to tell my plans & swap opinions about them, but I don't like them to get around."[9]

In beginning *A Tramp Abroad*, he had dutifully listed his three "purposes" on the first page and then had turned his back on them to plunge into the deeper purpose of which he was unaware—that of clarifying his feelings about the legendary past. He did so by making legends themselves the ever-recurring subject of his first nineteen chapters. He recited, paraphrased, discussed, burlesqued, and invented legends. He even translated Heinrich Heine's poem on the legend of the Lorelei.

He was led into the subject by stumbling in a Frankfurt shop upon F. J. Kiefer's *The Legends of the Rhine from Basle to Rotterdam*, a collection published in Mainz for the tourist trade, in French and English translations as well as in the original German. It was a book that, as he expressed it in two elemental but rather contradictory

---

7. Paine (ed.), *Mark Twain's Letters*, I, 349.
8. Smith and Gibson (eds.), *Mark Twain–Howells Letters*, I, 248.
9. *Ibid.*, 249.

metaphors, "has charmed me nearly to death" and "fed me in a very hungry place" (11, 12).

He used four of Kiefer's legends in *A Tramp Abroad*: Kiefer's "Frankfort: Foundation of the City" is the source of the story about the naming of Frankfurt in Chapter 1. Kiefer's "The Knave of Bergen" is copied verbatim in Chapter 1. Kiefer's "Lorelei" is extensively quoted and paraphrased in Chapter 16. And Kiefer's "George of Frankenstein" provided him an old plot, which he would use for modern purposes in the "Legend of the 'Spectacular Ruin'" in Chapter 17.

Twain recited three legends of the Neckar River, apparently gathered from sources other than Kiefer: that of Götz von Berlichingen (Chapter 12), "The Legend" of the wives of Weibertreu (Chapter 12), and "The Cave of the Specter" (Chapter 15). Three legends of the Neckar he invented himself: "The Legend of the 'Spectacular Ruin'" (Chapter 17), "The Legend of Dilsberg Castle" (Chapter 19), and "Legend of the Castles" (Appendix E). To this list illustrating Twain's preoccupation with the legendary should be added an American tale—"Baker's Bluejay Yarn," with its prologue (Chapters 2 and 3).

It is the "Bluejay Yarn," with its prologue, and the three invented legends that exhibit Mark Twain's dreamwork. One of the four, "Legend of the Castles," is built around money worries rather than the problem of his role as a writer and so need not be discussed.

In the prologue to "Baker's Bluejay Yarn," Twain remembers how fascinated he had been with German legends and fairy tales when he had stayed in Heidelberg the previous May. "I had been reading so much of this literature," he explained, "that sometimes I was not sure but I was beginning to believe in the gnomes and fairies as realities."

One afternoon [he continued] I got lost in the woods about a mile from the hotel, and presently fell into a train of dreamy thought about animals which talk, and kobolds, and enchanted folk, and the rest of the pleasant legendary stuff; and so, by stimulating my fancy, I finally got to imagining I glimpsed small flitting shapes here and there down the columned aisles of the forest. It was a place which was peculiarly meet for the occasion. It was a pine wood, with so thick and soft a carpet of brown needles that one's footfall made no more sound than if he were treading on wool; the tree-trunks were as round and straight and smooth as pillars, and stood close together; they were bare of branches to a point about twenty-five feet above ground, and from there upward so thick with boughs that not a ray of sunlight could pierce through. The world was bright with sunshine outside, but a deep and mellow twilight reigned in there, and also a silence so profound that I seemed to hear my own breathings. (21–22)

This paragraph from the second chapter of *A Tramp Abroad* introduces the theme of the first third of the book. The theme is the contest between imagination and observation, and between the realms that each has created—a legendary past and an actuality perceived in the modern way.

The language of the paragraph is perfectly tuned to evoke the silent and solitary world of the imagination and to inhabit it with enchanted forms. In tone and function it is the exact opposite of the dueling chapters. Its spell is soon broken by the intrusion of an observer:

When I had stood ten minutes, thinking and imagining, and getting my spirit in tune with the place, and in the right mood to enjoy the supernatural, a raven suddenly uttered a hoarse croak over my head. It made me start; and then I was angry because I started. I looked up, and the creature was sitting on a limb right over me, looking down at me. I felt something of the same sense of humiliation and injury which one feels when he finds that a human stranger has been clandestinely inspecting him in his privacy and mentally commenting upon him. I eyed the raven and the raven eyed me. Nothing was said during some seconds. Then the bird stepped a little way along his limb to get a better point of observation, lifted his wings, stuck his head far down below his shoulders toward me, and croaked again—a croak with a distinctly insulting expression about it. If he had spoken in English he could not have said any more plainly than he did say in raven, "Well, what do *you* want here?" I felt as foolish as if I had been caught in some mean act by a responsible being, and reproved for it. (22–23)

The emotions the narrator feels here are bizarre. What is he ashamed of? He has simply been daydreaming in a quiet woods, yet the raven's squawk makes him feel humiliated and guilty. Something deeper is the matter, and the dreamwork continues to furnish clues: The raven with his "keen bright eye" now becomes "the adversary" and is thrice so named. He is joined by another raven: "The two sat side by side on the limb and discussed me as freely and offensively as two great naturalists might discuss a new kind of bug. The thing became more and more embarrassing. They called in another friend. This was too much. I saw that they had the advantage of me, and I concluded to get out of the scrape by walking out of it. They enjoyed my defeat as much as any low white people could have done" (23).

At the least, what we have here is a drama of competition between the realm of dreams and the realm of scientific observation. The ravens—those "naturalists" discussing the meditative human being as if he were "a new kind of bug"—represent not only the vernacular character but the scientific intellect as well. Taine, it will be remembered, characterized his historical approach as that of a "naturalist" who regarded his subject "the same as the metamorphosis of an insect." The drama further allows us to guess that a year after Mark Twain had "insulted" America's romantic writers he began *A Tramp Abroad* seeking atonement. If not exactly a convert to romanticism, he had at least become sympathetic to the aims and methods of the writers he had made fun of. It was as if he must put himself in their place and suffer as they had suffered before he could make progress toward reestablishing a viable literary theory. Turning the tables might ease his conscience; now it fell to *his* part to immerse himself in the realm of the legendary and then be mocked by a parade of three "low white people."

"Baker's Bluejay Yarn," the minor American classic for which Mark Twain's meditations were prologue, seems to have as little to do with his current state of mind as with his current time and place. The yarn is about a California bluejay who is taught the "absurdity of the contract" of "trying to fill up a house with acorns" by dropping them through a knothole in the roof. Could it not, however, at one level of Twain's imagination, concern his anxieties over beginning still another book? Considering that he had left half a dozen unfinished books in his wake, considering his current ambivalence between contesting literary realms, and considering the tenuousness of his "plans," he has, in proposing to write *A Tramp Abroad*, indeed made an absurd contract. The house may be the empty book that he has to fill, and the acorns the hundreds of notes he has made on his recent travels. One by one, he has dropped them into his notebook, where, still unorganized, they lie like the acorns, "scattered all over the floor."

Mark Twain's first invented legend—that of "Dilsberg Castle"[10]— involved the author in a deep rumination on the past and a final

10. *Ibid.*, 249–50. Although "The Legend of Dilsberg Castle" appears in *A Tramp Abroad* two chapters after the invented "Legend of the 'Spectacular Ruin,'" he composed "Dilsberg" first.

recoil from it. The actual town of Dilsberg, which Twain visited, was a living museum. Girt by walls and perched on a hilltop above "the troublous world," Dilsberg had not, except for the erosion of time, changed for centuries. Its seven hundred inhabitants carried on age-old tasks—flailing, spinning, coopering, and goose herding. With its "narrow, crooked lane which had been paved in the Middle Ages," it was quaint and picturesque, a "snug town," "very still and peaceful"; yet there were jarring notes. The once grand castle had crumbled; the well had gone dry; and because of generations of inbreeding, the town had become an "idiot factory."

A four-hundred-year-old linden in the ruined castle's courtyard inspired this meditation:

That tree has witnessed the assaults of men in mail,—how remote such a time seems, and how ungraspable is the fact that real men ever did fight in real armor!—and it had seen the time when these broken arches and crumbling battlements were a trim and strong and stately fortress, fluttering its gay banners in the sun, and peopled with vigorous humanity,—how impossibly long ago that seems!—and here it stands yet, and possibly may still be standing here, sunning itself and dreaming its historical dreams, when to-day shall have been joined to the days called "ancient." (177–78)

And having dreamed himself deeply into the past of this ruined castle, Mark Twain invented a legend most melancholy and horrid: Long ago, Dilsberg Castle was occupied by a festive company, among whom were Conrad von Geisberg, a young knight, and Catharina, his betrothed and niece of the lord of the castle. When the revelers' talk turned to the castle's haunted chamber, Conrad shuddered: It was said that anyone sleeping in the chamber would not awaken for fifty years. The company, amused at Conrad's distress, were determined to make the "superstitious young man" sleep in the haunted room. They succeeded with the help of Catharina, who, through cajolery and tears, finally won Conrad's consent.

While Conrad was sleeping in the chamber, under the influence of a draught, the company carried out an elaborate practical joke: They moved his bed to a decrepit room, replaced his clothes with rags, and disguised themselves; and when he awakened, they convinced him that he had indeed slept for fifty years and that meantime Catharina had died of grief and was buried under the linden.

When Catharina deemed that the joke had gone far enough, she and the others threw off their disguises. "'Ah, 'twas a gallant jest!'

she cried. 'How real was thy misery for the moment, thou poor lad! Look up and have thy laugh, now!' "

But Conrad could not be disabused. He recognized no one and continued to regard himself as an old man cut off from all former associations. After two years of mourning beside Catharina's imaginary grave, he died. "Then Catharina sat under the linden alone, every day and all day long, a great many years, speaking to no one, and never smiling; and at last her long repentance was rewarded with death, and she was buried by Conrad's side."

"Dilsberg" presents a different aspect of the past from that presented in the forest meditation preceding the bluejay yarn. In the woods outside Heidelberg, one imagined legendary talking animals and enchanted folk, creatures that had never lived except in fancy; and that was pleasant enough. But at Dilsberg Castle, one was surrounded by evidence that generations of "vigorous humanity" had peopled the place and now were dead. The past was a haunted chamber that turned the young to old, the living into dead. There was danger in the past. It could envelop a sensitive imagination and sicken it. That realization, coupled with the feeling that he had been an intruder in Heidelberg's enchanted forest, put an end to Mark Twain's dalliance with Germany's legendary past and propelled him by recoil to an opposite position, where he embraced the modern American values of science, technology, and business enterprise. In so doing, he broke out of the murky tunnel of irresolution and ambivalence that he had been traveling through for more than a year and won his way to a clear definition of his role as a writer vis-à-vis Europe, the past, and the romantic tradition. Such is the import of his invented legend of the "Spectacular Ruin."

At first glance, "Legend of the 'Spectacular Ruin' " seems a slight and playful piece, little more than an excuse for springing a miserable pun on the reader: The tumbledown castle on the Neckar is not remarkable; it is called "spectacular" because its ancient owner manufactured spectacles. On second glance, it *is* an artful story, simply told but dense with nuances.[11]

11. Pascal Covici, Jr., has made an extensive analysis of the elements of parody and burlesque in the "Legend of the 'Spectacular Ruin' " (*Mark Twain's Humor* [Dallas, 1960], 118–22, 251–54). Franklin R. Rogers states that the legend foreshadows *A Connecticut Yankee* (*Mark Twain's Burlesque Patterns* [Dallas, 1960], 86). Robert Regan agrees with him and, in his further analysis, finds that "this little fable has much to recommend it" (*Unpromising Heroes* [Berkeley, 1966], 138–41).

The legend tells how Sir Wissenschaft (Science), "a poor and obscure knight out of a far country," sought the German emperor's reward for killing a dragon that had been spreading disease, fire, and famine across the land. When he presented himself, people made fun of his ragged, ridiculous appearance. The emperor sarcastically advised him to hunt hares instead of the dragon that had already slain so many heroic knights. But Sir Wissenschaft's confidence was unshakable. He only asked, "Were any of these heroes men of science?" The people laughed, for science was despised in the Middle Ages; but Sir Wissenschaft remained unruffled. "He said he might be a little in advance of his age, but no matter,—science would come to be honored, some time or other."

The next morning, refusing a spear and carrying only the fire extinguisher he had invented for the occasion, he easily dispatched the dragon. "This man had brought brains to his aid. He had reared dragons from the egg, in his laboratory, he had watched over them like a mother, and experimented upon them while they grew. Thus he had found out that fire was the life principle of a dragon; put out the dragon's fires and it could make steam no longer, and must die."

As his reward, Sir Wissenschaft refused to consider one of the emperor's daughters and instead asked for "the monopoly of the manufacture and sale of spectacles in Germany." Although dismayed by the request, the emperor granted it. Sir Wissenschaft proved his good will by lowering the price of his product so that a "crushing burden was removed from the nation." In gratitude, the emperor decreed that everyone should buy and wear the monopolist's spectacles.[12]

This story of the ragged knight's perfect success on both the technological and commercial fronts is a precipitation of attitude that announces the emergence of a new Mark Twain in what may be his best-known avatar. Where did all the ideas making up this new attitude come from? It is impossible to say. Mark Twain's reading in Taine was certainly influential, as he himself admitted some years later. In 1871, when he first read Carlyle's *French Revolution*, he had been a Girondist; but by 1887, "being influenced & changed, little by

---

12. Clemens was struck with the popularity of spectacles in Germany: "I would rather be a spectacle-maker in Germany than anything else.—These people might possibly get along without clothes, or Bibles, or even beer, but they've got to have spectacles." Frederick Anderson, Lin Salamo, and Bernard L. Stein (eds.), *Mark Twain's Notebooks and Journals* (3 vols. completed; Berkeley, 1975), II, 64.

little, by life & environment (& Taine & St. Simon),"[13] he was, he wrote Howells, a sans-culotte. Perhaps there is something of John T. Lewis, the courageous black who stopped the runaway horse, in Sir Wissenschaft. The ragged, comical appearances of both of them conceal unexpected powers; both heroes prevail against dangerous beasts; both gain the admiration of their social superiors; and both are substantially rewarded.

At any rate, the characterization of Sir Wissenschaft vitalizes and unifies the cluster of ideas that make up the new attitude. Those ideas are that the strategies used in the past for coping with mankind's problems are outmoded, as is the old hierarchical social structure; that the modern champion will depend not on privilege or tradition but on scientific thinking and business enterprise; and that through his efforts the modern champion will win riches for himself and benefits for mankind.

The new Mark Twain took the spotlight for a decade and a half. He was the social critic who measured a country's civilization not by its history but by its technology and enterprise. Touring England in 1879 and incensed at British contempt for things American, he wrote in his notebook: "We shall presently be indifferent to being looked down upon by a nation no bigger & no better than our own. We made the telegraph a practical thing; we invented the fast press, the sewing machine, the sleeping and parlor car, the telephone, the iron-clad, we have done our share for the century."[14] (He added: "Nobody writes a finer & purer English than Motley, Howells, Hawthorne & Holmes," thus putting a nation's writers on a par with its inventors.) Three years later, he described the American South as debilitated by "Walter Scottism"—that is, by the popularity there of Scott's romances, with their "fantastic heroes and their grotesque 'chivalry' doings and romantic juvenilities." Southerners had the chance to benefit from the "permanent services to liberty, humanity, and progress" resulting from the French Revolution's breaking the "chains of the *ancien régime* and of the Church"; but along "comes Sir Walter Scott with his enchantments, and by his single might checks this wave of progress, and even turns it back; sets the world in love with dreams and phantoms; with decayed and swinish forms of religion; with decayed and degraded systems of government; with the sillinesses and emptinesses, sham grandeurs, sham gauds,

---

13. Smith and Gibson (eds.), *Mark Twain–Howells Letters*, II, 595.
14. Anderson, Salamo, and Stein (eds.), *Mark Twain's Notebooks and Journals*, II, 348.

and sham chivalries of a brainless and worthless long-vanished society."

The result for the Deep South was a confusion of modernity with a sickly romanticism, but from St. Louis northward that confusion did not exist. There one saw instead "all the enlivening signs of the presence of active, energetic, intelligent, prosperous, practical nineteenth-century populations. The people don't dream; they work."[15] The new Mark Twain bravely invested hundreds of thousands of dollars in developing his and other people's inventions during the 1880s and early 1890s. What if most of the money disappeared down a rat hole? His hopes stayed high. He expected to become "one of the wealthiest grandees in America."[16] The new Mark Twain remodeled Sir Wissenschaft slightly in 1885 for his reappearance in *A Connecticut Yankee*, where, as Hank Morgan, he would modernize King Arthur's England. When the author, in the writing, found out to his chagrin how resistant the past was to being changed, he was not quite the same new Mark Twain by the time he finished the book in 1889. And by 1894, when his sanguine sallies into the commercial arena had bankrupted him, the venturesome Mark Twain had given way to a more introverted successor.

But to return to the Mark Twain who had just invented Sir Wissenschaft in Munich in 1879. Although there is apparently nothing about literary theory in the "Spectacular Ruin," perhaps the ragged hero and his adventures may be taken as metaphors for Mark Twain and his new understanding of his literary role. Both Sir Wissenschaft and Mark Twain were foreigners and nobodies in Germany. (In Germany and Switzerland, Mark Twain found that he was "utterly unknown" and that if he went into a bank he "must stand around & wait with Tom Dick & Harry—& lucky if not received at last with rude impertinence.")[17] Both of them were tramps abroad.[18] But Sir Wissenschaft, in spite of his modest appearance, had a powerful secret in his science and his fire extinguisher. Armed

---

15. Samuel Clemens [Mark Twain], *Life on the Mississippi,* Author's National Edition: The Writings of Mark Twain (25 vols.; New York, 1907–18), IX, 309, 346, 347, 421.

16. Paine (ed.), *Mark Twain's Letters,* II, 534.

17. Anderson, Salamo, and Stein (eds.), *Mark Twain's Notebooks and Journals,* II, 163.

18. Mark Twain was aware of the double meaning of his travel book title: "I perceived that in using the word Tramp I was unconsciously describing the walker as well as the walk." Hamlin Hill (ed.), *Mark Twain's Letters to His Publishers* (Berkeley, 1967), 109–10n.

with them, he had no use for the traditional spear. "Out of compassion . . . a decent spear was offered him, but he declined, and said, 'spears were useless to men of science.' " Might not Mark Twain's Tainean theory and method be *his* powerful secret? In Germany he had been offered an alternative in the legendary and romantic way of imagining and writing. He felt obliged to consider the offer but finally rejected it.

His rejection was emphatic and exultant. For much of nineteen chapters he had been moseying around Heidelberg and along the Neckar River, mooning over antiquities and legends. In the last six of these chapters he had used the fiction that he and his party were riding a raft down the Neckar, from Heilbronn to Heidelberg, the better to observe the life along its banks and the fabled ruins on its cliffs. As a signal that he had finished his sentimental excursion, and was glad of it, he smashed the raft at the end of Chapter 19. Confident that he could steer the raft, which was "slashing down with the mad current," he relieved the pilot of his pole and aimed the raft at the archway of a downstream bridge: "We went tearing along in a most exhilarating way, and I performed the delicate duties of my office very well indeed for a first attempt; but perceiving, presently, that I really was going to shoot the bridge itself instead of the archway under it, I judiciously stepped ashore. The next moment I had my long-coveted desire: I saw a raft wrecked. It hit the pier in the center and went all to smash and scatteration like a box of matches struck by lightning." Thus, in a flurry of energetic images and gleeful expressions, he put an end to both his meanderings along the Neckar and his preoccupation with legends.

What he turned to in the next chapter is beyond theory. It is a celebration of the American vernacular and a revival of the spirit that had gotten *Huckleberry Finn* off to a great start in 1876. More than a celebration, it is a kind of morality play, remarkably complex, full of echoes of the Christian story, and designed to prove the salvational power of the vernacular. Its title might well be CHOLLEY ADAMS, THE VERNACULAR CHRIST.

The place is Baden-Baden, along whose streets Mark Twain, Harris, and the Reverend Mr. _____, an old friend from America newly met, are walking and chatting. Appearing on the scene like the apotheosis of an American is "a fine, large, vigorous young fellow, with an open, independent countenance . . . and . . . clothed from head to heel in cool and enviable snow-white linen." The "stately snow-white" youth turns out to be Cholley Adams, a western New

Yorker, who at his father's behest has been studying veterinary science in Germany for two years. Hungry for the sound of American speech, he attaches himself to the minister. When the minister asks him if he is homesick, he responds, " 'Oh, *hell*, yes!' " Oblivious to the minister's signs of distress and aching "to lisp once more the sweet accents of the mother tongue," Cholley "limbered up the muscles of his mouth and turned himself loose,—and with such a relish!"

"Yes indeedy! If *I* ain't an American there *ain't* any Americans, that's all. And when I heard you fellows gassing away in the good old American language, I'm _____ if it wasn't all I could do to keep from hugging you! My tongue's all warped with trying to curl it around these _____ forsaken wind-galled nine-jointed German words here; now I *tell* you it's awful good to lay it over a Christian word once more and kind of let the old taste soak in."

Cholley is " 'homesick from ear-socket to crupper, and from crupper to hock joint,' " because his "old man" had promised to let him come home and then had reneged on his promise. He

"never said why; just sent me a hamper of Sunday-school books, and told me to be good, and hold on a while. I don't take to Sunday-school books, dontchuknow,—I don't hanker after them when I can get pie,—but I *read* them anyway. . . . I buckled in and read all of those books, because he wanted me to; but that kind of thing don't excite *me*, I like something *hearty*."

" 'Well, _____ it ain't any use talking,' " he sums up; " 'some of these old American words do have a kind of bully swing to them; a man can *express* himself with 'em,—a man can get at what he wants to *say* dontchuknow.' "

The episode ends when the minister, who has been distressed by Cholley's hearty backslapping and vulgar eloquence, gives in to Cholley's earnest invitation to join him for supper. The "Reverend's heart was not hard enough to hold out against the pleadings,—he went away with the parent-honoring student, like a right Christian, and took supper with him in his lodgings, and sat in the surf-beat of his slang and profanity till near midnight." The minister has not tried to change Cholley's speech and is himself converted, so to speak, for he "brought away a pretty high opinion of Cholley as a manly young fellow."

Mark Twain potently commends the vernacular style here. Language and action that are frank, familiar, and vivid satisfy man's urgent need for communication, for communion. Conversely, formalities, unfamiliar language, and pious artificialities frustrate understanding. Mark Twain had been right to make fun of poets for using such phrases as *yonder squalid peasant* and *lives sublime*. Taine had been right about the way formal language starved the human spirit and the way homely language nourished it.

Another dictum of Taine's—his formula for assessing the soul of a people—controls the next chapter and a half (Chapters 21 and 22) of *A Tramp Abroad*. The subject is the German character, and the method is a detailed examination of the customs and artifacts displayed in Baden-Baden and the Black Forest.

Thereafter, Mark Twain's apparent purpose was simply to fill up the book. The next section, on Switzerland (Chapters 25 to 46), is not without its high spots; but there is no probing of national character, and his five weeks of experience in that country (out of sixty-nine weeks of travel) are inflated to make up half the book.

Although he seems to have completed the Switzerland chapters by the end of May, he could not finish the "infernally troublesome book"[19] until January, 1880. At that point, having written the required number of pages, though having covered less than half of his European travels, he chopped the manuscript off like a piece of sausage of the requested weight and sent it to his publisher.

He returned immediately to the writing of *The Prince and the Pauper*, a book he was prepared to take up again by the repossession of his Tainean theory and method. Unfortunately, he found little room in his historical novel to exercise the American vernacular.

19. Smith and Gibson (eds.), *Mark Twain–Howells Letters*, I, 290.

# PART III

# Mark Twain's Tetralogy: Training Is Everything

# CHAPTER 8

# The Hopeful View: *The Prince and the Pauper*

*My idea is to afford a realizing sense of the exceeding severity of the laws of that day by inflicting some of their penalties upon the king himself & allowing him a chance to see the rest of them applied to others—all of which is to account for certain mildnesses which distinguished Edward VIs reign from those that preceded and followed it.*

—Twain to Howells, March, 1880

LIFE, DARWIN DECLARED IN the first pages of his *Origin of Species,* is shaped by "two factors: namely, the nature of the organism, and the nature of the conditions."[1] Of course, we say now. Heredity and environment. With us, the idea has become a cliché; but in the nineteenth century, when people first began mulling it over, it was radical enough. It ended by establishing in the Western mind a new concept of personality and society.

Mark Twain probably had not read Darwin's assertion by the time he began *The Prince and the Pauper* (his copy of *Origin of Species* was published in 1884), but he had read his Taine. And even Lecky, who believed that humans were gifted with intuitive moral perceptions independent of experience, advised readers in his preface that he would present moral histories, "showing in what respects they were the products or expressions of the general condition of society."[2] Holmes, in his *Autocrat,* was even more explicit about the influence of environment. Personality, he declared, was formed by "organization [heredity], education, condition." "Education," he continued, "is only second to nature. Imagine all the infants born this year in Boston and Timbuctoo to change places!"[3] What created a Bostonian, Holmes implied, was not heredity but Boston itself.

1. Morse Peckham (ed.), *The Origin of Species by Charles Darwin: A Variorum Text* (Philadelphia, 1959), 78.
2. W. E. H. Lecky, *History of European Morals from Augustus to Charlemagne* (London, 1910), ix.
3. Oliver Wendell Holmes, *The Autocrat of the Breakfast Table* (Boston, 1892), 88–89, Vol. I of Holmes, *The Works of Oliver Wendell Holmes,* 13 vols.

From such sources, and from myriad others, for the idea was in the air, Mark Twain was assembling his notion that (as he would come to phrase it in *A Connecticut Yankee*) "training is everything." When in *The Prince and the Pauper* he used it to explain how Edward's character was transformed through retraining, it was to cheerful purpose. He had already begun *Huckleberry Finn* with the same hopeful view that heartfelt experience could modify ingrained attitude; but after his 1882 trip into the post-Reconstruction South, that hope, as it applied to the writing of the rest of *Huckleberry Finn*, was dead. In *A Connecticut Yankee*, his revived hope that the citizens of Arthur's England might be retrained was fiercely at odds with his conviction that they could not be. In *Pudd'nhead Wilson* there was no longer a hope of retraining, his acquiescence in determinism was complete, and in the subsidence of conflict, he wrote a surprisingly serene and sympathetic novel.

*The Prince and the Pauper* was influenced by Taine's *Ancient Regime* and by French history in general. Mark Twain was obliged to Taine not only for his scientific method of recalling history and for his social vision but for numerous historical details, including those having to do with the court of Louis XIV, which he applied to his English setting. This French influence has been overlooked by scholars, perhaps because French history seems an unlikely source for a novel about English royalty. Unlikely though it is, its influence was seminal.

The idea for *The Prince and the Pauper* was suggested to Mark Twain by his reading Charlotte M. Yonge's *The Little Duke*,[4] a romance of political intrigue set in tenth-century France. That was in the summer of 1876. On February 5, 1878, Twain reported that he had been "studying for" *The Prince and the Pauper* "off & on, for a year and a half"[5]—that is, ever since he had read Yonge's romance. His plan for the novel as we know it was not, however, put down until the fall of 1877; and it was only then that the reading for it and the writing of it began. His working notes, with their references to English history and literature, were written between late 1877 and February, 1881.[6]

4. Howard G. Baetzhold, *Mark Twain and John Bull* (Bloomington, Ind., 1970), 48.

5. Dixon Wecter (ed.), *Mark Twain to Mrs. Fairbanks* (San Marino, Calif., 1949), 218.

6. Samuel Clemens [Mark Twain], *The Prince and the Pauper*, ed. Victor Fischer and Lin Salamo (Berkeley, 1979), 3–4, 345–72, Vol. VI of the Works of Mark Twain. Further

What *was* he reading during that first year when he was "studying for" *The Prince and the Pauper*? The answer is French history and historical fiction. Here is the bibliography he sent Mrs. Fairbanks on August 6, 1877:

I cannot quite say I have read *nothing*. No, I have read half of Les Miserables, two or three minor works of Victor Hugo, & also that marvelous being's biography by his wife. I have read Carlyle's wonderful History of the French Revolution, which is one of the greatest creations that ever flowed from a pen. I followed that with Mr. Yonge's recent "Life of Marie Antoinette." . . .

I followed that with "In Exitu Israel," a very able novel by Baring-Gould, the purpose of which is to show the effect of some of the most odious of the privileges of the French nobles under *l'ancien regème* [*sic*], & of the dischurching of the Catholic Church by the National Assembly in '92. I preceded this with one of Dumas's novels, "The Taking of the Bastille" & another which illustrated the march of the rioters upon Versailles, the massacre upon the Champ de Mars, the frightful scenes of the 10th of August & 2ᵈ of September & c.

I followed all these with a small history of France in French & a story by Madame de Genlis, also in French, neither of which cast much light upon my subject or amounted to much. I would have done well to stop with Carlyle & Dumas. The others only confuse one—except some chapters in Taine's "Ancient Regime," a book I forgot to mention.

He ended by noting that he was currently reading X. B. Saintine's "Picciola" in French.[7]

The context of this reading list makes the list doubly interesting. It suggests that Mark Twain's feelings about his "subject" were troublesome and heavily repressed. The paragraph immediately preceding the quoted passage begins this way: "I wonder what you've been reading, my charming sister. I haven't been reading *any*thing. Too busy. One mustn't read when he has not anything to do. It distracts." The tone here is the curiously girlish and gossipy one that he often assumed in his letters to Mrs. Fairbanks. The "I haven't been reading *any*thing" conceals a guilty secret he was dying to tell. But before he could get to it, he had to go through a series of contortions: Reading "burns intellectual fuel" that should be saved for writing. The writer should be "dead to everything *but* his work." The writer should not read, should not receive letters or

---

references to *The Prince and the Pauper* are indicated by parenthetical page numbers in the text.

7. Wecter (ed.), *Mark Twain to Mrs. Fairbanks*, 207–208.

telegrams, should have no social life, "no seductive pleasures . . . dividing his mind." The least distracting place for a writer is prison, as John Bunyan, Sir Walter Raleigh, and Miguel de Cervantes found out. If only he could be "so circumstanced," he could "weave his fancies & continue his work in his head" without interruption. Therefore, "[i]f it were not for Livy and the cubs, this sun should not set before I would kill somebody in the second degree." Only after this tortuous preliminary was he able to confess, "I cannot quite say I have read *nothing.*"[8]

What are we to make of the reading list and of Mark Twain's ambivalence about displaying it? To begin with, the "subject" of his reading is obviously the ancient regime and the French Revolution. Moreover, it is likely that he originally planned to write a "Prince and Pauper" with the French Revolution as a central event. If such is the case, we can guess why he abandoned his plan: He could not settle on the meaning of the Revolution. His reading failed to assure him that the benefits of the Revolution had been worth the terror and the bloodshed. The problem of the French Revolution, which, as Walter Blair has asserted, became "a living part of Clemens's thought"[9] from 1877 on, troubled him deeply. By the spring and summer of 1879, when he was staying in Paris, reading Carlyle again, and visiting historical spots, his ambivalence toward the "hideous but beneficent French Revolution"[10] was extreme and would spread to an obsessive preoccupation with French immorality as he saw it—a view he got "from their books & their history."[11]

His attitude toward the French Revolution would change: In *A Connecticut Yankee* he praised "the ever-memorable and blessed Revolution." Nevertheless, his ambivalence lingered even in that book. What the people of King Arthur's England needed, the Yankee declared, "was a Reign of Terror and a guillotine"; but the Yankee shrank from the job. He was "the wrong man" for it. Instead he would work out "a peaceful revolution."[12] A peaceful revolution is

8. *Ibid.*, 207.

9. Walter Blair, *Mark Twain and Huck Finn* (Berkeley, 1960), 178.

10. Samuel Clemens [Mark Twain], *A Tramp Abroad*, Author's National Edition: The Writings of Mark Twain (25 vols.; New York, 1907–18), III, 267.

11. Frederick Anderson, Lin Salamo, and Bernard L. Stein (eds.), *Mark Twain's Notebooks and Journals* (3 vols. completed; Berkeley, 1975), II, 322.

12. Samuel Clemens [Mark Twain], *A Connecticut Yankee in King Arthur's Court*, ed. Bernard L. Stein and Henry Nash Smith (Berkeley, 1979), 157, 229, Vol. IX of the Works of Mark Twain.

what, in a sense, Mark Twain would be able to work out in turning away from France and choosing the England of Edward VI for his setting.

Mark Twain did not, however, leave his cargo of French history behind him when he crossed the Channel. That history, and particularly *The Ancient Regime*, informs *The Prince and the Pauper* in matters large and small.

The royal court in *The Prince and the Pauper* is more French than English, a fact that has apparently gone unnoticed since 1881. In that year a British reviewer, probably Edmund Sheridan Purcell, pointed out that "the absurd description of the young King's levee" was concocted from something the author "must have read somewhere about the ceremonies of the bedchamber introduced by Louis XIV."[13] The description referred to is of "the weighty business of dressing" Tom Canty, the supposed Edward VI, in Chapter 14. Among the ceremonies is the passing of the royal shirt from "the Chief Equerry in Waiting" through the consecutive hands of thirteen noble courtiers, until "what was left of it" was put on Tom (157). That ceremony was undoubtedly inspired by several pages from Taine's *Ancient Regime*, Book II, Chapter 1, describing Louis XIV's matutinal toilet, of which this is a sample:

There is quite a formality in regard to this shirt. The honor of handing it is reserved to the sons and grandsons of France; in default of these to the princes of the blood or those legitimated; in their default to the grand-chamberlain or to the first gentleman of the bedchamber. . . . At last the shirt is presented and a valet carries off the old one; the first valet of the wardrobe and the first *valet-de-chambre* hold the fresh one, each by a right and left arm respectively, while two other valets during this operation, extend his dressing-gown in front of him to serve as a screen. The shirt is now on his back.[14]

In like manner, Chapter 7 of *The Prince and the Pauper* depends on the same section of *The Ancient Regime*. Wrote Taine: "And I have not mentioned the infinite detail of etiquette, the extraordinary ceremonial of the state dinner, the fifteen, twenty, and thirty beings busy around the king's plate and glasses, the sacramental utterances

---

13. E. Purcell, "Review, *Academy*," in Frederick Anderson (ed.), *Mark Twain and the Critical Heritage* (New York, 1971), 90.

14. Hippolyte Taine, *The Ancient Regime*, trans. John Durand (Gloucester, Mass., 1962), 106. Further references to *The Ancient Regime* are indicated by parenthetical page numbers in the text.

of the occasion, the procession of the retinue" (109). In order to dine, Tom is "conducted with much state to a spacious and ornate apartment . . . half filled with noble servitors." A chaplain says grace, and my lord d'Arcy, First Groom of the Chamber, the Lord Chief Butler, the Lord Great Steward, and the Lord Head Cook stand by (97–98). Like Louis XIV, Tom has his taster. Altogether, Taine reported, Louis had "[t]hree hundred and eighty-three officers of the table" (95). Mark Twain was not to be outdone. He upped the ante to "three hundred and eighty-four" (98).

Mark Twain's Frenchifying of the English court borders on the mischievous. He drew characters and events from Hume when it pleased him and overlaid them with details and ceremonies from *The Ancient Regime* when he needed a comic or dramatic effect. He apparently got part of the idea for Chapter 14 from Hume. His pertinent working note is "Tom's great servants—320H. Put these around him in the beginning."[15] Page 320 of the third volume of Hume's *History of England* begins a chapter titled "Edward VI"; and although there are no "servants" mentioned on the page, there are the names of the sixteen executors appointed by the dying Henry VIII to rule "the king and kingdom" until Edward achieved his majority.[16] At one point in Chapter 14, Mark Twain responded to the information with proper solemnity. He brought the "body of illustrious men named by the late king as his executors" into Tom's presence "to ask Tom's approval of certain acts of theirs" and then ended by listing the signatures of the first seven of the executors as copied with slight variations from Hume: "the Archbishop of Canterbury; the Lord Chancellor of England; William Lord St. John; John Lord Russell; Edward Earl of Hertford; John Viscount Lisle; Cuthbert Bishop of Durham—" (159). However, this episode occurs *after* the Archbishop of Canterbury and the Lord High Admiral (John Viscount Lisle) have stood in the line of noble servants to pass Tom his shirt and hose.

The executors entrusted, as Hume wrote, with "the whole regal authority" (320) would not, in the court of Edward VI, act as servants, though some of them (such as the Earl of Hertford, Chamberlain) might oversee certain areas of maintenance. Domestic du-

15. Appendix A, "Mark Twain's Working Notes," in Clemens, *The Prince and the Pauper,* 350.

16. David Hume, *The History of England* (4 vols.; Boston, 1849), III, 320. Further references to *The History of England* are indicated by parenthetical page numbers in the text.

ties within the English court were managed by an effective administrative unit peopled by trained servants generally of nonnoble
blood.[17] The household of Louis XIV was quite another matter, as
Taine pointed out. At Versailles, hundreds of titled nobles were at
the same time the king's guests and his household servants. When
Taine counted the pedigreed nobility working in the service of the
court, he found "68 almoners or chaplains, 170 gentlemen of
the bedchamber or in waiting, 117 gentlemen of the stable or of the
hunting train, 148 pages, 114 titled ladies in waiting . . . , without
counting 1400 ordinary guards . . . verified by the genealogist"
(100). In making the Archbishop of Canterbury and the Lord High
Admiral members of the bucket brigade that hands Tom his apparel,
and in giving Tom's table servants the titles Earl and Lord, Mark
Twain is clearly reflecting the practices of the ancient regime rather
than those of the Tudor court.

Other borrowings from Taine are visible in *The Prince and the Pauper.*
Tom Canty's weariness with the elaborate rituals of the court—his
sense of being "fettered by restrictions and ceremonious obser-
vances" (169)—remind us of Taine's pitying the Louis whose courtly
duties are "an incessant daily performance . . . imposed on them
like a heavy, gilded ceremonial coat"(104). Mark Twain's Chapters 17
and 18, describing the activities of the displaced "company of tat-
tered gutter-scum and ruffians, of both sexes, . . . blind mendicants, . . . crippled ones" (191), depend on Taine's Book V, Chapter 3, with its "[v]agrants, every species of refractory spirit, . . .
mendicants, foul, filthy, haggard, and savage" (380), as well as on
Hume and James Anthony Froude. It "was not infrequent," wrote
Taine, "to see fifteen or twenty of these 'invade a farm-house to
sleep there, intimidating the farmers and exacting whatever they
pleased' " (384). Twain's twenty-five vagrants "invaded a small farm
house and made themselves at home while the trembling farmer
and his people swept the larder clean to furnish a breakfast for
them" (204). And there is the whimsical possibility that Mark Twain
drew the first name for Miles Hendon, his brave soldier and Ed-

17. Mark Twain may have been misled by the phrase *royal household,* used by
historians in his time and ours, which in the twelfth century did refer to the English
king's servants, as well as to his ministers and agents, but which by Henry VIII's time
referred to the king's administrative officers and advisers. Nevertheless, Henry's
royal household is never described as undertaking menial duties. G. R. Elton, *England Under the Tudors* (London, 1959), 11–13.

ward's protector, from these two sentences in the first pages of *The Ancient Regime:* "The benefactor, the conservator at this time is the man capable of fighting, of defending others, and such really is the character of the newly established class. The noble, in the language of the day, is the man of war, the *soldier* (miles), and it is he who lays the second foundation of modern society" (6).

But of greater significance than the details borrowed from *The Ancient Regime* is the vision of society in *The Prince and the Pauper*, which, if not borrowed from Taine, corresponds with his view. Both men not only see their societies as polarized into the two levels of the deprived and the privileged, but both treat each level with equal particularity. As well as detailing the opulent and ceremonious court life, both writers spend scores of pages designed to make the reader realize the desperation of the lives of slum dwellers, peasants, and laborers, many of whom become beggars, thieves, and felons. Such close and particular attention to the lives of the miserable is quite foreign to Froude's and Hume's histories of England, from which Mark Twain drew matters of fact. Hume especially, with his eighteenth-century penchant for abstraction, concentrates almost totally on the words and deeds of royalty, the machinations of the nobility, the meetings of Parliament, and the fortunes of diplomacy and war. Only occasionally does Hume turn his attention to the "common people" and their "grievances" (355).

In choosing Taine's vision over Hume's, Mark Twain was able to write his first modern novel. *The Prince and the Pauper* reflects both the techniques and the tenets of science-based realism—both the care for detailing significant aspects of environment and the recognition that people are formed by their environments.

To illustrate Mark Twain's modernization in *The Prince and the Pauper*, we might compare that novel with his previous one, *The Adventures of Tom Sawyer*, an old-fashioned book. In *Tom Sawyer* there is no program for describing the visible aspects of "the poor little shabby village of St. Petersburg" and its culture. What details are vouchsafed—a sidewalk here, a gate there—are rare and incidental. But in *The Prince and the Pauper* our Tainean historical novelist knows he has to furnish the reader's imagination with the appearances of his chosen time and place. He calls the reader's attention to the plaster, beams, panes, and door hinges of houses; to the gilded gates and granite lions guarding Westminster Palace; to the flat black caps, clerical bands, and blue gowns of the Christ's Hospital boys; to the gilt nails that fasten the crimson velvet to the gold-tasseled halberd staves; to the crutches of the crippled, the eye-patches and string-tied dogs of the blind, and the cant words of the ruffians; to the pail, cup, pots, basin, bench, and stool in the hermit's earth-floor hut; to the hedges, gardens, and sculptured columns of a nobleman's estate; and, pervasively, to the resplendent robes of the nobility and the rags of the poor.

Tom Sawyer's author felt free to introduce him *in medias res*, without past or parents. Tom Canty's author, knowing that a person is the product of past experiences, gave this Tom a detailed case history in a chapter called "Tom's Early Life." There he explained how Tom, though raised in a wretched tenement by a drunken father and an ignorant mother, was secretly educated by a good priest, read books about the lives of princes, pretended that he himself was a prince, and organized his playmates into a royal court. Only with such training could he later be credibly mistaken for a real prince.

When it comes to the psychological transformations that Tom Canty and Prince Edward undergo in their switched environments, there is nothing to compare them to in *Tom Sawyer*. They are exceedingly well done, and their mirror-image symmetry is pointed up by elegant touches: Both boys are thought to have gone mad from too much reading and study; both boys on their first night after the switch dream of their former familiar conditions and awaken with dismay to their new, strange surroundings; each boy is given some comfort by a sympathetic "sister"; Tom's first royal meal is touchingly parodied in Edward's first meal in Miles Hendon's quarters; and the courtiers' elaborate respect for Tom is mocked by the vagabonds' derision for Edward when they enthrone him as "Foo-foo the First."

Tom's adaptation to the duties and privileges of royalty is understandably easier than Edward's to the insults and deprivations of pauperdom. Tom's first request of his "father," Henry VIII, is to be returned to "the kennel where I was born and bred to misery" and to leave "these pomps and splendors whereunto I am not used" (79–80). But like Huck Finn before him, who got so he could stand going to school and living in a house, Tom begins to adjust to, even enjoy, his situation. Later that day, when he manages to phrase a courtly sentence, he congratulates himself for having learned from books "some slight trick of their broidered and gracious speech withal" (91). By the third day of his kingship, "he was getting a little used to his circumstances and surroundings; . . . the presence and homage of the great afflicted and embarrassed him less and less sharply with every hour that drifted over his head" (169–70); and on the fourth day, "the poor little ash-cat was already more wonted to his strange garret . . . than a mature person could have become in a full month" (181). By the time of his coronation procession, "his heart swelled with exultation" at the sight of worshipful crowds "and he felt that the one thing worth living for in this world was to be a king, and a nation's idol" (301). He becomes so intoxicated with pride that he denies his own mother, who unexpectedly steps out of the crowd to accost him. Immediately thereafter, he is eaten with remorse and his "grandeurs were stricken valueless" (305); he regains his humility, seeks out his mother, and is rewarded by the true king.

Edward's adjustment to poverty and insolence is much harder but, finally, more spiritually ennobling. Unlike Tom, who comes to deny his own past, Edward never forgets that he is the prince and, on the death of his father, the king of England. "My person is sacred," he screams at the guard who has thrown him, dressed in Tom's rags, out of the palace grounds, "and thou shalt hang for laying thy hand upon me!" (66). He later resolves to hang the jeering boys of Christ's Hospital and to have Tom, his usurper, hanged, drawn, and quartered for treason when he is restored to his throne. He will not allow Miles Hendon to sit in his presence until he has knighted Miles; and when, as an apparent tramp, he does let a charitable peasant woman, who has fed him, sit at her own table, he prides himself on his "gracious humility" (221). A turning point comes when, after several weeks of preserving his autocratic identity in spite of perils and humiliations, he witnesses with horror the kind of punishment he has impulsively wished on people who have crossed him. "That which I have seen," he says, turning away from the fire in which two women are burning for the crime of being Baptist, "will never go out from my memory"; and he resolves that the laws that have "shamed the English name, shall be swept from the statute books" (283, 284). Restored to his throne, and having learned compassion through suffering, he becomes a merciful monarch.

*The Prince and the Pauper* is more "realistic" in technique and theory than *Tom Sawyer*, but that does not mean that Mark Twain's second novel was better than his first. *Tom Sawyer* is too mythic and subjective to be called realistic, yet many readers are likely to find it realer than *The Prince and the Pauper*. What—in spite of the latter novel's "realism," its elegant structure, and its canny psychology—is the matter with it?

Language for one thing. In his working notes, Mark Twain copied a few dozen words and phrases from *Henry IV*, Part I, and hundreds from *Ivanhoe, Kenilworth,* and *Quentin Durward,* by way of practicing sixteenth-century English. Perhaps if he had reversed the ratio, there would be more Shakespearean vigor and pith in his characters' language—more vivid speeches like this of Miles Hendon to Tom's father: "If thou do but touch him, thou animated offal, I will spit thee like a goose!" (134). Instead, generally, he vaguely imitated Scott, who was himself shamming, or produced locutions that smacked melodramatically of the popular stage of his own time, as in another speech of Miles Hendon: "I have lost thee, my poor little mad master—it is a bitter thought—and I had come to love thee so! No! by book and bell, *not* lost. Not lost, for I will ransack the land till I find thee again. Poor child, yonder is his breakfast—and mine, but I have no hunger now—so, let the rats have it—speed, speed! that is the word!" (153). Unfortunately, the stilted dialogue is too often matched by a fake-quaint narrative style. The archaic idioms and genteel abstractions that Mark Twain somehow felt obliged to use in his storytelling give his images a sepia-toned distance and unreality. How can one feel Edward's pain and outrage under the vicious beating he gets from Tom Canty's father and grandmother when the author says, "Between them they belabored the boy right soundly" (115)? When Tom as king, looking out of his throne-room window, feels sorry for three people harassed by a mob, Mark Twain loftily describes his emotions this way: "The spirit of compassion took control of him, to the exclusion of all other considerations"; and anticipating the entrance of the three people, Tom "turned his eyes upon the door with manifestations of impatient expectancy" (171, 172). It is hard to believe that the author of "Old Times on the Mississippi" could write such polite jargon.

Another problem of the book is the way Mark Twain monkeys with history. Uncritical readers might not mind the Frenchifying of the court, the inflicting of certain seventeenth-century laws on six-teenth-century vagabonds, or the burning of Baptists at the stake before Baptists had come into existence. But it must occur to many readers that the climactic episode, of high moment and total pub-licity, could not have happened. The episode is, of course, the ragged Edward's bursting into Westminster Abbey when Tom is about to be crowned and, after many public consternations, doubts, tests, and proofs, succeeding in his demand that he be crowned instead. For authenticity's sake, Mark Twain could have arranged a behind-the-scenes restoration.

Then, the inevitability of the novel's ideas and action reduces suspense. Beginning as he did with a clear plot outline, instructed as he was in a historian's technique for recovering the past, and delighted as he was with his theory about the formative power of environment, Mark Twain did not in the process of filling in his outline have much room for adventuring.

Finally, the novel is less than convincing because (as he would in general come to understand) it was about a foreign land and not his own; it was the product of research rather than of a lifetime of unconscious absorption. But in the larger picture the novel is important because it introduces the theme that continued to preoccupy him in *Huckleberry Finn, A Connecticut Yankee,* and *Pudd'nhead Wilson*—that of the power of training.

CHAPTER 9

# Crisis: *Huckleberry Finn*

*Why, where was you raised? Don't you know what a feud is?*
—Chapter 18

*All I say is, kings is kings, and you got to make allowances. Take them all around, they're a mighty ornery lot. It's the way they're raised.*
—Chapter 23

WHEN WE COMPARE *The Prince and the Pauper* to *Tom Sawyer*, we see evidence of Mark Twain's modernization, of his having begun to use certain approaches and techniques derived from the new age of science. When we compare *Huckleberry Finn* to *Tom Sawyer*, we witness another remarkable advancement. A part of the later novel's spell comes from Mark Twain's consummately skillful use of what Taine called "the characteristic detail, the animating fact, the specific circumstance, the significant, convincing and complete example." I do not, however, intend to pursue questions of modernization or technique in *Huckleberry Finn*. As a more fitting salute to that Promethean novel, I will try to deal with two of the major forces at work in it.

One force is Mark Twain's early ideal and hope that human beings could come to know and love one another if they could rid themselves of prejudice. The other force is his later conviction that society trained people in blind and unbreakable habits of attitude and behavior that, though regarded as respectable and even admirable, were pernicious.

Both forces were nourished by one part or another of Mark Twain's reading in science and in its philosophers, especially in Paine, Holmes, Darwin, Lecky, and Taine. His early ideal is consonant with realism's finest concept—that, in Taine's words, one "enters into the mind of another" through the evidences, sympathetically observed, of everyday life. His later conviction was based on the scientific view that environment and training inform a person's moral character.

In their succession the two forces worked a change in his attitude toward the subject that preoccupied him for two decades—the cruel and irrational custom of imposing inferior status on certain human beings because of caste, race, or slavery and the kind of revolution needed to destroy the custom. In the latter part of the novel he finally gave in to a determinism that was less explicit than in *What Is Man?* but just as severe. He tried to counter his pessimistic determinism by making a villain of the customs and attitudes of the tyrannical Old World and, particularly in the Wilks episode, to place hope in the ideals of the democratic New World; but the strategy failed.

The two forces were born out of historical contradictions that Mark Twain, more than any other writer of his time, experienced with painful intimacy. One was the contradiction between the rootless West and the established East. Another, between North and South, was for him extremely complex, not only because he had roots in both areas but because his perceptions regarding them underwent a spasm of change. Yet another was the contradiction between past and present as he understood it. The past meant superstition, ceremony, tradition, and tyranny. The present meant science and technology and, along with them, an experimental and egalitarian view of life that promised to fulfill the social ideals of the American and French revolutions. His rededication to the present in *A Tramp Abroad* was sorely puzzled by his observation in 1882 that the South, in its Walter Scottism, had been reclaimed by the past.

The effect upon him of these historical contradictions was intensified through the two different ways he had been raised. One way was as the free and easy perennial summer guest on his aunt and uncle's farm, where slave children were his playmates and black Uncle Dan'l was his surrogate father. The other was as the child of respectable, strict, and unaffectionate parents in Hannibal, that town with its "aristocratic taint."[1]

The lessons of these two upbringings were brought home to him in his maturity by two piercingly contradictory experiences. One was his being anointed by his surrogate mother, former slave Rachel Cord, in 1874. That experience directed the part of *Huckleberry Finn* written in the summer of 1876, roughly through Chapter 16. The other was his riverboat trip down the Mississippi from St. Louis to New Orleans and back up to St. Paul in the spring of 1882. Observing the post-Reconstruction South's obsessive harking back to the Civil War and its determination to deprive freed blacks and their

---

1. Charles Neider (ed.), *The Autobiography of Mark Twain* (New York, 1959), 28.

descendants of their civil rights, he became convinced that the war had been a tragic exercise in futility. Its divisiveness mocked the notion that "union" had been preserved; and in its purpose of "freeing the slaves," it was a failed revolution. In a camouflaged way he said as much: The Grangerford-Shepherdson feud can be read as a metaphor for the Civil War; and the "evasion"—Tom Sawyer's elaborate attempt to keep Jim imprisoned in the Phelps cabin knowing that Jim is a freed man—is, as indeed certain scholars have shown, an allegory for the continuing subjugation of emancipated blacks.

The Civil War and all it entailed had been, and in a measure remained, an embarrassment to Mark Twain. It lurked in his mind like a nagging question he was not privileged to answer. His feelings about slavery and about the Civil War and its aftermath while he was writing *Huckleberry Finn* were deep and intense, but several considerations inhibited their free expression. To begin with, he had not been much concerned about slavery when he had lived with it; nor, as war clouds gathered, did he have a settled conviction about secession. As a citizen of a slave state that did not secede, he saw Missourians in 1861 join both the northern and southern armies and was himself, as he tells us in "The Private History of a Campaign That Failed" (1885), strong alternately for the Union and the Confederacy. In lighting out for the Territory at the beginning of the war, he absented himself from the historical process that dealt with slavery and emancipation, secession and Reconstruction. His withdrawal was more than geographic. The focus of his journalism during the war is almost unrelentingly local; and in *Roughing It*, describing his activities from 1861 to 1866, there is no significant allusion to the war.

Once back in the States and a resident, successively, of New York City, Buffalo, and Hartford—and soon a member of the Nook Farm community and of the *Atlantic Monthly* crowd, with their abolitionist histories—he became northernized. At some stage in this process, it must have occurred to him that as a one-time southerner he had something special to tell his readers. It had to do not with the principle of civil equality that abolitionists had fought for but with the possibility of a white person's and a black person's freely sharing their feelings with each other.

He had himself learned about sharing feelings from his "faithful and affectionate good friend, ally and adviser . . . 'Uncle Dan'l,'" the middle-aged slave on his Uncle John Quarles's farm near Florida,

Missouri. Dan'l's "sympathies were warm and wide and [his] heart was honest and simple and knew no guile." This open and loving person furnished Mark Twain with a ready-made Jim. In memory and spirit he also gave Mark Twain "his welcome company" into Twain's old age.[2]

To say that the theme of shared feeling "occurred" to Mark Twain is probably inaccurate. Judging from its tentative and tardy development in the novel, it was more of an upwelling. One of the subterranean pressures at work was surely Twain's memory of Rachel Cord's laying on of hands two years before, as he told about it in "A True Story." The complete title—"A True Story Repeated Word for Word as I Heard It"—is disarming, for it points only toward "Aunt" Rachel's story of her past as a slave and not at all to the story that surrounds it—that of Mr. C's awakening, conversion, and dedication.

The setting of Mr. C's story is the porch of the Cranes' hilltop farmhouse, the time early evening, the season summer, and the year 1874. Mr. C and unnamed others are sitting on the porch while Rachel sits "respectfully below our level, on the steps—for she was our servant, and colored."[3] As was his habit, Mr. C chaffs Rachel without mercy and is rewarded with such outpourings of laughter from Rachel as leave her breathless. Charmed with her invariable jollity, Mr. C wonders out loud how she could have lived so long without knowing trouble. Rachel's suddenly serious reaction surprises Mr. C, "and it sobered my manner and speech too." Rachel "faced fairly around now" and tells the thoughtless Mr. C a couple of things he should have known—that she had been born a slave and knew "all 'bout slavery, 'case I ben one of 'em my own se'f" and that she loved her family as much as white people love theirs. Her husband, she asserts, "was lovin' an' kind to me, jist as kind as you is to yo' own wife. An we had chil'en—seven chil'en—an' we loved dem chil'en jist de same as you loves yo' chil'en. Dey was black, but de Lord can't make no chil'en so black but what dey mother loves 'em an' wouldn't give 'em up, no, not for anything dat's in dis whole world" (266).

Rachel's story begins in 1852, when she and her family were put up for sale in Richmond by their mistress. Weighed down with

2. *Ibid.*, 6.

3. Samuel Clemens [Mark Twain], *Sketches New and Old*, Author's National Edition: The Writings of Mark Twain (25 vols.; New York, 1907–18), XIX, 265. Further references to "A True Story" are indicated by parenthetical page numbers in the text.

chains and forced to stand on the auctioneer's platform, where they were inspected and handled by prospective buyers, they were sold one by one until only Rachel and her young son were left: " 'You shan't take him away,' I says; 'I'll kill de man dat tetches him!' I says. But my little Henry whisper an' say, 'I gwyne to run away, an' den I work an' buy yo' freedom.' Oh, bless de chile, he always so good! But dey got him—dey got him, de men did; but I took and tear de clo'es mos' off of 'em an' beat 'em over de head wid my chain; an' *dey* give it to *me*, too, but I didn't mine dat" (268). Of all her family, Rachel saw only Henry again; and that was at or near the end of the war, when Henry, who had escaped to the North and then, as a young man, had returned to search for his mother, arrived at a Union army base in North Carolina where Rachel was cook. Once Rachel had identified Henry by means of scars on his wrist and forehead, the two were joyfully reunited.

"I do believe," mused Huckleberry, when he overheard Jim "moaning and mourning" for the wife and children he had left behind, that "he cared just as much for his people as white folks does for their'n. It don't seem natural, but I reckon it's so."[4] It took Huck weeks of close living with Jim to come to that conclusion. How can Mark Twain suggest that Mr. C had a profound change of heart in the few minutes it took Rachel to tell her story? One way, of course, is through the reader's assumption that Mr. C feels the same sequence of emotions that the reader does—uneasiness, outrage, pity, suspense, and joy. The art with which Mark Twain relays Rachel's story is consummate. His vernacular rendering of Rachel's speech and the story's pathos and melodramatic form are designed to invite the white reader's condescension, a condescension that is liable to be replaced by empathy and humility.

Another way that Mark Twain signals Mr. C's conversion is by carefully describing Rachel's movements as they appear to Mr. C. The porch becomes a stage, and Rachel's unconscious actions become symbols possessing great delicacy and power. At first, though of "mighty frame and stature" (265), Rachel respectfully sits on the steps below the white folks; but as she begins to tell of being placed on the auctioneer's platform, Mr. C observes that she "had gradually risen, while she warmed to her subject, and now she towered

---

4. Samuel Clemens [Mark Twain], *Adventures of Huckleberry Finn*, Mark Twain Library edition (Berkeley, 1985). Further references to *Huckleberry Finn* are indicated by parenthetical page numbers in the text.

above us, black against the stars" (267). She begins to move about the porch, acting out her story, standing even taller, and taking on a commanding presence. When she tells how she read the riot act to skylarking young blacks using her army kitchen for their dance hall, she says: "My eye was jist a-blazin'! I jist straightened myself up, so,—jist as I is now, plum to de ceilin', mos'," and "Well, I jist march' on dem niggers,—so, lookin' like a gen'l" (271).

The dignity and authority that Rachel takes on are striking; but even so, they hardly prepare the reader for the audacious way she manipulates Mr. C's person in the thrilling penultimate paragraph, where the story of Rachel and the story of Mr. C merge.

Among the black dancers that Rachel shooed out of her kitchen was her unrecognized son Henry. Henry had more than an inkling that the red-turbaned guardian of the kitchen was his mother; and after a sleepless night, he returned while Rachel was preparing the officers' breakfast.

I was a-stoopin' down by de stove [she explains to Mr. C],—jist so, same as if yo' foot was de stove,—an' I'd opened de stove do' wid my right han',—so, pushin' it back, jist as I pushes yo' foot,—an' I'd jist got de pan o' hot biscuits in my han' an' was 'bout to raise up, when I see a black face come aroun' under mine, an' de eyes a-lookin' up into mine, jist as I's a-lookin' up clost under yo' face now; an' I jist stopped *right dah*, an' never budged! jist gazed, an' gazed, so; an' de pan begin to tremble, an' all of a sudden I *knowed*! De pan drop' on de flo' an' I grab his lef' han' an' shove back his sleeve,—jist so, as I's doin' to you,—an' den I goes for his forehead an' push de hair back, so, an' "Boy!" I says, "if you an't my Henry, what is you doin' wid dis welt on yo' wris' an' dat sk-yar on yo' forehead? De Lord God ob heaven be praise', I got my own ag'in!" (272)

She pushes Mr. C's foot, gazes long into his face, bares his wrist and forehead, and declares that she has got her own again. What can this astonishing ritual mean except that Mr. C has been singled out to receive the special understanding that comes with accepting the role of surrogate son to former slave Rachel Cord?

Mr. C, one guesses, is a compressed Samuel Clemens. It is not likely that Clemens' hatred for slavery and his ingenuous and total respect for the humanity of blacks were sudden acquisitions, though the development and realization of those convictions may have been completed in the act of writing "A True Story." Certainly, from that time on, Samuel Clemens carried those convictions with him.

From "A True Story," Mark Twain took both the main plot and

theme for the first part of *Huckleberry Finn*. Henry's determination to escape from slavery and earn money to buy his mother's freedom is similar to Jim's plan to run away to a free state, there to work and save money to buy his wife and two children out of slavery. As for theme, what Mr. C learns in a flash about the equal humanity of blacks is akin to Huck's growing love for Jim; and the sense of ritual and commitment with which "A True Story" ends is perhaps echoed at the end of Chapter 15, where Huck "could almost kissed" (105) Jim's foot before humbling himself to him. A less dramatic link is that the fulfilling life within Rachel's loving family (before that life was wrecked on the auctioneer's block) is re-created between Jim and Huck. For Huck, life with Miss Watson had been "tiresome and lonesome" (4), with pap it was "dreadful lonesome" (31), but joined with Jim on Jackson's Island, Huck happily reports, "I warn't lonesome now" (51); and a few days later, when the two return to their snug cavern after a busy day of exploring, he says simply, "We got home all safe" (62). Jim and Huck have become a family, one whose values, writes Robert Shulman, are nourished by "[g]enuine feelings of joy and grief, real laughter and tears, the authentic language of the heart."[5]

The family of Huck and Jim could not survive the dark vision of humanity that Mark Twain's 1882 river trip impressed on his mind. What he saw in the post-Reconstruction South, and especially what civil rights activist George Cable told him, convinced him that the theme of Jim and Huck's shared feelings was an idle dream. He saw that people were disposed to live by such circumscribed and ceremonial habits of mind that they were much more likely to make nonpersons out of outsiders than to discover their humanness. His vision led him into a state of irony, a condition that he suffered as well as turned into literature; and because his suffering was intense, it led him to concoct the anodyne of a deterministic philosophy: People are "the way they're raised" (200).

The first expression of that post-river-trip philosophy appears in Chapter 18, the second of the two Grangerford chapters. Therein lies a problem, for according to Walter Blair's chronology in "When Was *Huckleberry Finn* Written?" both of the chapters "probably were

5. Robert Shulman, "Fathers, Brothers, and 'the Diseased': The Family, Individualism, and American Society in *Huck Finn*," in Robert Sattelmeyer and J. Donald Crowley (eds.), *One Hundred Years of Huckleberry Finn* (Columbia, Mo., 1985), 328.

written two years before the river trip—during Twain's period in Hartford in 1879 and 1880."[6] Blair's hypothesis is stated here with appropriate qualification, but Twain scholars have generally accepted it as canon. Unfortunately, that acceptance has kept us from observing those evidences within the two chapters of a major watershed in Mark Twain's conceptual life; it has also kept us from appreciating the crisis that his Deep South visit must have been.

In questioning Blair's chronology, I have found support in a colleague's study; but since that study is as yet unpublished, I will present here only my own quite different analysis. I will bring to bear certain facts concerning Mark Twain's knowledge of feuds recently assembled by Edgar Branch and Robert Hirst, as well as two new approaches to the problem: a look at moments in Mark Twain's ideological life during the several years he was writing *Huckleberry Finn* and a search for differences of tone and texture within the two chapters.

We have been properly impressed with Blair's meticulous research in establishing that Group A and part of Group B of Twain's working notes for *Huckleberry Finn* (published in DeVoto's *Mark Twain at Work*) "were written between mid-November, 1879, and mid-June, 1880."[7] We need to have been more tentative, as Blair himself was, about the inference that the two chapters were written in the same period. The case for tentativeness is mandated by two facts that canonical scholars seem to have overlooked. One is that Blair's analysis—his careful work with watermarks and inks—is of the notes, not the manuscript. The manuscript for Chapters 17 and 18 is not extant. The other fact is that the notes do not have much to do with the chapters or, indeed, with the novel as we know it.

A close examination of Blair's data and analysis leads inescapably to the conclusion that nothing in the notes requires that Chapter 18 be written before the river trip. If, instead, we begin with the hypothesis that Chapter 18 was written *in response to* the river trip, nagging anomalies clear up.

Why should Mark Twain have reminded himself in mid-April, 1882, while anticipating his river trip, to "ask about old feuds" at New Madrid, Missouri, except to gather material for a chapter he planned to write? Why, when he reminisced with Horace Bixby on

6. Walter Blair, "When Was *Huckleberry Finn* Written?" *American Literature*, XXX (1958), 12.

7. *Ibid.*, 6.

his return trip upriver, did he misremember a feud that he came near witnessing in 1859 as being between a Missouri "tribe" and a Kentucky "tribe"? The feud had been between two families on the same side of the river; in *Huckleberry Finn* the families are back on the same side of the river.[8] Perhaps Twain temporarily misplaced the families because the last feud he had written about—in "Simon Wheeler, Detective" (1877–1878)—involved a Kentucky family and a Missouri family.

How could Mark Twain have written the description of the area of Jim's hideout in Chapter 18, with its geographical details—a point, a swamp, an island, and a creek—"clearly represented" on the two maps of the Mississippi River that he had ordered and received from the Army Corps of Engineers in April, 1882, unless he had consulted the maps?[9] How else explain the striking similarities in the descriptions of the Grangerford-Shepherdson feud and of the Darnell-Watson feud in *Life on the Mississippi*—similarities not only of incident but of phraseology—unless the compositions were, in Arthur Pettit's term, "symbiotic"?[10] Consider these parallels: The causes of both feuds are lost in the dim past. When Huck asks Buck Grangerford who did the first shooting, Buck replies, "Laws, how do I know? it was so long ago" (146). The steamboat passenger who tells about the Darnell-Watson feud says, "Nobody don't know now what the first quarrel was about, it's so long ago."[11] Like the feuders in *Huckleberry Finn*, the Darnells and Watsons "didn't hunt for each other, but when they happened to meet, they pulled and begun. Men would shoot boys, boys would shoot men" (208–209). Each pair of feuding families attended the same church, the male members carrying guns. In church, Grangerford and Shepherdson men "took their guns along, so did Buck, and kept them between their knees or stood them handy against the wall" (147). Churchgoing Darnell and Watson "men and boys would lean their guns up

8. Edgar Branch and Robert Hirst, *The Grangerford-Shepherdson Feud* (Berkeley, 1985), 34, 41–42, 51, 90. Branch and Hirst's careful study has provided me bits of evidence for the post-river-trip composition of Chapter 18, although the authors themselves generally attempted to work within Blair's chronology.

9. *Ibid.*, 37–41, 90–91.

10. Arthur Pettit, *Mark Twain and the South* (Lexington, Ky., 1974), 200.

11. Samuel Clemens [Mark Twain], *Life on the Mississippi*, Author's National Edition: The Writings of Mark Twain (25 vols.; New York, 1907–18), IX, 208. Further references to *Life on the Mississippi* are indicated by parenthetical page numbers in the text.

against the wall, handy" (209). The climaxes of both feuds occur at landings, with their woodpiles of steamboat fuel. In *Huckleberry Finn*, Buck and a nineteen-year-old comrade take shelter from Shepherdson bullets by crouching behind the woodpile. When they are outflanked, they make a futile attempt to escape death by jumping into the river; "and as they swum down the current the men run along the bank shooting at them and singing out, 'Kill them, kill them!' " (153). In *Life on the Mississippi*, "a young man of nineteen," similarly outflanked, in like manner abandons his woodpile for the river; "and as he swum along down stream, they followed along the bank and kept on shooting at him" (209–210). Such strong parallels suggest that the accounts of the two feuds were written in response to the same creative stimulus and therefore at about the same time.

Things begin to fall into place, and if we take one more step our hypothesis will mature into a well-grounded theory. That step is to look elsewhere for the working notes for Chapter 18. The notes labeled Groups A and B will not do. There is nothing in them about the feud; nor is there any detail of incident that reappears in the chapter.

It is not hard to spot the working notes. They lie in the pages of Mark Twain's notebook, in the stenographic record of his and Bixby's reminiscences about feuds, shared on the decks of *The City of Baton Rouge* as it paddled upstream from New Orleans in May, 1882. Here are the details that reappear in Chapter 18. And here is Bixby's story about the two families, "armed with shotguns," who "used to attend church on the line (part of church in Tenn. part in Ky.) . . . & neither party would allow the other to cross the line in that church."[12] So far as the carefully examined record shows, it was in this conversation with Bixby that Mark Twain first heard about the feuding churchgoers.

Our thinking of the two Grangerford chapters as a unit has prevented us from seeing not only that parts of them were written at different times but that they were written in response to different creative and conceptual impulses. It is extremely unlikely, for example, that when Mark Twain wrote the first half of Chapter 17, perhaps as early as 1876, he intended to feature the feud.[13] The half

12. Frederick Anderson, Lin Salamo, and Bernard L. Stein (eds.), *Mark Twain's Notebooks and Journals* (3 vols. completed; Berkeley, 1979), II, 567–69.

13. "[R]ecent work on the [Iowa-California] edition of *Huckleberry Finn* suggests that in 1876, Mark Twain may well have written as far as the first mention of Harney

chapter was written in the midst of an eight-year period when he was celebrating a series of little revolutions that promised to solve the problem that his "subject" had raised. People of different castes, races, and predispositions had been brought together through lightning flashes of sympathy and love. There were Mr. C and Rachel Cord, Huckleberry and Jim, John T. Lewis and the white folks at Quarry Farm, Prince Edward and the Baptist women. In every case the human heart was opened in spite of the forbidding forces of tradition and training.

More strikingly to the point is the triumph of love and enlightenment over the deadly tradition of feuding in "Simon Wheeler, Detective," which Mark Twain wrote in late fall and winter, 1877–1878. Hale Dexter, a young Kentuckian, arrives in Guilford, Missouri, with a commission from his father to kill Hugh Burnside, member of the family that the Dexters have been feuding with for generations. Without learning their names, he meets Hugh and Hugh's beautiful sister Clara and falls in love with Clara. When he discovers Hugh's identity as the brother of the woman he loves, he renounces his promise to his father. " 'Thank God,' he breathes, 'I shall never be a murderer, now.' "[14] Judge Griswold of Guilford is a harder case. Not directly involved in the feud, but a generation older than Hale and Hugh, a friend of Hale's father, and a Kentuckian by birth, he understands the code of honor: The feud "cannot end till one house is extinct" (316). He abets Hale Dexter in his plan to kill Hugh. Judge Griswold is a severe person, in appearance much like Colonel Grangerford, but with one soft spot. He idolizes his sixteen-year-old daughter, Milly, though he "never kissed and never petted her" (314). When he is told that Milly has been saved from "horrible mutilation and death" by an unknown hero who curbed her runaway horse (exactly as John T. Lewis had done), "[h]e showed strong excitement—an unusual thing for him; he even trembled like a girl. Evidently the hidden great deeps of his nature had been touched at last" (387). When he discovers that the young hero is

---

Shepherdson in Chapter 18." Branch and Hirst, *The Grangerford-Shepherdson Feud*, 84. That the second half of Chapter 17 and the first part of Chapter 18 compose a compositional unit with the first half of Chapter 17 seems to me a questionable assumption, however, in light of marked differences of tone, purpose, and characterization among the three sections.

14. Franklin R. Rogers (ed.), *Mark Twain's Satires and Burlesques* (Berkeley, 1968), 341. Further references to "Simon Wheeler, Detective" are indicated by parenthetical page numbers in the text.

Hugh Burnside, he immediately takes steps to save Hugh from the bullet that he mistakenly thinks Hale is still intending for him.

The theme of "Simon Wheeler, Detective" could be called the power of love over stubborn tradition; and in Simon Wheeler's dream of heaven, Mark Twain's faith in that power is raised to a social philosophy. At the gate of heaven, Wheeler sees people of various "denominations"—Quaker, Mohammedan, Catholic, Baptist, Buddhist, and so on—being assigned to their particular places in heaven. Without a denomination of his own, Wheeler is afraid he will be rejected. He apologetically explains to the Beautiful Personage, "I didn't know any better, your honor . . . , and I went a-blundering along and loving everybody just alike, niggers and Injuns and Presbyterians and Irish." "Rise up, Simon Wheeler!" intones the Beautiful Personage. "The gates of heaven stand wide to welcome you! Range its barred commonwealths as free as the angels, brother and comrade of all its nations and peoples" (436–37).

Written within the period of this ecumenical philosophy, and more specifically within a year or two of Twain's showing love's way of ending a feud, the first half of *Huckleberry Finn*'s Chapter 17 may well have been prologue to the love story of Sophia Grangerford and Harney Shepherdson, wherein Huck would play Cupid and the clans become reconciled. Such a speculation is supported by a tonal and structural parallel between the two works. Both begin with chilling references to the feud. In both, the chill soon evaporates in the warm glow of hospitality and family love.

At any rate, the mind that conceived Chapter 18 was radically changed from the one that wrote the first half of Chapter 17. Something of that change of mind, and of Mark Twain's change of purpose, can be guessed from the two descriptions of Grangerford, his family, and his house. In the first of the two chapters he is Saul, a "fine and handsome" gray-haired man of about sixty. He smokes a corncob pipe, as does everyone in the family except the two young women. He and his family laugh easily and like to talk. What they say has an affectionate, down-home ring to it (for example, "take this little stranger and get the wet clothes off from him" [134]). One enters their house by climbing "three log doorsteps" (133).

In Chapter 18 Saul has been promoted to Colonel Grangerford. Although his appearance is striking, it can hardly be called handsome. His body is gaunt; and his thin, pale face, with "the thinnest kind of lips, the thinnest kind of nostrils, . . . and the blackest kind of eyes, sunk so deep back that they seemed like they was looking out of caverns at you" (142), has the aspect of a death's-head. His hair is black. The suit he wears is "so white it hurts your eyes to look at it" (142). His appurtenance is not a corncob pipe but a silver-headed mahogany cane. He is reserved and formal, as are his family. In contrast to their midnight laughter and talk over corn-beef, corn-pone, and buttermilk in the previous chapter is the Granger-fords' morning ceremony, in which sons and daughters rise from their chairs and courteously bow when the Colonel and his lady descend the stairs to join the family at breakfast. "Our duty to you, sir, and madam" intone Tom and Bob, raising their glasses of bitters; and in return the Colonel and Mrs. Grangerford bow "the least bit in the world" (143) and murmur their appreciation. Their house has become a mansion; at least it provides lodging for numerous guests for five or six days at a time and a ballroom for their dances.

This opening description leads into a chapter whose desperate ironies are precisely those of Mark Twain's post-river-trip vision. In elevating the Grangerfords into the aristocracy, he not only created an ironic contrast between the style of their living and the sordid-ness of their killing and dying but, in doing so, made them into a full-blown example of the Walter Scottism that he concocted in response to his southern visit. He first expresses that Scottism in Chapter 40 of *Life on the Mississippi,* where, after making fun of the "maudlin Middle-age romanticism" (309) of certain examples of sham-castle architecture, he sets up a grisly antiphony between a quotation in his text and its footnoted rejoinder. The quotation, from the prospectus of a Kentucky women's college, states that "the Southern [is believed] to be the highest type of civilization this continent has seen" (310). The footnote, consisting of extracts from current news sources, details the results of feuds and vendettas between and among "highly connected" southerners—some with titles of general, major, captain, and professor—who have at each other with shotguns, pistols, clubs, axes, and butcher knives, leaving eight dead and several wounded. There is as little punctilio among these wellborn murderers as between the Grangerfords and Shepherdsons, who were not above shooting from ambush or gunning down unarmed opponents.

Consider, too, Buck Grangerford's countering Huck's question, "What's a feud?" with "Why, where was you raised? Don't you know what a feud is?" (146) and then cheerfully reciting the insane catechism of feuding as taught him by family tradition. It is Mark Twain's first expression in fiction of the pessimistic side of his idea that training is everything. It is not likely to have preceded those first hints of pessimistic determinism that appear in his river-trip notebooks. The time for its emergence would be closer to that of his first formal statement of determinism in a talk he gave to the Hartford Monday Evening Club in February, 1883.

Consider also Huck's description of the churchgoing feuders who sit with guns between their knees while listening admiringly to a sermon on brotherly love. In its moral topsy-turviness it is of a piece with Huck's believing that what accounts for his loving Jim and wanting to free him is that he "was brung up wicked" (269) and that there is no accounting for Tom's wanting to free Jim, since Tom "was respectable and well brung up" (292). All three passages point to a society that has rationalized a tradition that denies (at the same time giving lip service to) the doctrine of brotherly love. The vision of that society—one that was to trouble Mark Twain for the rest of his life—was, I will try to show, quickened by his southern trip.

Before we turn to Mark Twain's experiences on his 1882 visit to the South, we need to assess an earlier experience that would make certain aspects of that visit bewildering and even painful. That earlier experience—"a solid week of unpareleled [*sic*] dissipation"—was his involvement in the "Citizens Reception and Grand Reunion of the Army of the Tennessee" in Chicago in November, 1879. His excitement while he mingled with the several hundred veterans of Grant's army in the Tennessee campaigns and listened to toasts and speeches in honor of Grant and the Union cause was absolutely intense. Four of the speeches, he wrote to Howells, "carried away all my wits & made me drunk with enthusiasm." The music of Robert Ingersoll's speech, he declared,

will sing through my memory always as the divinest that ever enchanted my ears. And I shall always see him as he stood that night on a dinner table, . . . the most beautiful human creature that ever lived. "They fought that a mother might own her own child"—the words look like any other print, but Lord bless me, he borrowed the very accent of the angel of mercy to say them in. . . . Imagine what it was like to see a bullet-shredded old battle-flag reverently unfolded to the gaze of a thousand middle-aged soldiers. . . . And imagine what it was like when Grant, their first commander, stepped into view while they were still going mad over the flag—& then right in the midst of it all, somebody struck up "When we were Marching through Georgia." Well, you should have heard the thousand voices lift that chorus & seen the tears stream down. If I live a hundred years I shan't ever forget these things—nor be able to talk about them.[15]

Samuel Clemens' vicarious induction into the Army of the Tennessee surely marks a climax in his northernization. It seems also to have directed his imagination to the spot near the Kentucky-Tennessee border where he had stranded Huck and Jim three years before. He wrote to Howells about the reunion on November 17, the day he returned to Hartford from Chicago; the next day he switched from the black ink he had been using to the violet ink he used in writing his notes for the resumption of *Huckleberry Finn*.[16] Unfortunately, his exulting in the end of slavery and the triumph of the Union cause robbed his theme of its tension. The revolution he had been seeking had, he must have felt, indeed taken place. There was no longer much point to writing about a feud or its reconciliation or about freeing a slave. This slackening of tension can help explain a remarkable aspect of the 1879–1880 notes: how inchoate they are and how little they have to do with the novel as we know it.

Clemens' three weeks below the Mason-Dixon line in the spring of 1882 restored whatever degree of tension his theme had lost and added more thereto than he could easily handle. He had not visited the Deep South for twenty-one years. During that time, deeply resented and staunchly resisted changes had been imposed on the South; and a quite different set of changes, cheerfully enough accepted, had taken place in Samuel Clemens. He went as a stranger to a strange land, an "inexperienced stranger," an "ignorant, near-sighted stranger," with "untrained and vacant mind" (329, 337).

Before leaving, he apparently turned to two books to help bring him up-to-date. "War Diary of Gen. Geo. H. Gordon. Gen Dick Taylor's book," he wrote in his notebook in April, 1882. Both Union general Gordon's *A War Diary*, which told about the corruption of Federal officers and crews on Mississippi River ships, and Confederate general Taylor's *Destruction and Reconstruction*, with its indictment of Reconstruction policies, would have chastened his northern pride.[17] His journalist's and pilot's curiosity about battles on and

---

15. Henry Nash Smith and William M. Gibson (eds.), *Mark Twain–Howells Letters* (2 vols.; Cambridge, Mass., 1960), I, 280–81.

16. Blair, "When Was *Huckleberry Finn* Written?," 7.

17. Anderson, Salamo, and Stein (eds.), *Mark Twain's Notebooks and Journals*, II, 462; Alan Gribben, *Mark Twain's Library: A Reconstruction* (2 vols.; Boston, 1980), I, 268, II, 689.

along the Mississippi—as evidenced in the several, often lengthy entries in his river-trip notebooks—brought him a new understanding of the inglorious realities of whizzing bullets and bursting shells.

Even so, he was unprepared for the South's consuming interest in the Civil War seventeen years after its cessation. People in the North, he wrote in *Life on the Mississippi,* no longer talked about the war, partly because so few of them had experienced its "dread realities." "The case is very different in the South. There, every man you meet was in the war; and every lady you meet saw the war. The war is the great chief topic of conversation. . . . In the South the war is what A.D. is elsewhere; they date from it. . . . It shows how intimately every individual was visited, in his own person, by that tremendous episode. It gives the inexperienced stranger a better idea of what a vast and comprehensive calamity invasion is than he can ever get by reading books at the fireside" (336–37). In Vicksburg, "the materials furnished by history" ignited his imagination and led to this description of an early morning bombardment of that besieged city: "[A]ll in a moment come ground-shaking thunder-crashes of artillery, the sky is cobwebbed with the criss-crossing red lines streaming from soaring bomb-shells, and a rain of iron fragments descends upon the city, descends upon the empty streets— streets which are not empty a moment later, but mottled with dim figures of frantic women and children scurrying from home and bed toward the cave dungeons—encouraged by the humorous grim soldiery, who shout, 'Rats, to your holes' and laugh" (278). A survivor's story about church services in besieged Vicksburg reminds us of the mixture of menace and piety in the Grangerfords' church: "I've seen service stop a minute, and everybody sit quiet—no voice heard, pretty funeral-like then—and all the more so on account of the awful boom and crash going on outside and overhead; and pretty soon, when a body could be heard, service would go on again. Organs and church music mixed up with a bombardment is a powerful queer combination" (281).

The source of the cannon thunder—the source of the shells and of the iron rain that poured down on Vicksburg—was General Grant's Army of the Tennessee. Within three years, Mark Twain had identified himself first with the northern victors and then with the southern victims. He had gone from being ineffably thrilled at hearing a thousand exultant voices singing "While We Were Marching Through Georgia" to declaring that the activity of Union troops in the South was a "calamity" and an "invasion."

Mark Twain's ability to feel the indignity and terror of Vicksburg's bombarded citizens at the same time not giving an inch in his conviction that slavery was an abomination was one of the unbearable ironies he suffered. He made it bearable by denying the connection between Union victory and the end of slavery, a connection he had himself celebrated. The Civil War and slavery became for him separate issues, separate horrors. From 1882 on, he was moved to make an abstraction of war and paid little attention to its political issues. It was so absurd and dehumanizing as to be unproductive of any real political benefit. What war *did* show about human beings was their dismaying ability to lust for the destruction of the other side. At the same time, he saw slavery as incurable by edict so long as the attitudes (as encouraged under "white redeemer" state governments) of the enslaver and the enslaved persisted.

Where does Mark Twain announce these grave ideas? We might, to begin with, glance at "The Private History of a Campaign That Failed" (1885)—his apologia for defecting after a couple of weeks in the Confederate militia. Here the urgent moral issue for him was neither slavery nor secession but the soldier's duty, which he defined as "the killing of strangers against whom you feel no personal animosity; strangers whom, in other circumstances, you would help if you found them in trouble, and who would help you if you needed it." And in "The War Prayer" (1905; reprinted and distributed as a tract by Vietnam War protesters), there is a war going on whose cause is never mentioned. The message of "The War Prayer" is that to pray for the success of one side is to pray for the suffering and destruction of the other; it is to pray that God will help us "to tear their soldiers to bloody shreds . . . ; to lay waste their humble homes with a hurricane of fire; . . . to wring the hearts of their unoffending widows with unavailing grief." And with the same mocking irony that he used in describing the churchgoing feuders who listened to a sermon on brotherly love, he concluded his prayer with, "We ask it, in the spirit of love, of Him who is the Source of Love."[18]

In *A Connecticut Yankee* (1889), Mark Twain hints that the Civil War was a mistake, especially in regard to its "abolishing" slavery. He dared make the hint, perhaps, because in writing about white slaves

18. Samuel Clemens [Mark Twain], *The American Claimant and Other Stories and Sketches*, Author's National Edition: The Writings of Mark Twain (25 vols.; New York, 1907–18), XXI, 225; Janet Smith (ed.), *Mark Twain on the Damned Human Race* (New York, 1962), 67.

in sixth-century England, he ran little risk of being fully understood. In midnovel, where Hank Morgan, who has become the Boss of England, is traveling with a group of pilgrims, he comes across a band of slaves chained together and forced to march, though with manacled hands and fettered feet. The plight of the slaves is most pitifully described. A young woman carrying her child is whipped when she stumbles from fatigue. Later, she is sold and separated from her husband: "They had to be torn apart by force; the girl had to be dragged away, and she struggled and fought and shrieked like one gone mad." Hank Morgan is not quick enough in averting his gaze. The picture of the anguished couple is printed on his mind, "and there it is to this day, to wring my heart-strings whenever I think of it." As Boss, Hank could have issued his own emancipation proclamation, but he declined: "I wanted to stop the whole thing and set the slaves free, but that would not do. I must not interfere too much and get myself a name for riding over the country's laws and the citizens' rights roughshod. If I lived and prospered I would be the death of slavery, that I was resolved upon; but I would try to fix it so that when I became its executioner it would be by command of the nation."[19] He wanted, in other words, to change people's hearts before he changed their heartless laws. In the meantime, he would avoid confrontation and conflict at all costs; presumably, he preferred the pitiable costs of gradualism to the terrible costs of imposing righteous principle on an unready society.

Finally, Mark Twain speaks his mind through his accounts of the Darnell-Watson feud and the Grangerford-Shepherdson feud. We may speculate that at some level of his imagination Mark Twain intended both feuds as metaphors for the Civil War. Our speculation is aided by Edgar Branch and Robert Hirst's pinpointing the identical locations of the two feuds. Both of them took place on a tongue of land south of New Madrid, surrounded on three sides by the oxbowing Mississippi River and the state of Missouri.[20] Less than ten miles long, this tongue of land is neatly bisected by the leapfrogging Kentucky-Tennessee border. The Watsons (and Shepherdsons) lived north of the border and the Darnells (and Grangerfords) south of it. Although Mark Twain makes no reference to the fact, it could

19. Samuel L. Clemens [Mark Twain], *A Connecticut Yankee in King Arthur's Court,* ed. Bernard L. Stein and Henry Nash Smith (Berkeley, 1979), 246, Vol. IX of the Works of Mark Twain.

20. Branch and Hirst, *The Grangerford-Shepherdson Feud,* 38, 76, 90, 90–91, and *passim.*

not have escaped his attention that the miniterritory to the north of the line remained loyal to the Union whereas the one south of it was part of the secession. He chose to locate both feuds in this microcosm of the conflict between North and South.

In doing so, he emphasized (if we may continue our speculation) a tragic irony of the Civil War. The idea of armed and ready-to-kill families, in either feud, worshiping on opposite sides within the same church building is, in realistic terms, preposterous, though it grips the imagination. Taken as a symbol of the pattern of worship and war-waging during the intersectional hostilities of 1861 to 1865, it is loaded with ironic meaning. In this bitter conflict, in which sometimes even blood relatives were pitted against one another, neither side had the comfort of regarding the other as heretical. Millions of families on both sides worshiped weekly in churches of the same Christian faith. Both sides, Lincoln reminded the nation in his Second Inaugural Address, "read the same Bible, and pray to the same God; and each invokes His aid against the other."

Our subject at the moment is the unbearable ironies Mark Twain suffered as a result of his trip south in 1882 and the shifts he made to bear them. In *Huckleberry Finn*, his principal shift was to seek the anesthetic of determinism. His determinism has a two-leveled base. At bottom is his deistic conviction, derived from Paine, "that the universe is governed by strict and immutable laws." Overlying and informing that conviction is what he learned from Taine about history's being directed by race, surroundings, and epoch; from Holmes about the automatic mechanisms of mind and body; and from Darwin about conscience's being shaped by society's expectations. If what one witnessed was cruel and absurd and unreformable, it was, after all, a working out of the laws of nature, society, and behavior and not one's own responsibility.

Mark Twain's determinism in *Huckleberry Finn* is strongly discernible in the feuding chapter; it is strenuously resisted in the Wilks episode, and it totally rules the evasion. In each case, the deterministic forces are equatable with Walter Scottism, a notion developed in *Life on the Mississippi*—still another book (except for the "Old Times" section) conceived and written during the long period when the composition of *Huckleberry Finn* was stalled.

It was Mark Twain's contention that the popularity of Sir Walter's novels in the South had caused southerners to fall in love with Scott's romantic version of the Middle Ages, with its chivalry, pageantry, and titles. Worse, it led them to embrace the worn-out social and political creed that said that it was right for one person to lord it over another.[21]

As a social phenomenon, Walter Scottism can be classed under "epoch," the third of Taine's forces influencing the development of a people. Far from being an indigenous and modern historical current, however, it was not only a European import but a revival of a set of attitudes that presumably died out with the American and French revolutions. In the stream of epochs, the South was the victim of a curious historical eddy.

Mark Twain developed his Walter Scottism in those chapters of *Life on the Mississippi* having to do with his nine days in New Orleans, when "he was almost constantly with [George Washington] Cable."[22] He had met Cable in Hartford the previous year. He had read Cable's *Madame Delphine* and *The Grandissimes,* in the latter of which, according to Louis D. Rubin, Jr., Cable "produced some of the most trenchant criticism of racism ever to be written by a Southerner."[23] During Clemens' visit, Cable was gestating the incredibly candid commencement address he would soon give at the University of Mississippi, in which, among other upbraidings, he railed against the South's "stupid wickedness of exalting and abusing our fellow humans class by class and race by race instead of man by man."[24] Mark Twain depended on Cable's ideas for his impressions of southern life. In Cable, he wrote, "the South has found a masterly delineator of its interior life and history. In truth, I find by experience, that the untrained eye and vacant mind can inspect it and learn of it and judge of it more clearly and profitably in his books than by personal contact with it." If, he continued, on being guided through New Orleans, you have "Mr. Cable along to see for you,

---

21. Although hardly the single force shaping the South, the novels of Scott did have their influence: "And even Walter Scott was bodily taken over by the South and incorporated into the Southern people's vision of themselves. If it is not strictly true that, as H. J. Eckenrode has it, his novels (which one Yankee bookseller said he sent below the Potomac by the trainload) 'gave the South its social ideal,' it is unquestionable that they did become the inspiration for such extravaganzas as the *opéra bouffe* title of 'the chivalry,' by which the ruling classes, including the Virginians, habitually designated themselves." W. J. Cash, *The Mind of the South* (New York, 1941), 67–68.

22. Arlin Turner, *Mark Twain and George W. Cable* (East Lansing, Mich., 1960), 7.

23. Guy A. Cardwell, *Twins of Genius* (East Lansing, Mich., 1953), 81, 123; Louis D. Rubin, Jr., *George W. Cable* (New York, 1969), 108.

24. Arlin Turner, "George W. Cable's Revolt Against Literary Sectionalism," *Tulane Studies in English,* V (1955), 22.

and describe and explain and illuminate, . . . you have a vivid *sense* as of unseen or dimly seen things—vivid, and yet fitful and darkling." As guide and interpreter, Cable was "an inspired and enlightened long-sighted native" (329).

The two men would have much in common. Both were raised to take slavery for granted, and both had come to regard slavery as an abomination. Instructed, as he undoubtedly was by Cable, in the post-Reconstruction South's efforts in keeping blacks segregated, disenfranchised, poorly educated, impoverished, and obsequious, Mark Twain would admire Cable's courage in his fight to win full citizenship for black freedmen. Indeed, in what he wrote about the South in *Life on the Mississippi*, he agreed minutely with what Cable had been saying in his novels and essays, except for one demurral. Both men saw the South as industrially backward, as unwholesomely in love with a past literature and ignorant of modern writing, and as given over to archaic and unjust social and political forms. As the cause of these ills, Cable pointed to slavery and the slaveholding mentality; Mark Twain pointed to Walter Scottism.

Mark Twain was as explicit as if he were actively debating with Cable: "Enough is laid on slavery, without fathering upon it these creations and contributions of Sir Walter." Nor was he finished: "Sir Walter had so large a hand in making Southern character, as it existed before the war, that he is in great measure responsible for the war. . . . The Southerner of the American Revolution owned slaves; so did the Southerner of the Civil War; but the former resembles the latter as an Englishman resembles a Frenchman. The change of character can be traced rather more easily to Sir Walter's influence than to that of any other thing or person" (348). Mark Twain's argument here is elliptical. My guess is that by the "Southerner of the Revolution" he meant Thomas Jefferson and his kind, who, though slave owners, were dedicated to the ideal of equality and worked to abolish slavery. If that kind of southerner had prevailed, if Scott had not corrupted the South by creating "reverence for rank and caste," the South would have phased slavery out and the Civil War have been avoided. Such a might-have-been scenario would be agreeable to someone who regarded both slavery and the war as horrid mistakes.

Nevertheless, Twain's fulminations on Walter Scottism sound evasive next to Cable's ringing denunciations of slavery and subjugation. Is Twain's reluctance to censure slavery here a sign of moral timidity? It is true that Twain was not Cable's kind of single-minded Christian soldier. Still, by substituting Walter Scottism for slavery as the cause of the South's backwardness, he by no means avoided the risk of offending southern readers.

My guess is that Mark Twain's Walter Scottism is both an attempt to avoid the pain of ambiguous moral judgments—of having to make monsters of good people who believed in slavery—and a philosophical attempt to discover the cause in history and human nature of all tyrannies, including slavery. We must remember that he had spent several years reading, thinking, and writing about his "subject" and that he would continue to do so. At the heart of both *Huckleberry Finn* and *A Connecticut Yankee* is Mark Twain's sincere, one might say impassioned, search for the sources of social evil. *Huckleberry Finn* is not, after all, about the *institution* of slavery. At the plot level it is about a black slave who seeks freedom and a white boy who, in helping him, hopes he will not be mistaken for an abolitionist. At the philosophical level it is about everybody's enslavement—to training, to accommodation, to human nature, and to a medieval disease capable of infecting modern societies.

In the Wilks episode, Mark Twain attempted to separate Walter Scottism from slavery. His aim there is to contrast the sets of mind of people who ruthlessly lord it over others and of people who have been taught to care for one another, and to engineer a clash between the two. In Chapter 23, which immediately precedes the Wilks episode, he thematically outlines his problem. The middle of Chapter 23 is given to Huck's discourse on kings. Kings are "a mighty ornery lot." Selfish, treacherous, and remorseless, they take delight in lying and breaking contracts, in confounding people's expectations and understanding. From the subject of kings and their crimes, Mark Twain abruptly switches to the other end of the social and moral scale—to Jim's mourning his separation from his family, to Huck's realizing that Jim "cared just as much for his people as white folks does for their'n," and to Jim's infinite remorse at having struck his daughter for not obeying a command she could not hear. It is a parable of the need and cost of human sympathy.

In the tyrannies that Mark Twain concerned himself with—of kings over subjects, slave owners over slaves, and adults over children—the element that separated top from bottom was, as he saw it, not so much structural as emotional. Sympathetic feeling was rarely, if ever, directed downward, nor were love, concern, or fellowship much practiced among members of the upper level. Being in charge, having to exercise control over others, limited and distorted the emotions. Among parents and guardians, those emotions ranged from sentimentality to exasperation, with disapprobation as a kind of norm. Among kings, the privilege of emotional self-gratification led to unspeakable perversions of justice. It was only at the lower level that feelings could be shared and, in being shared, sometimes richly developed.

In the Wilks episode, Mark Twain gives us a classless (except for the slaves) community, which, untouched by Walter Scott, corresponds to the revolutionary ideal that men in their natural goodness and reasonableness may live amiably together in the American garden as long as they are free of pernicious European influences. Wilks-town is a tiny republic of shared feeling and mutual concern. Invading it are the king and the duke, who exhibit the traits of Huck's kings—remorseless exploitation, clever selfishness, and hypocrisy.

The Wilks episode, which comprises about a sixth of the novel, is melodrama; it serves us the familiar and reassuring myth of evil confounded. In the simplicity and optimism of its moral outlook, it is a far cry from the dark and troubled vision of two previous episodes—the Grangerford-Shepherdson feud and the Sherburn-Boggs affair among the Bricksvillites. We can guess how troubled that vision is by what happens to Huck's consciousness, and to his author's. In witnessing the incidents around Buck's death, Huck is traumatized: "I wished I hadn't ever come ashore that night to see such things. I ain't ever going to get shut of them—lots of times I dream about them" (153). In witnessing the murder of Boggs, he goes into shock. His eyes are wide open; he catches every detail ("I seen where one of the bullets went in" [187]), but he is emotionally numb. He has been pushed beyond where he knows how to feel. Mark Twain's own disgust with the mindless animality of the Bricksvillites shows in his imagery—loafers roost and scratch and chaw and gnaw. It shows, too, in his sicking the river on the town, just as the loafers had sicked dogs on a wallowing sow. "Such a town as that has to be always moving back, and back, and back, because the river's always gnawing at it" (183).

In those episodes, Huck seems to be the only sane and decent person, a moral minority of one, albeit in shock. Things are radically different in the Wilks episode. The citizens of Wilks-town, numerically an overwhelming majority, are kind and decent. It is the king and the duke, no longer amusing rascals but proper villains, who are the anomaly; and though they are clever and ruthless, they will not prevail. Huck returns to being the emotionally vivid person we used to know, reacting to experiences within his ken. For the one time in the book, he becomes an active hero; and far from being implicitly a critic of society, he defends its most cherished values—femininity and property. His sincerity and dedication cannot be doubted. His decision to help the Wilks girls by stealing the money back from the king and duke comes as the result of a painful psychological transformation—from thoughtless mockery to shame and penitence—identical to the one where in Chapter 15 he humbled himself to Jim.

Wilks-towners have been called gullible. I would prefer to say that in their openness and good will, they are vulnerable. Guileless and sympathetic, when they greet, as they think, Peter's English brothers, who had hoped to see Peter alive, the greeter speaks "soft and gentle" (209); and all "gethered around, and sympathized with them, and said all sorts of kind things to them" (210). When friends gather at the Wilkses for supper that evening, they show their good will by playing out a little drama of appreciation: "Mary Jane . . . said how bad the biscuits was, and how mean the preserves was, and how ornery and tough the fried chicken was—and all that kind of rot, the women always do for to force out compliments; and the people all knowed everything was tip-top, and said so—said 'How *do* you get biscuits to brown so nice?' and 'Where, for the land's sake *did* you get these amaz'n pickles?'" (220–21). In another act of friendship, the men guests stay all night to sit with the corpse. And when it comes to finding a friendly family in the nearby countryside who will take Mary Jane in on a moment's notice, Mr. Lothrop, the Apthorps, and the Proctors appear to have been equally willing. Down-home neighborliness, rather than gullibility, is their principal trait.

Moreover, in the benevolent republic of Wilks-town, there is a healthy balance of heart and head. Countervailing the uncritical generosity of the townspeople is the judicious skepticism of the town's natural aristocrats—Dr. Robinson and lawyer Levi Bell; and countering the townspeople's hot impulse to take revenge on foreigners who have used them is the lawyer's cool logic. When the real Wilks brothers show up and make their claim, Robinson and Bell assemble the two sets of claimants and the townspeople in "a big room in the hotel" (251) and conduct a "general investigation" (252) to determine which pair are imposters. When, after several fruitless hours of investigation, the people, convinced that all four are frauds, shout, "Le's duck 'em! le's drown 'em! le's ride 'em on a rail!" (256) lawyer Bell's firm leadership and rationality prevail; and no violence is done.

It must have given Mark Twain refreshment to contemplate the myth of an Edenic American community, to leave behind him the horrors of Bricksville, to simplify his social vision, to see again that what was wrong with America was the persistence or invasion of European tyranny. It can hardly be doubted that the king and the duke are made to stand for that tyranny. Rootless, nameless, and lawless, their American selves are overlain with a series of European identities. In explaining the king and duke's villainous behavior to Jim, Huck simply lumps them with "all kings"; they are part of "the breed" (199). Later he realizes that it would be useless to tell Jim that they are not the genuine articles: "It wouldn't a done no good; and, besides, it was just as I said: you couldn't tell them from the real kind" (201).

As the "real kind" of tyrants, they expropriate Jim and Huck's territory—their raft—and take away their civil rights. Huck and Jim cannot speak their minds except in whispers to each other, and they have no voice in the king and duke's decision to continue south. Their freedom of movement is severely restricted. Jim is tied hand and foot when the raft stops at towns, and in the end he is committed to the prison of the Phelps cabin.

As tyrants of the raft, the king and the duke represent a historical European threat. As the Wilks girls' bogus English uncles, however, they perhaps represent an up-to-date threat as well, one that—if the novels of Mark Twain's fellow cosmopolite Henry James are to be taken seriously—was currently troubling the American psyche. That threat was to Americans who, in their ingenuousness, generosity, and prosperity, were liable to be victimized by unscrupulous, money-hungry, pedigreed Europeans or by Europeanized Americans.

As much satisfaction as Mark Twain must have gotten out of his melodrama, there are signs of his uneasiness. Concerning one form of tyranny, namely slavery, monarchic England had not in modern times practiced it; but the United States had. Both Twain's effort to put monarchy in a polarized position vis-à-vis democracy and his bafflement are evident, I believe, in Huck's bantering dialogue with fourteen-year-old Joanna Wilks.

It begins with Joanna's asking Huck (whom she knows as her

English "uncle's" valet), "Did you ever see the king?" Huck's response is: "Who? William Fourth? Well, I bet I have—he goes to our church." Huck then confides to the reader, "I knowed he was dead years ago, but I never let on" (221).

Joanna is not likely to have said *king*. If there is anything an American teenager would have known about Europe "years" after the death of William IV in 1837, it is that a young queen sat on England's throne. But Joanna's author's campaign to make a villain of monarchy would be undermined if he allowed Joanna to ask about Queen Victoria, in whose reign England's democratization was a steady progress. He rather lamely attempted to continue the campaign when Joanna later asks, "How is servants treated in England? Do they treat 'em better'n we treat our niggers?" and Huck replies, "No! A servant ain't nobody there. They treat them worse than dogs" (223).

The Wilks girls treat their slaves kindly enough. True to the values of the melodrama, it is the heartless king who sells the Wilks slaves, "the two sons up the river to Memphis, and their mother down the river to Orleans." It is the Wilks girls who nearly "break their hearts for grief" over the sale, and their indignant neighbors who "come out flatfooted and said it was scandalous to separate the mother and children that way" (234). Nevertheless, the Wilks girls, and Wilks-towners in general, presented a paradox that could not be fitted into the moral terms of the melodrama—they were good people who kept slaves.

Mark Twain's three days in Hannibal on the upriver leg of his trip in 1882 made him "feel like a boy again." He passed along Hannibal's streets "seeing the town as it was, not as it is" (393), and from the boyhood memories that flooded his mind, he filled four chapters of *Life on the Mississippi*. Some of those memories would certainly be of his parents, John and Jane Clemens, respectable people who kept slaves.

John Marshall Clemens was in his son's memory "a proud man, a silent austere man," a man of rectitude without the capacity for showing affection.[25] His self-esteem was based more on his family origins in Virginia, whose "symbols of gentility" he cherished, than on his meager success as shopkeeper in Kentucky and Missouri

25. Neider (ed.), *The Autobiography of Mark Twain*, 23.

and, just before his death in 1847, as justice of peace.[26] Jane Lampton Clemens was a quite different person. Lively and talkative, she had "a heart so large that everybody's grief and everybody's joys found welcome in it and hospitable accommodation." She was compassionate, yet her notion of parenting seemed to require that she save her affection for people outside her family and for stray animals. Mark Twain wrote about her autobiographically as about an esteemed person he had observed but was not close to. So little was Sam the child used to loving words and caresses, so total was the "atmosphere of reserve" he was raised in, that when Livy fell in love with him, her "prodigal affections in kisses and caresses and . . . endearments" were an astonishment to him.[27] His mother, he said, "figures as Tom Sawyer's Aunt Polly"; and one remembers that a burden of *Tom Sawyer* is the inability of Tom and his aunt to communicate with each other in any important way. When Aunt Polly knocks Tom sprawling to the floor with a disciplinary blow, and then finds out that he was not guilty after all, she cannot apologize but goes silently "about her affairs with a troubled heart" while Tom fantasizes "himself lying sick unto death and his aunt bending over him beseeching one little forgiving word."[28]

Two stories about Jane Clemens and slaves define the poles of compassion and discipline. The first is of "a little slave boy" from Maryland whose singing so irritated young Sam that he begged his mother to shut him up. "Poor thing," she explained, "when he sings it shows that he is not remembering, and that comforts me. . . . He will never see his mother again; if he can sing I must not hinder it, but be thankful for it."[29] The second is of saucy house slave Jennie's insubordination. Jane attempted to whip Jennie, but Jennie wrenched the whip from Jane's hand. Summoned, John Clemens bound Jennie's wrists together and flogged her with a cowhide.[30]

"[K]ind-hearted and compassionate" as his mother was, Mark Twain wrote in his autobiography:

26. Dixon Wecter, *Sam Clemens of Hannibal* (Boston, 1952), 31.

27. Neider (ed.), *The Autobiography of Mark Twain*, 25, 185.

28. Samuel L. Clemens [Mark Twain], *The Adventures of Tom Sawyer; Tom Sawyer Abroad; Tom Sawyer, Detective*, ed. John C. Gerber, Paul Baender, and Terry Firkins (Berkeley, 1980), 54, Vol. IV of the Works of Mark Twain.

29. Neider (ed.), *The Autobiography of Mark Twain*, 6–7.

30. Albert Bigelow Paine, *Mark Twain: A Biography* (3 vols.; New York, 1912), I, 17.

I think she was not conscious that slavery was a bald, grotesque and unwarrantable usurpation. She had never heard it assailed in any pulpit but had heard it defended and sanctified in a thousand; her ears were familiar with Bible texts that approved it but if there were any that disapproved it they had not been quoted by her pastors; as far as her experience went, the wise and the good and the holy were unanimous in the conviction that slavery was right, righteous, sacred, the peculiar pet of the Deity and a condition which the slave himself ought to be daily and nightly thankful for. Manifestly, training and association can accomplish strange miracles.[31]

Think of the moral tension implicit in this half paragraph! Between Mark Twain's mature perception that slavery was a grotesque usurpation and his mother's unreformable conviction that slavery was right and sacred, there is a prodigious moral chasm. Twain had crossed that chasm at the pain of leaving his mother and gentlefolk like her on the other side. In order to grapple deeply with the problem of slavery, he had not only to stand where his humanity and enlightenment bade him but to remember with a certain understanding, and even love, the good people who remained where he had been. In *Huckleberry Finn,* such people are represented by the Wilks-towners, who, though slaveholders, were the salt of the earth, and by Tom's Aunt Sally and Uncle Silas Phelps, who were as "kind as could be" to Jim, the runaway slave they kept prisoner; Silas would pray with Jim, and Sally would see that "he was comfortable and had plenty to eat" (309). In neither representation does Twain seek the relief of rhetorical irony.

The result of Mark Twain's visits in New Orleans, where Cable showed him the South of the present, and in Hannibal, where he conjured up the South of the past, was, it seems to me, twofold. In a nation where racism was so widely, and in large part unconsciously, persisted in, where Twain's special respect and love for blacks was an oddity, he felt a moral loneliness. By the same token, he decided that Jim could not really be freed. Nor was it simply his southern experiences that need have convinced him. They could have reminded him how colored folks in the North were kept in their place. There was Aunt Rachel, for example, who was constrained to sit "respectfully below" the level of the white folks on the Cranes' porch. Then there was John T. Lewis, another of the Cranes' drudges. Come to think of it, Jim had a son named John, who could well have been born in 1835, the year of John T. Lewis' birth.[32]

31. Neider (ed.), *The Autobiography of Mark Twain,* 30.
32. Smith and Gibson (eds.), *Mark Twain–Howells Letters,* II, 915.

Suppose that Jim had succeeded in escaping north and ended up by settling his family in Elmira, New York; it could have been his son's privilege, when he had grown into free manhood, to work for the Cranes and thereafter dress in rags, haul manure, and every year go deeper in debt.

Mark Twain's moral loneliness resulted from his failure to grow up, or stay grown up, in the expected way in Hannibal. In that town, Mark Twain recalled, "there were grades of society—people of good family, people of unclassified family, people of no family. Everybody knew everybody and was affable to everbody and nobody put on any visible airs; yet the class lines were quite clearly drawn and the familiar social life of each class was restricted to that class. It was a little democracy . . . ; yet you perceived that the aristocratic taint was there." To the classes listed, he might well have added two others: slaves and children. Slaves in the Hannibal region, he said, were treated decently. Sam Clemens was treated as decently as any slave, one supposes, and about as affectionately. For affection he went to Uncle Dan'l, on his uncle's farm, where "[a]ll the negroes were friends of ours, and with those our own age we were in effect comrades."[33] The great difference between him and his black friends and comrades and, indeed, between him and Uncle Dan'l, is that he would outgrow his inferior status. He would be privileged to join his parents, his uncle, and decent people like them in their masterly roles and in their social anesthesia. That he could not, that he remained loyal to the friends he left behind, at the same time obliged to the generation that nurtured him, accounts for some of the puzzling currents and countercurrents in the evasion chapters.

Those currents subside if we join Mark Twain in his hopeless view of the plight of the emancipated black in the South of 1882. Besides presenting that view, he did his best to distract us from it. I doubt that his dual strategy was deliberate. I take the evasion chapters to be the work of unconscious genius, with which the critical sense, standing aside in modest bewilderment, had little to do. Considering the tensions and contradictions he was working within, those chapters are a monument to his creative stamina.

Louis Budd was the first to develop the idea that *Huckleberry Finn* reflected "the context Twain was living and writing in" as well as the context of his memories of Hannibal and the Mississippi River. In

33. Neider (ed.), *The Autobiography of Mark Twain*, 5, 6.

his 1962 study, *Mark Twain: Social Philosopher*, Budd observed that Twain's emphasis on violence and lawlessness was a comment not on the South of 1845 but on that of the 1880s, when "the Negro's civil rights crumbled before massive pressure." Nine years later, Neil Schmitz more specifically declared, "Jim's situation at the end of *Huckleberry Finn* reflects that of the Negro of the Reconstruction, free at last and thoroughly impotent, the object of devious schemes and a hapless victim of constant brutality." In substantial agreement with Schmitz, but without reference to him, Richard Gollin and Rita Gollin subsequently demonstrated that Jim's plight in the evasion "constitutes a paradigm for the condition of the emancipated Negro at the time Twain wrote the novel, legally free but nevertheless imprisoned by his ignorant need to trust in white good will, betrayed by the peculiar sense of propriety even of those best-intentioned whites, and because no one's property, ending in a worse state than before." More recently, Charles H. Nilon, without reference to either Schmitz or the Gollins, made the same general interpretation of the evasion: "Twain suggests that, like Jim, black people in the post-Reconstruction South were losing a sense of selfhood and often were forced to see themselves as inferior. Jim's losses suggest that the consequences of the 'evasion' were complex and serious, as serious perhaps as the effects of chattel slavery had been."[34]

If we read the evasion as an allegory of the plight of the black in the post-Reconstruction South, Tom Sawyer emerges as the type of contemporary southerner who, wrapped in his sense of principle and tradition and drawing moral strength therefrom, was determined to reverse the gains that freed slaves had made during Reconstruction and to see that they stayed in positions of social and psychological inferiority.

He is, to begin with, the very embodiment of Walter Scottism. Mark Twain begins his grumbling about Walter Scottism in *Life on the Mississippi* by ridiculing the southern penchant for making practical buildings look like castles. In Baton Rouge, he explains, "Sir Walter Scott is probably responsible for the Capitol building; for it is not

34. Louis J. Budd, *Mark Twain: Social Philosopher* (Bloomington, Ind., 1962), 95–106; Neil Schmitz, "Twain, *Huckleberry Finn*, and the Reconstruction," *American Studies*, XII (Spring, 1971), 60; Richard Gollin and Rita Gollin, "*Huckleberry Finn* and the Time of the Evasion," *Modern Language Studies*, IX (Spring, 1979), 10; Charles H. Nilon, "The Ending of *Huckleberry Finn*: 'Freeing the Free Negro,'" *Mark Twain Journal*, XXII (Fall, 1984), 27.

conceivable that this little sham castle would ever have been built if he had not run the people mad, a couple of generations ago, with his mediaeval romances. The South has not yet recovered from the debilitating influence of his books. Admiration of his fantastic heroes and their grotesque 'chivalry' doings and romantic juvenilities still survives here." From the Louisiana capitol building he turns his attention to a couple of "female colleges." One of them has a building that resembles "the old castles of song and story, with its towers, turreted walls, and ivy-mantled porches"; the other is advertised in such romantic terms that Twain's sardonic response is, "What, warder, ho! the man that can blow so complacent a blast as that, probably blows it from a castle" (308–10).

Tom Sawyer does his best to transform Jim's cabin into a castle. All the "regulations" having to do with the freeing of prisoners from castle dungeons must be applied in Jim's case. Jim must throw plates bearing messages out of his window, the way the "Iron Mask always done" (302). The foundation of Jim's "fortress" must be dug through with case knives in imitation of the prisoner of the "Castle Deef" (304). Jim must have a rope ladder, since escaping prisoners tie rope ladders to castle battlements for descent to the moat. Jim's cabin, it is true, lacks a moat, but "[i]f we get time, the night of the escape, we'll dig one," Tom declares (299).

"Romantic juvenilities" are the least baneful of Walter Scottism's manifestations. Is the Tom Sawyer of the evasion solidly enough constructed to stand for its most dangerous aspect—the taking on of the power and authority to lord it over others? He is indeed. Tom is by far the most powerful personality in the last quarter of the book. When, in his store clothes, he strides across the Phelpses' yard to present himself to his aunt and uncle as a stranger from Ohio, "[h]e warn't a boy to meeky along up that yard like a sheep; no, he come ca'm and important, like the ram" (285). Impressed, the Phelpses pay him the deference they would an adult. His ability to control everyone's perceptions of reality is prodigious. He has Silas "mooning around" (316) in bewilderment, thinking he must have done what he cannot remember doing, and Sally "just a trembling all over" (318) with frustration at her inability to count spoons. In a cool and masterful way, he twice convinces Nat, the slave who brings Jim his food, that what Nat has seen and heard and felt in the cabin is a delusion of his bewitched imagination. Having convinced Nat that he is a victim of witchcraft, Tom compounds his deceit by offering to take care of the witches. For the offer, Nat is abjectly grateful: "Will you do it, honey?—will you? I'll wusshup de groun' und' yo' foot, I will!" (311). Tom imperiously overrules Huck's practical plans for freeing Jim. Tom's methods are sanctioned by the "authorities" (299), by "regulations" (301), by the "custom in Europe" (300). An evasion has to go by "the rules"; "right is right, and wrong is wrong." "Full of principle," grumbles Huck (307).

Tom has no intention of freeing Jim. On the contrary, he makes every effort to prolong his captivity and to deprive him of such minuscule dignities, privileges, and comforts as he has. Tom refers to Jim not as an escaping slave but as a prisoner, and all of Tom's inventions and requirements mire Jim more deeply in that role. Tom wants to string out Jim's imprisonment for generations "and leave Jim to our children to get out." Jim would come to like his subjugation "better and better the more he got used to it" (310). When, at length, Tom feels forced to stage Jim's escape, he insists on announcing the event to the Phelpses through "nonnamous letters" and ominous pictures, because "if we don't *give* them notice there won't be nobody nor nothing to interfere with us" (332). In response to the letters, fifteen gun-toting farmers gather at the Phelps plantation; and as a result of the shooting that follows, Jim's attempt to escape is indirectly but effectively prevented.

What if the three of them had safely gained the raft? It was Tom's plan to run Jim "down the river, on the raft, and have adventures plumb to the mouth of the river, and then tell him about his being free" (360). Thereafter, Jim would be shipped back to St. Petersburg, where he would be met with a torchlight procession and a brass band. Putting together the hackneyed analogy of life as a river and Mark Twain's mocking images of afterlife, we are permitted to conclude that with Tom in charge, Jim would have to die and go to heaven for his freedom.

Huck's role in the allegory is that of the person of good will who would like to believe the South had the best interest of freed blacks at heart and who was disturbed at evidences to the contrary but was reluctant or powerless to interfere. More dismaying than Huck's hands-off policy is the dulling of his emotions. In his complacency with Tom's cruel schemes, in his finding some of them rather entertaining ("there warn't ever anything could a worked better" [310] than Jim's nearly getting his teeth mashed out when he bit on the piece of brass candlestick in the corn pone), he is simply not the Huck who wrestled with himself before he could humble himself to Jim or the one who decided to go to hell for him.

Jim's role as the subjugated is obvious enough; and yet, since the novel may be said to end happily, we perhaps need to be reminded how psychologically devastating Mark Twain felt that subjugation to be. Jim has been so acquiescent in the role of prisoner, so industrious in carrying out Tom's crazy requirements, that the role of prisoner dominates his personality. When, at the end, he understands that he is free, he is "pleased most to death," *not* with his freedom but with the forty dollars Tom gives him "for being prisoner for us so patient, and doing it up so good" (360). Jim's freedom has become insignificant. It is celebrated by no one, not Jim, not Huck, and especially not the author. There is no mention of Jim's rejoining his family. Instead, he will go out west with Tom and Huck to have "adventures amongst the Injuns" (361). He will become a boy.

As plain as it is to me that one effect of the evasion is to satirize the principle and practice of white supremacy, I cannot claim that the problem of the novel's ending has been solved. The allegory *is* there, but Mark Twain took such pains to cover it over that it is not likely to be seen by the casual reader.[35] There are rather elaborately developed episodes that point away from the allegory. Some of Tom and Huck's activities, such as the construction of the witch pie and the gathering of vermin, are distractingly detailed and make the boys seem so childish that for the time being they slip out of their symbolic roles. The contrast between mild, unworldly Silas and his practical, energetic wife is portrayed with richness and economy, but it has no connection with the deeper meaning. The episodes in which Tom drives his aunt nearly insane, first with evidences that she has lost her common sense, then by populating her house with snakes, and finally through threatening letters, are, one might say, thoroughly done; yet they are not only beside the point but rather distasteful as comedy. They are an act of revenge by the author on members of his parents' generation, for reasons validated in his own emotional economy but not made pertinent to the relationship between Tom and his aunt. They, along with other passages featuring bugs, rats, and snakes (Tom wants Jim to take a rattlesnake for a pet, for then the snake "will let you wrap him around your neck and put his head in your mouth" [325]), are comparable to "The Battle of the

---

35. A brilliant discussion of elements in the evasion "ordinarily held in tension" but seeming "to pull apart before our eyes" is to be found in Forrest G. Robinson, *In Bad Faith: The Dynamics of Deception in Mark Twain's America* (Cambridge, Mass., 1986), 173–80.

Sand-Belt" chapter in *A Connecticut Yankee,* in that all are bizarre expressions of the author's rage over certain miscreated aspects of human nature that will not let his stories come out right.

Then there is Mark Twain's keeping from the casual reader, just as Tom keeps from Huck, news of Jim's having been freed. The multitude of ironies generated between the fact of Jim's freedom and Tom's words and actions in the evasion chapters are the private property of the author. They may be appreciated only by the retrospective and inquisitive reader, the kind whom Mark Twain specifically threatened with prosecution, banishment, and death.

Mark Twain half concealed his allegory of the evasion because it expressed a deep moral and philosophical conflict, the product of his southern visit, which he had not come to terms with. In the world where he had become northernized, he developed the optimistic view that in spite of great pressures to conform, a person might undergo a profound and heroic change, a revolution of the emotions, a stirring of the "hidden great deeps" of one's nature. Huckleberry could humble himself to Jim and never be sorry for it. Jim could change from a superstitious darky to a man who hungered for freedom and audaciously planned to achieve it. In visiting the South, in seeing it through his eyes and Cable's, Mark Twain lost that view. It seemed to him that people were so conditioned by training and tradition that they could not change. Worse, they justified dark deeds and mean motives with ceremonious language. It was a judgment not on the South but on human nature; and therefore neither indignation nor condemnation was appropriate, but a kind of resignation.

To achieve that resignation, he began constructing his determinism, a philosophy based on what he had read in Paine, Holmes, Darwin, and Taine about the laws, processes, and mechanics that ruled behavior. He began moving from the heroic old world of moral drama to one that made only mechanical sense. In what he wrote during the year following his river trip, there are signs of that move.

In *Life on the Mississippi* he recalled that while he was chatting with his brother Henry in New Orleans, "the water which was to make the steam which should cause [the boiler explosion that would kill Henry] was washing past some point fifteen hundred miles up the river" (170). His stopover in Hannibal "carried me back more than a generation in a moment, and landed me in the midst of a time when the happenings of life were not the natural and logical results of great general laws, but of special orders, and were freighted with very precise and distinct purposes" (398). In mid-June, 1882, he constructed a conversation between two Negro deckhands to prove that men were no more responsible for their crimes than a fox for "stealing" or a rattlesnake for "murder."[36] In February of the next year he delivered a paper before the Hartford Monday Evening Club in which he anticipated *What Is Man?* by "denying that there is any such thing as personal merit; maintaining that man is merely a machine."[37]

The story of the Grangerford-Shepherdson feud conveys Mark Twain's reluctant acknowledgment that human beings are, as Darwin, Holmes, and Taine seemed to say, capable of being trained in such perverse ways as to lose the good of their humanity. The Grangerfords are an example of Darwin's theory that consciences can be trained to embrace as sacred duty what generally would be called wickedness—in their case, the killing of Shepherdsons. In so doing, they have abandoned reason in favor of what Holmes called "automatic and instinctive principles" and what Taine identified as the substratum of "violent and destructive instincts" in human nature.

The evasion is neatly bracketed by two of Huck's soliloquies, which say that training is everything. In the first, Huck is trying to adjust himself to the idea that Tom Sawyer "was actuly going to help steal [Jim] out of slavery. . . . Here was a boy that was respectable and well brung up; and had a character to lose; and folks at home that had characters; and he was bright and not leather-headed; and knowing and not ignorant; and not mean, but kind; and yet here he was, without any more pride, or rightness, or feeling, than to stoop to this business, and make himself a shame, and his family a shame, before everybody. I *couldn't* understand it no way at all. It was outrageous" (292–93). Eight chapters later, in the denouement, Huck is reassured by Aunt Polly that "Tom was right about old Miss Watson setting Jim free in her will; and so, sure enough, Tom Sawyer had gone and took all that trouble and bother to set a free nigger free! and I couldn't ever understand before, until that minute and that talk, how he *could* help a body set a nigger free with his bringing up" (358). Mark Twain misuses Huck here to deliver his

---

36. Anderson, Salamo, and Stein (eds.), *Mark Twain's Notebooks and Journals*, II, 434–35, 493–95.

37. Samuel Clemens [Mark Twain], *What Is Man? and Other Philosophical Writings*, ed. Paul Baender (Berkeley, 1973), 4, Vol. XIX of the Works of Mark Twain.

own philosophy and its attendant ironies. In Huck's trust in the laws of behavior, in his sense of security in them, he is not the Huck we used to know.

More to the point is the uncompromised orthodoxy of Tom's views on slavery and on the power of training to instill that orthodoxy. Perhaps the problem with the evasion is the deterministic philosophy behind it. That philosophy says that in Tom there can be no change of heart. Worse, it says that Huck's and Jim's changes of heart were the author's mistake; they are to be forgotten. In the post-Reconstruction roles that Jim and Huck have slipped into, heroic changes of heart are not appropriate. Action in the evasion is dictated by the laws of behavior, laws of "training and association" that govern society with mechanical precision. In a society under such law, no blame can be placed and no one can triumph. The world of the evasion is without sin, and without redemption.

# CHAPTER 10

# Warring Views: *A Connecticut Yankee*

*Training—training is everything; training is all there is* to *a person.*
—Chapter 18

ONCE FINISHED WITH *Huckleberry Finn* in the summer of 1883, Mark Twain was pleased to put it out of his mind in favor of other projects. He returned to the manuscript (not to be published in the United States until February, 1885) more than a year later in search of platform material for his reading tour with George Cable. The selections he considered indicate that the determinism of the evasion had not become a fixed attitude. "Make a whole reading from Huck," he advised himself in his notebook; and other entries include "All right, I'll *go* to hell," "Call *this* a gov't.?" and two reminders to use "A True Story."[1] His resignation was being replaced by his more characteristic indignation.

The process continued. Early in January he wrote Livy of an incident he had observed on a train in southern Illinois: "A small country boy, a little while ago, discussed a negro woman in her easy hearing distance, to his 17-year old sister. 'Mighty good clothes for a nigger, *hain't* they? *I* never see a nigger dressed so fine before.' She *was* thoroughly well & tastefully dressed, & had more brains & breeding than 7 generations of that boy's family will be able to show."[2] His notebook response was to jot down an idea for a story, a kind of revenge fantasy, in which a revolution would have taken place: "America in 1985. (Negro supremacy—the whites under foot.)" The notion lingered in his mind; and in 1887 he set down a more elaborate set of notes, which began: "1910. In the South, whites of both sexes have to ride in the smoking car (& pay full fare,) the populous & dominant colored man will not ride with them."[3]

---

1. Robert Pack Browning, Michael B. Frank, and Lin Salamo (eds.), *Mark Twain's Notebooks and Journals* (3 vols. completed; Berkeley, 1979), III, 61, 91, 83, 89.

2. Dixon Wecter (ed.), *The Love Letters of Mark Twain* (New York, 1949), 225.

3. Browning, Frank, and Salamo (eds.), *Mark Twain's Notebooks and Journals*, III, 88, 358.

His indignation restored, could Mark Twain have been uneasy with the way *Huckleberry Finn* had turned out? We may speculate that two subsequent works were, in some part, attempts to arrive at different meanings from the one produced by the evasion.

If readers are disappointed with the way Huck's decision to go to hell for Jim—surely one of the glories of our literature—is obscured and diminished by the tomfoolery of the last quarter of the novel, they should be pleased with the "corrected" arrangement of similar elements in "The Private History of a Campaign That Failed" (1885). Here the hilarity, horseplay, and floundering of the raw recruits is the long prologue to the brief and serious climax—the shooting of the stranger and the author's understanding that he "was not equipped for this awful business" of war. Mark Twain's determination to desert so as to avoid the guilt and anguish of killing, his diffidence in his decision, his knowing that "war was intended for men, and I for a child's nurse," that those who stayed and fought were turned "from rabbits into soldiers," is remarkably similar to Huck's lonely decision in the face of reigning social, moral, and religious values to go to hell for Jim.[4] In "Campaign," however, it comes, as the high point should, at the end.

*A Connecticut Yankee,* conceived during the reading tour when *Huckleberry Finn* was much on his mind and lips, "plotted out" a year later in December, 1885, and begun the following year, was an attempt to return upriver from the "absolute South" where his previous book had ended.[5] He *had* made the return trip in *Life on the Mississippi* and was exhilarated by the contrast between the tradition-bound, backward-looking South and the vigorous, industrial, and egalitarian area along the upper reaches of the Mississippi. Here the tradition had been of slaveless farms and servantless households, of town meetings and granges, of individual enterprise and progress. Now it was an "amazing region, bristling with great towns," a land not only of "vast manufacturing industries" but of newspapers, libraries, schools, colleges, and churches, of telephones, telegraph, fire departments, and railroads. In "all these

4. Samuel Clemens [Mark Twain], *The American Claimant and Other Stories and Sketches,* Author's National Edition: The Writings of Mark Twain (25 vols.; New York, 1907–18), XXI, 255, 258.

5. Browning, Frank, and Salamo (eds.), *Mark Twain's Notebooks and Journals,* III, 78, 86, 176–77; Samuel Clemens [Mark Twain], *Life on the Mississippi,* Author's National Edition: The Writings of Mark Twain (25 vols.; New York, 1907–18), IX, 308.

Upper-River towns one breathes a go-ahead atmosphere which tastes good in the nostrils."[6]

Although his purpose in writing *A Connecticut Yankee* was murky at first, its germ was surely the contrast between the two regions he visited on his river trip; and as that purpose developed, it turned into his all-out attempt to master his subject—something he had failed to do in his previous novel, where the problem of men's willingness to inflict and suffer slavery and tyranny remained unsolved. Unfortunately, instead of resolving anything in his projected novel, he was doomed to repeat the cycle of responses he had already gone through, running more or less from sympathy and hope to indignation and finally despair, the last deadened by a deterministic philosophy. His main advance in *A Connecticut Yankee* would be to bring his deep musings closer to the surface, to be more explicit about the nature of his subject and more willing to give voice to his determinism.

*A Connecticut Yankee* begins rapidly and superbly. In the opening pages, the atmospheres of both the nineteenth and sixth centuries are evoked, as is the touching bewilderment of Hank Morgan, the Yankee superintendent of Hartford's Colt arms factory, who is tumbled backward in time and eastward in space to King Arthur's England. Mark Twain's early intention seems to have been simply to exploit the dramatic and humorous possibilities in the Yankee's displacement—in his "anomalous position in King Arthur's kingdom [where he was] a giant among pigmies, a man among children, a master intelligence among intellectual moles."[7] After Hank is made the king's minister, with the title of "The Boss," he intends to use his power at first simply to contrive such amenities as will make his Robinson Crusoe life bearable (100) and later to "grow up with the country" as another of history's adventurers operating within "the shelter of its long array of thrones" (109). It is not until Chapter 13 that Hank becomes zealous to reform England. Seeing in the oppression of "freemen," who make up the large majority of England's

6. Clemens, *Life on the Mississippi*, 420–31.

7. Samuel Clemens [Mark Twain], *A Connecticut Yankee in King Arthur's Court*, ed. Bernard L. Stein and Henry Nash Smith (Berkeley, 1979), 113, Vol. IX of the Works of Mark Twain. Further references to *A Connecticut Yankee* are indicated by parenthetical page numbers in the text.

population, "France and the French, before the ever-memorable and blessed Revolution" (157), he resolves to effect a bloodless revolution through "educating his materials" (160). (Chapter 10, detailing the social and technological changes going on under cover, was written a year and a half after Chapter 13.)

The novel's many flaws—its inconsistencies of tone and its failure to realize Hank Morgan as the practical, unsentimental blacksmith, horse doctor, and shop superintendent he is introduced as, presenting him instead as being endowed with Mark Twain's sophistication in show business, journalism, and history—make the novel an artistic disappointment. Yet, if we were to cull out of the middle third of the novel (Chapters 13–30) those passages where Mark Twain struggles to find the causes and cure for tyranny and slavery, we might see him as worthy of amateur standing in the nascent sciences of sociology and psychology.

Mark Twain looked to history for his case studies. A good deal of the history he used was, it is true, that of France and England of the eighteenth century—a fact he did not apologize for, since it seemed to him that the tyranny of the ancient regime epitomized the tyranny of Europe as far back as King Arthur's century, that if any inhumane prerevolutionary law or custom "was lacking in that remote time, its place was competently filled by a worse one" (45). From Taine's *Ancient Regime*, for example, he borrowed the detail of French peasants' not being allowed to protect their crops from the nobles' hunting parties (557). From Taine's work and from Carlyle's *French Revolution* and Madame du Barry's *Memoirs* he gathered descriptions he applied to Morgan le Fay's dungeons (560). From Lecky's *History of European Morals* he drew information that a suicide's property was confiscated by the English crown (557). And from Charles Ball's *Fifty Years in Chains* (about American slavery) he gathered details for his slave traders' cruelties (561).

In his choice of episodes from history (and the ones mentioned are only samplings), he was inspired by Taine. He was, to begin with, searching out such specific and graphic evidences as would give a sense of actuality to history. Mark Twain had absorbed Taine's advice that to represent the life of a time gone by, one must deal in homely details. If "I would govern this country wisely," the Boss declares, "I must be posted in the details of its life, and not at second hand but by personal observation and scrutiny" (240). Thus inspired, he later determines to disguise myself as a freeman of a peasant degree and wander through the country a week or two on foot. This would give me a chance to eat and lodge with the lowliest and poorest class of free citizens on equal terms. There was no other way to inform myself perfectly of their every-day life and the operation of the laws upon it. If I went among them as a gentleman, there would be restraints and conventionalities which would shut me out from their private joys and troubles, and I should get no further than the shell. (274–75)

Besides detailing "every-day life," the episodes are Tainean in that their display of cruelties and horrors is bound to stimulate the reader's sympathetic imagination.

What are some of Mark Twain's case studies of tyranny and slavery? The following abstracts may give an idea.

### Morgan le Fay and Her Page

Morgan le Fay, the beautiful, heartless queen of a small realm, while entertaining the Boss, stabbed a page to death because he stumbled and "fell lightly against her knee." Later, when the Boss upbraided her for her crime, she angrily responded: "Crime, forsooth! Man, I am going to *pay* for him." Morgan le Fay regarded her response as generous, since the law permitted her to kill the page but did not require payment for his life.

Comment: "She was a result of generations of training in the unexamined and unassailed belief that the law which permitted her to kill a subject when she chose was a perfectly right and righteous one" (190, 207–208).

### The Gallant Young Husband and Wife

A "young giant" is, at the Boss's command, released from the rack, where, refusing to confess that he had killed a stag in Morgan le Fay's royal preserve, he had been tortured for hours. The man's wife confided to the Boss that she had been praying for her husband's confession so that his summary execution would end his tortures. The husband had refused to confess because if he were convicted his estate would be confiscated and his widow and child would be penniless.

Comment: Even under the most heartless tyranny, true manhood and womanhood can persist. The husband stood by his wife and child "like a man"; the wife's caring only that her husband's suffering should end "humbles a body to think what your sex can do when it comes to self-sacrifice" (199–203).

## THE COMPANY OF PILGRIMS AND THE SLAVE

A company of pilgrims—"a pleasant, friendly, sociable herd; pious, happy, merry"—witnessed a slave trader's disciplining a young female slave carrying a baby. Her fault was her reeling with fatigue during a long march. The slave trader "snatched the child from her, and then made the men slaves who were chained before and behind throw her on the ground and hold her there and expose her body; and then he laid on with his lash like a madman till her back was flayed, she shrieking and struggling the while, piteously. . . . All our pilgrims looked on and commented—on the expert way in which the whip was handled."

Comment: The pilgrims "were too much hardened by life-long every-day familiarity with slavery to notice that there was anything else in the exhibition that invited comment. This is what slavery could do, in the way of ossifying what one may call the superior lobe of human feeling; for these pilgrims were kind hearted people, and they would not have allowed that man to treat a horse like that" (241, 245–46).

## KING ARTHUR AND THE SMALLPOX HUT

A peasant family—father, mother, two young daughters, and three grown boys—had suffered a series of calamities. First, the three sons, falsely accused of cutting down certain fruit trees, had been thrown into the lord's dungeon. Shorthanded, the peasant family were nevertheless expected to be as efficient in harvesting the lord's crops as in previous years. Unable to keep up with the work, they were daily fined; to pay the fines, they had to give their own crops to the lord. Starving and in rags, the family contracted smallpox. When King Arthur and the Boss, themselves disguised as peasants, entered the "smallpox hut," the husband and one daughter were dead; the mother and the other daughter were dying. Full of compassion and careless of the disease or of the curse the Church had put on the family, Arthur climbed into the loft and carried the girl down so that she could die in her mother's arms.

Shortly thereafter, mother and daughter dead, Arthur and the Boss latched the hut's door behind them. They were slipping away in the midnight darkness when they heard the three sons approach the hut. Arthur insisted that since the three young men had broken out of the dungeon, he and the Boss were "bound in duty to lay hands upon them and deliver them again to their lord."

Comment 1: Arthur's risking his own life in reuniting the diseased and dying mother and daughter "was heroism at its last and loftiest possibility, its utmost summit. . . . He was great, now; sublimely great."

Comment 2: Arthur's callousness in insisting that the three sons be apprehended and returned to their cruel lord resulted from his being "born so, educated so, his veins were full of ancestral blood that was rotten with this sort of unconscious brutality, brought down by inheritance from a long procession of hearts that had each done its share toward poisoning the stream" (328–38).

## THE LORD'S DEATH AND THE AVENGING MOB

The cruel lord was murdered and his manor house burned down. The "lord's liveried retainers proclaimed an instant crusade" against the relatives and friends of the smallpox family "and were promptly joined by the community in general." The mob hanged or "butchered" eighteen people. One member of the mob, a charcoal burner named Marco, later confessed to the Boss, "I helped to hang my neighbors for that it were peril to my own life to show lack of zeal in the master's cause." When the Boss averred that the murdered lord "got only what he deserved," and that "[i]f I had my way, all his kind should have the same luck," Marco momentarily threw off his abject manner and, although aware that the Boss might be a spy, nevertheless heartily agreed with him.

Comment: "There it was, you see. A man *is* a man, at bottom. Whole ages of abuse and oppression cannot crush the manhood clear out of him" (338–46).

What can one say about such case studies? To begin with, our social psychologist obviously refused to pick bland cases. As was his habit, he searched out or thought up extremes of human behavior. It was his way of testing a philosophy. The first two world views he had absorbed—Calvinism and deism—were simple and comprehensive. The first having failed and the second failing, he was looking for a third—one that would be simple, comprehensive, and infallible. He would construct it, finally, in the determinism of *What*

*Is Man?*. In the meantime, still in the process of building and testing, he was reluctant to give up certain cherished beliefs embedded in the old views. He was fervently hoping to find evidence of man's secular redeemability, of his "manhood," of his primal goodness; but in seeming to find it, even magnifying it in celebration, he could not represent it as prevailing. It cropped up here and there, usually in domestic acts of courage and self-sacrifice, but without political force.

Without completely realizing it, Mark Twain found himself in a conflict among three concepts of personality. The earliest was that implied in the psalmist's answer to his own question—"What is man that thou art mindful of him?"—that answer being, "Thou hast made him a little lower than the angels." In spite of countless evidences in the human record that man was far from angelic, that idea persisted into the eighteenth century (and beyond), when one of the ideals of the American and French revolutions was that man's natural goodness and reasonableness, stifled and perverted by tyranny, would, if man were freed, enable him to build a just society. The second concept of personality that Mark Twain responded to was a current one that regarded humans as dominated by sentiment. One's emotions—limited in number but pure—were guides for personal conduct and, when expressed, were socially useful. People were humanized through imparting their own emotions and in sympathizing with others' emotions, thus creating communities of, say, suffering or indignation or joy. Mark Twain was rather too well equipped as a sentimentalist. It was his habit to regret his overactive "conscience"; and in *A Connecticut Yankee*, he declared, "If I had the remaking of man, he wouldn't have any conscience" (209–10). The third concept was one being developed in the behavioral sciences—that man is an organism conditioned by past experiences and responding in predictable ways to current stimuli. All three of these concepts come together, for example, when the Boss frees the young giant from the rack because "I could not let this horror go on; it would have killed me to see it," and then sends him and his wife to the Man Factory, "where I'm going to turn groping and grubbing automata into *men*" (201, 203).

The result of the contest among the three concepts of personality and between Mark Twain's dying and nascent philosophies is to give *A Connecticut Yankee* a vacillating motion—a series of surges and withdrawals—that discomfits the reader. He could, for example, immediately follow his declaration that "a man *is* a man, at bottom" with this startling sentiment: "Well, there are times when one would like to hang the whole human race and finish the farce" (348). Basically, the conflict is between an idealistic, sentimental view of man and a clinically behavioristic view, precisely the views represented by the Young Man and the Old Man, respectively, in *What Is Man?*. In that latter work, Mark Twain, having separated the two views and having discredited the former as a fallacy of youth's witless optimism, serenely recited the infallible tenets of his determinism. In *A Connecticut Yankee*, still subject, in man's behalf, to surges of hope and pity and indignation, he exposes us to the swirling thoughts and feelings of a social philosopher in spiritual transition.

In spite of the turbulence, he managed certain balanced statements in which he got to the heart of the problem of tyranny and slavery as he saw it. One of those statements concerns King Arthur's performance as a judge. On the whole, the Boss honored and respected Arthur. "He was a wise and humane judge," he declared, "and he clearly did his honest best and fairest—according to his lights." His lights, however—"his rearing"—required him to give his sympathy to persons of high degree and withhold it from persons of low degree.

It was impossible that this should be otherwise. The blunting effects of slavery upon the slaveholder's moral perceptions are known and conceded, the world over, and a privileged class, an aristocracy, is but a band of slaveholders under another name. . . . One needs but to hear an aristocrat speak of the classes that are below him to recognize—and in but indifferently modified measure—the very air and tone of the actual slaveholder; and behind these are the slaveholder's spirit, the slaveholder's blunted feeling. They are the result of the same cause, in both cases: the possessor's old and inbred custom of regarding himself as a superior being. (285)

It becomes clearer, now, that Mark Twain's unwillingness to focus on the institution of slavery in *Life on the Mississippi* and *Huckleberry Finn*, his apparent lack of abolitionist satisfaction in seeing slavery outlawed, came from a painful understanding that the root of slavery is the custom of one's "regarding himself as a superior being," and that the root is more difficult to abolish than the institution.

The last third of *A Connecticut Yankee* (Chapters 31–44) suffers from authorial fatigue and impatience. The Boss's humiliation of Dowley, the enterprising and hospitable blacksmith, is meanspirited; the plotting in the long episode where the Boss and Arthur are slaves is dime-novel stuff; the brief description of England's transformation under civilization is marred by tasteless jokes; the circumstances of the interdict and its consequences are sketchily drawn; and the Battle of the Sand-Belt is a nightmare. Exhausted by the contest of philosophies and disgusted with determinism's putative victory, the author wanted only to end the novel.

The fullest expression of his determinism appears in Chapter 18, just after Morgan le Fay righteously announces that she is going to pay for the page she has stabbed to death:

Oh, it was no use to waste sense on her. Training—training is everything; training is all there is *to* a person. We speak of nature; it is folly; there is no such thing as nature; what we call by that misleading name is merely heredity and training. We have no thoughts of our own, no opinions of our own: they are transmitted to us, trained into us. All that is original in us, and therefore fairly creditable or discreditable to us, can be covered up and hidden by the point of a cambric needle, all the rest being atoms contributed by, and inherited from, a procession of ancestors that stretches back a billion years to the Adam-clam or grasshopper or monkey from whom our race has been so tediously and ostentatiously and unprofitably developed. (208)

At last! After mulling the idea over for a decade or more, he has said it full out—"Training is everything." It is a major precipitation of attitude.

The statement seems forthright enough; yet, as we read it over, certain troublesome words stick out. What, to begin with, does he mean by *nature* in "there is no such thing as nature"? Does he mean human nature? Probably not. *Nature* here, I judge, means what "the creation" meant to Tom Paine in his last paragraph in "Chapter IX" of *The Age of Reason:*

Do we want to contemplate [God's] power? We see it in the immensity of the creation. Do we want to contemplate his wisdom? We see it in the unchangeable order by which the incomprehensible whole is governed. Do we want to contemplate his munificence? We see it in the abundance with which he fills the earth. Do we want to contemplate his mercy? We see it in his not withholding that abundance even from the unthankful. In fine, do we want to know what God is? Search not the book called Scripture, which any human hand might make, but the scripture called Creation.[8]

8. Harry Hayden Clark (ed.), *Thomas Paine: Representative Selections* (New York, 1944), 258.

Mark Twain was willing, finally, to declare what he had long suspected, that nature was no scripture, no blessed medium through which God spoke his power and wisdom in regulating the universe or his goodness and mercy toward men. In this sense, nature for him had vanished. Instead of nature's being a benevolent system, it was an inane process; instead of its being a gift from above, it was the arena for an evolution controlled by the laws of heredity and environment, an evolution that, after a billion years, resulted in the unprofitable outcome called man.

The "training is everything" statement was written in 1887; and though its deterministic tone is nearly unmitigated (he did insist that there was "one microscopic atom in me that is truly me"), his declaration did not crystallize his thinking in the rest of the novel, as his ambivalence testifies. But by 1891, he would pen his declaration that the Christian and "all other religions" (undoubtedly including his deism) "are lies and swindles."

*Heredity, transmitted,* and *inherited* are the other troublesome words. In the first place, Twain's inserting heredity into the equation creates a paradox. In one sentence, training is everything; but in the next, training is apparently only half of everything, since it shares its place with heredity. The paradox does make sense of a sort: Although Mark Twain was willing enough to give heredity equal billing with environment in their act of determining personality, heredity was to him an afterthought. His interest in heredity was casual; his interest in training was consuming.

As casual as his interest was in heredity, could Mark Twain have entertained the notion that opinions and attitudes are genetically transmitted? We now regard that notion as not only ignorant but mischievous, and we hope that we misunderstand him when he writes that our thought and opinions "are transmitted to us," as well as "trained into us," but a further search in the novel quenches that hope. Perhaps his phrase *inherited ideas* (111) is ambiguous in its context, but we remember that his explanation for Arthur's warped sense of justice was that "his veins were full of ancestral blood that was rotten with this sort of unconscious brutality" (338); and elsewhere in the novel he declared: "Old habit of mind is one of the toughest things to get away from in the world. It transmits itself like physical form and feature" (256).

In defense of Mark Twain's misled thinking in this matter, we may point out that such statements are extremely rare in his work.

I find none before *A Connecticut Yankee* and perhaps one or two borderline cases after. It is true that several times, especially in *What Is Man?*, he mulled over the inheritability of traits and instincts; but they are not the same as attitudes and opinions.

We may point out too that the notion that attitudes and beliefs are transmittable was commonly held and even "scientifically" supported in his time. In the history of ideas, one remembers that the Lamarckian theory of the inheritance of acquired characteristics, intellectual as well as physical, was discredited and replaced by Darwin's theory of natural selection; but in actuality the two theories jostled each other for several decades. Lamarckism, or the theory of "progressive heredity," had its proponents among scientists (Ernst Haeckel, for example) even into the twentieth century. They were joined by prestigious interpreters of science. Herbert Spencer based his theory of human progress on the conviction that "mental characteristics could be inherited as well as physical ones," and Taine saw a nation's character as developing through progressive heredity: "Man, forced to accommodate himself to circumstances, contracts a temperament and character corresponding to them; and his character, like his temperament, is so much more stable, as the external impression is made upon him by more numerous repetitions, and is transmitted to his progeny by a more ancient descent." Oliver Wendell Holmes could have his Dr. Kittredge in *Elsie Venner* seriously declare, "Everybody knows that Catholicism or Protestantism is a good deal a matter of race. Constitution has more to do with belief than people think for."[9]

Considering the popularity and authority of the notion of progressive heredity, it is no wonder that Mark Twain was infected by it. The wonder is that the infection was so trivial. As he continued to think about heredity he became more tentative and ended by reflecting Darwin's uneasiness in the matter of "inherited habit" or instinct. One cannot be sure, Darwin stated, if animals act from reason or from "inherited habit"; moreover, some reasoned acts "become converted into instincts and are inherited," whereas other instincts are products of natural selection. The Old Man in *What Is Man?* similarly defines *instinct* as "inherited habit" and concludes that the

9. Richard Hofstadter, *Social Darwinism in American Thought* (Philadelphia, 1945), 26; Hippolyte Taine, *History of English Literature*, trans. H. Van Laun (New York, 1880), 24; Oliver Wendell Holmes, *Elsie Venner* (Boston, 1892), 317, Vol. V of Holmes, *The Works of Oliver Wendell Holmes*, 13 vols.

term *instinct* "confuses us; for as a rule it applies to habits and impulses which had a far-off origin in thought, and now and then breaks the rule and applies itself to habits which can hardly claim a thought-origin."[10]

Darwin accepted heredity as a fact, but he also understood that "[t]he laws governing inheritance are for the most part unknown"; and he was therefore chary in his speculations on the subject.[11] Similarly with Mark Twain. Indeed, as a novelist, he appears to have made a special effort to prevent his readers from assuming that any specific trait of his characters was genetically inherited. His main characters are presented as having parents whom we know nothing of (Tom Sawyer, Jim, Hank Morgan, Roxy) or as being altogether different from their parents or parent (Tom Canty, Huckleberry Finn, and Roxy's Tom). There is no hint that any character physically resembles a parent. There is nothing in Twain's fiction like Howells' double cameo of the identical profiles of Squire Gaylord and his daughter Marcia in *A Modern Instance,* suggesting that for all her youth, beauty, and femininity, Marcia has inherited some of her father's character. In fact, Twain positively mocks the idea that physical resemblance depends on heredity. Tom Canty, the pauper, and Edward, the prince, come from carefully separated bloodlines yet are identical in appearance. In *Pudd'nhead Wilson,* Chambers, the slave infant, is part Negro; and Tom, the aristocrat's baby, is pure white, yet Tom's father cannot tell them apart. In this matter of heredity, so invaded with supposition and myth, Mark Twain was admirably tentative.

10. Charles Darwin, *The Descent of Man in Relation to Sex* (2 vols.; New York, 1871), I, 45, 36–37; Samuel Clemens [Mark Twain], *What Is Man? and Other Philosophical Writings,* ed. Paul Baender (Berkeley, 1973), 190, Vol. XIX of the Works of Mark Twain.

11. Morse Peckham (ed.), *The Origin of Species by Charles Darwin: A Variorum Text* (Philadelphia, 1959), 86.

CHAPTER 11

# Resolution: *Pudd'nhead Wilson*

> *Training is everything. The peach was once a bitter almond; cauliflower is nothing but cabbage with a college education.*
>
> —Pudd'nhead Wilson's Calendar
>
> *[I]t seems to me by far the most probable view, that the peach is the descendant of the almond, improved and modified in a marvellous manner.*
>
> —Charles Darwin, *The Variation of Animals and Plants Under Domestication*, Chapter 10

MARK TWAIN'S REVULSION OVER the way his jaunty time-travel fantasy had turned into a nightmare is everywhere evident in the "Final P.S. by M.T." at the end of *A Connecticut Yankee*. That "Final P.S." completes the action begun in "A Word of Explanation," which precedes Chapter 1. The prefatory "Word" tells how the author, settled by a cozy fire on a rainy night, begins to read the "Yankee Historian's" tale of his sixth-century adventures. In the "Final P.S.," he finishes reading a few hours later, as day dawns. Gone is the coziness, gone the magic of his being "steeped in a dream of the olden time";[1] what he sees when he raises his eyes from the Yankee's manuscript is a world grown "gray and sad," and what he hears is "the exhausted storm . . . sighing and sobbing itself to rest" (491). Seeking out the Yankee, the author finds him, though healthy a few hours before, delirious and dying. "Such dreams! such strange and awful dreams, Sandy" (492), he raves, remembering the Battle of the Sand-Belt and all that led to it. "It was awful—awfuler than you can ever imagine; . . . death is nothing, let it come, but not with those dreams, not with the torture of those hideous dreams—I cannot endure *that* again" (493). Perhaps partly because of "those hideous dreams," Mark Twain was determined

---

1. Samuel Clemens [Mark Twain], *A Connecticut Yankee in King Arthur's Court*, ed. Bernard L. Stein and Henry Nash Smith (Berkeley, 1979), 48, Vol. IX of the Works of Mark Twain. Further references to *A Connecticut Yankee* are indicated by parenthetical page numbers in the text.

that *A Connecticut Yankee* would be his last book. "It's my swan-song," he wrote Howells in 1889, "my retirement from literature."[2]

As it turned out, he wrote as much as ever in the next four years—*The American Claimant*, for example, *Tom Sawyer Abroad*, *Pudd'nhead Wilson* and *Those Extraordinary Twins*, and a good deal of *Joan of Arc*. He wrote under trying circumstances, one of which—a cash-flow problem—drove him back to his pen. At the beginning of the period he had been confident that his investments in the Paige typesetter and in his publishing house, Webster and Company, would make him rich enough to join "the Vanderbilt gang"; but by 1891, they had made him so poor that he had to close his Hartford house and move with his family to Europe, where they could live more cheaply.[3] Both before and after moving to Europe, he suffered the distraction of business trips to New York, Washington, D.C., Chicago, and other cities; and in late 1890 he traveled twice to Keokuk, Iowa, the first time to visit his dying mother, the second time to attend her funeral. Livy's mother died a month after Sam's; and it was around that time that Jean, the youngest Clemens daughter, developed a "condition" later diagnosed as epilepsy. "I have fed so full on sorrows, these last weeks," Clemens wrote to Howells on November 27, 1890, "that I seem to have become hardened to them—benumbed."[4] Sickness dogged the family. For many months during 1891 and 1892, Clemens' writing arm was crippled with rheumatism; and that winter, in Berlin, he was in bed for three weeks with lung congestion. Livy had heart trouble, which it was hoped European doctors could treat; and Susy, the oldest daughter, was showing signs of neurasthenia.

Once the family was settled in a villa near Florence, in the fall of 1892, Mark Twain had time to fiddle with a ridiculous story about a pair of Siamese twins. Although the fiddling was interrupted by other writing, by a distraught correspondence with the manager of his failing publishing company, and by a business trip back to the States in the spring of 1893, he managed not only to develop his "howling farce" but to witness the birth, under his pen, of a kind of Siamese twin to it. As he explained the joint composition, his tale

2. Henry Nash Smith and William M. Gibson (eds.), *Mark Twain–Howells Letters* (2 vols.; Cambridge, Mass., 1960), II, 610.

3. Albert Bigelow Paine (ed.), *Mark Twain's Letters* (2 vols.; New York, 1917), II, 533–34.

4. Smith and Gibson (eds.), *Mark Twain–Howells Letters*, II, 633.

"changed itself from a farce to a tragedy, while I was going along with it. . . . But what was a great deal worse was, that it was not one story, but two stories tangled together." He completed the tangled stories in February, 1893; but it took him some months to see what was wrong and to perform "a kind of literary Caesarean operation" separating the farce, *Those Extraordinary Twins*, from the tragedy, *Pudd'nhead Wilson*.[5]

Such are the unlikely circumstances surrounding the creation of a masterpiece. Although *Pudd'nhead Wilson* is not likely to supplant *Huckleberry Finn* as Mark Twain's major work, it has an essential quality that the former novel lacks—a final coming to grips with the onerous subject that had preoccupied Twain for nearly two decades.

Circumstances would not seem to account for the extreme differences between *A Connecticut Yankee* and *Pudd'nhead Wilson*, especially in tone and management. While he was writing the former novel Mark Twain traveled little except between Hartford and Elmira, his winter and summer residences. His family life was fairly serene; and though his business affairs were sometimes hectic, his expectations of wealth were sanguine. Yet Mark Twain's vacillations on human nature in *A Connecticut Yankee* and his recourse to megalomaniac and nihilistic fantasies reflect anything but authorial composure. Although *A Connecticut Yankee* has been catalogued as an early example of American science fiction, it is the least scientific of his novels—and the one most disturbed by his impulses to mock and destroy and to create out of nothing. Countering his Tainean intention of being "posted in the details" of the peasants' "everyday life" and his moments of intense sympathy with the sufferings of the oppressed are episodes where the Boss, who has gained ascendance through the "magic of science," exults in his superiority. Standing on his platform (for example) and looking out over the crowd at the restoration of the holy fountain, he muses that "you could have walked upon a pavement of human heads to—well, miles" (267).

Style and imagery in *A Connecticut Yankee* betray the author's unease. Rockets do not simply ascend; instead, "a vast fountain of dazzling lances of fire vomited itself toward the zenith" (269). The

5. Samuel Clemens [Mark Twain], *Pudd'nhead Wilson and Those Extraordinary Twins*, ed. Sidney E. Berger (New York, 1980), 119. Further references to *Pudd'nhead Wilson and Those Extraordinary Twins* are indicated by parenthetical page numbers in the text.

Boss's hidden civilization is ominously enough "as substantial a fact as any serene volcano, standing innocent with its smokeless summit in the blue sky and giving no sign of the rising hell in its bowels" (128). Members of a reunited family do not merely rejoice but indulge themselves in "typhoons and cyclones of frantic joy, and whole Niagaras of happy tears" (214). The dynamiting of two mounted knights results in fifteen minutes of "a steady drizzle of microscopic fragments of knights and hardware and horseflesh" (318). When Dowley, the prosperous blacksmith, is humiliated by the Boss's outlay of wealth, he is "wilted, and shrunk-up, and collapsed; he had the aspect of a bladder-balloon that's been stepped on by a cow" (365). Such overheated language and such violent images betray the panic of an author relying on the proposition that manner is everything.

Turn from the perfervid prose of *A Connecticut Yankee* to the dense and lively language of *Pudd'nhead Wilson,* and it is as if you are reading a different author. In his newfound equanimity, Mark Twain created a kind of throwaway style, which, graceful and wise, tells his story with great efficiency and without obliging you to look for, or even be aware of, the layers of meaning beneath it. Read the first paragraphs describing Dawson's Landing, a river town below St. Louis, where the novel's action takes place. You see neat houses surrounded by flowers, a cat "asleep and blissful" on a window ledge, trees that furnish fragrance in spring and shade in summer, a quaint main street with its "little frame shops" and their creaking signs (3). The description is charming; it welcomes you. You may like this pretty town as much as you please. Never mind the glimpse of wilderness "enclosing the town" (3); never mind the litany of river names connecting Dawson's Landing to half a continent; never mind that Dawson's Landing is "a slave-holding town"; in sum, Dawson's Landing is "sleepy, and comfortable, and contented" (4).

In the next paragraphs, our genteel guide introduces us to the town's finest citizens, descendants of the First Families of Virginia. He speaks so politely of their virtues—courtesy, generosity, pride, and so on—and so respectfully of their sorrows at being childless that it may not occur to us that they are a dying tribe. Of the five households represented by the village aristocrats, three are of married couples. Two of the marriages—Judge York Driscoll's and his sister Rachel's—are sterile. The third marriage—that of the Judge's younger brother Percy—produced children who died in infancy; their "cradles were empty" (5). Mrs. Percy Driscoll finally gives birth to Thomas à Becket Driscoll, who survives; but since she dies a week later, Tom will be the only Driscoll of his generation. Besides the married couples, there are two aristocratic bachelors—Pembroke Howard, a lawyer, and Colonel Cecil Burleigh Essex. A child *is* born to the Colonel—in fact, on the same February first as Percy Driscoll's Tom—or rather it is born to his slave mistress Roxana, for the Colonel, a "formidable" member of the community, has washed his hands of Roxana and their son. Valet de Chambre, as Roxy names him, has no surname—"slaves hadn't the privilege" (9).

Such are the facts concerning the chief citizens of Dawson's Landing—given in the novel with nearly the same economy as I have tried for. But for Mark Twain's deftness of touch and disarming lightness of tone in introducing his proto-Faulknerian theme, the original has to be read.

Mark Twain's authorial self-possession in *Pudd'nhead Wilson* comes from his having lived through his spiritual crisis. The crisis was in part the conflict between his idealism and sentimentalism on the one hand and his determinism on the other. It was also in part his giving up his dream of immense wealth.

For more than a decade, his talismanic image had been that of Sir Wissenschaft, the knight who had killed the medieval dragon with science and had become rich by monopolizing the spectacles industry. The image had led him not only to strike out into new literary territory but to attempt to make a fortune in those industries having to do with reading and writing (that is, with spectacles)—the Kaolotype process for printing illustrations, the Paige typesetting machine, and his publishing house. He had fully expected to become a monopolist in two of the enterprises. The Kaolotype, he wrote to his brother Orion in 1880, "will utterly annihilate & sweep out of existence one of the minor industries of civilization, & take its place."[6] Ten years later, it was the typesetter that would swamp the market: "I claim yet, as I have always claimed, that the machine's market (abroad and here together,) is today worth $150,000,000, without saying anything about the doubling and trebling of this sum that will follow within the life of the patent."[7] Something of this monopolist supremacy surely invades *A Connecticut Yankee*, where the Boss is "a Unique" with colossal power (109).

6. Samuel C. Webster (ed.), *Mark Twain, Business Man* (Boston, 1946), 142.
7. Paine (ed.), *Mark Twain's Letters*, II, 533–34.

By the time he wrote *Pudd'nhead Wilson*, his dream of wealth had faded; he was, indeed, only a year or so from formal bankruptcy. His having lived in a succession of faintly seedy places and his having been "benumbed" by his sorrows dried up his fantasies of lordly separateness. He had come down to earth. His idealism and sentimentalism, which in their death throes had given him such a tussle in *A Connecticut Yankee*, were laid to rest. Taking their place was a healing determinism—healing because since things worked according to laws of their own and were therefore beyond his power to change them, he no longer had to play the role of the indignant moralist. No longer as a creator himself (and therefore with a professional interest in the Masterwork) did he feel obliged to change the creation or even to criticize it. He realized, perhaps, that what is plastic to the writer's touch is not the set past or the congealing present but the minds of future readers.

His revolution in *A Connecticut Yankee* had failed, and he saw the reason: He had depended too much on magic, not enough on science. He was in a real sense born again, but out of a religion rather than into one.

His new talismanic image was of David Wilson, a modest, patient man, quite different from either Sir Wissenschaft or his personification as Hank Morgan, the Connecticut Yankee. There are, it is true, similarities of circumstance between the careers of Hank and Pudd'nhead, as David came to be called; but they serve to emphasize the men's basic differences. Both men were transported to cultures less modern and less democratic than the ones they were raised in. Both found themselves out of place because of their sophistication. Here the similarities end.

David Wilson, of upstate New York, college educated and with a law degree, settled in Dawson's Landing, that contented and caste-ridden town, where he was immediately misunderstood. Intelligent and friendly, he had an ironic manner that was not appreciated by the community. On his first day in town, he made an absurd joke; and the citizens, judging from his straight face that he did not recognize his own absurdity, labeled him "Pudd'nhead." He might have been able to live his reputation down—for he became a useful member of the community—except that his principal friend, Judge Driscoll, showed people some of the ironical maxims that Pudd'nhead privately composed—statements such as "Nothing so needs reforming as other people's habits" (73) and "Few things are harder to put up with than the annoyance of a good example" (92). Since "irony was not for those people," they "read those playful trifles in the solidest earnest" and continued to regard him as a pudd'nhead. In summing up the effect of the Judge's intrusive action, Mark Twain composed a maxim worthy of heading a chapter: "That is just the way, in this world; an enemy can partly ruin a man, but it takes a good-natured injudicious friend to complete the thing and make it perfect" (25).

Unlike Hank Morgan, Wilson made no effort to change his comfortless environment. Unable to find clients for his law practice, he resigned himself for twenty-three years to being given work now and then as a surveyor or accountant. His enforced leisure, however, allowed him to become something that neither Sir Wissenschaft nor Hank Morgan ever became—a pure scientist. Neither for show nor for power, and with no interest in technological application, David Wilson "interested himself in every new thing that was born into the universe of ideas, and studied it and experimented upon it at his house" (7).

In the one activity that is detailed in the novel—his collection of fingerprints—we can see how carefully and indefatigably he worked. It was his pleasure to ask townspeople of all ages to put their fingerprints on three-by-five-inch glass plates, the five fingers of the right hand on one plate and those of the left hand on another. Pasted across the bottom of each plate was a strip of paper on which he wrote the name of the person, which hand, the day, month, and year—a task that he did not do "the next day or even the next hour, but in the very minute the impression was taken" (109). He took pride in never labeling a plate carelessly. It was his practice, moreover, to take a "series" of prints from each person—"two or three 'takings' at intervals during the period of childhood, these to be followed by others at intervals of several years" (9). He had wooden boxes made to carry and store his glass plates. He spent countless hours studying his prints; and the better to examine them, he often "made fine and accurate reproductions" of them and "then enlarged them on a scale of ten to one with his pantograph," thereafter making "each individual line of the bewildering maze of whorls or curves or loops . . . stand out bold and black by reinforcing it with ink" (105). In the twenty-three years that he pursued his study, he had taken the fingerprints of nearly every person in town, black and white. The two conclusions of his study were that each fingerprint is unique and that it does not change from birth to death. The fingerprint is a person's "natal signature" (108–109).

David Wilson's conclusions are precisely those of Sir Francis Galton, as published in his pioneering work, *Finger Prints*, in 1892; indeed, Anne P. Wigger has shown that Mark Twain depended on Galton's study for its exposition of fingerprinting methods as well as for its conclusions.[8] I believe he depended on it also to bolster his postdeistic philosophy. Certainly, Galton's book radically influenced his creative process. He obtained his copy of it on or shortly before November 10, 1892, while he was working on his twins story; and looking back, he remarked that "that accident changed the whole plot & plan of my book,"[9] inspiring him, it seems, to introduce "a stranger named Pudd'nhead Wilson, and a woman named Roxana" (120) and to begin building a tragedy on top of his farce.

Sir Francis Galton (1822–1911), like his cousin Charles Darwin, was one of those Victorians who, equipped with private incomes and scientific zeal, spent a lifetime studying nature's workings. He did research in meteorology, differential psychology, anthropometry, and genetics. (As geneticist he invented the word *eugenics*.) He was a tireless correspondent with fellow scientists; published something like two hundred items, fifteen of them books; and was honored with a dozen awards and degrees. In the Darwinian controversy, he was on his cousin's side; indeed, Darwin strengthened some of his own arguments in *The Descent of Man* with Galton's data. For his part, Galton remembered that the publication of the *Origin of Species* "made a marked epoch in my own mental development, as it did in that of human thought in general." Religious before, he found "the constraint of my old superstition [driven away] as if it had been a nightmare" upon reading the *Origin*.[10]

Galton began his study of fingerprints in 1888, not aiming to develop a tool for criminology but with the thought "that fingerprints might prove to be of high anthropological significance." He "examined large numbers of persons of different races to our own,

---

8. Anne P. Wigger, "The Source of Fingerprint Material in Mark Twain's *Pudd'nhead Wilson* and *Those Extraordinary Twins*," *American Literature*, XXVIII (1957), 517–21.

9. Paine (ed.), *Mark Twain's Letters*, I, 251.

10. D.W. Forrest, *Francis Galton: The Life and Work of a Victorian Genius* (New York, 1974), 84.

as Jews, Basques, Red Indians, East Indians of various origins, Negroes, and a fair number of Chinese," without discovering any correlation between race and fingerprints.[11] He fingerprinted people of various degrees of achievement and intelligence, again finding no characteristic differences: "I have prints of eminent thinkers and of eminent statesmen that can be matched by those of congenital idiots. No indications of temperament, character, or ability are to be found in finger marks, so far as I have been able to discover."[12]

As observed by Galton, the fingerprint is the ultimate in discrete identity, standing as it does for nothing but itself and its owner. As such, it marks an end point in the Darwinian revolution, which turned scientific attention from principles to processes, from classification to variation.

Eighteenth-century scientists and other thinkers were concerned with discovering what was essential and permanent in nature. In the inorganic realm, they were pleased to find it in the laws of nature, and in the organic realm, in species. A species to them was a divine abstraction, an Idea brought to earth at the creation (not many thousands of years before) and incarnated in individual forms of life. These forms might vary with one another but always within the bounds of species. As such, a species was fixed and permanent.

The belief in "fixity of species" persisted, and for readers in 1859 the mere title *Origin of Species* was likely to be a puzzle: What was the problem? God originated species. When they understood Darwin's vision—of infinite variation in the forms of life, of nature's "selecting" among the forms by destroying those less well adapted before they propagated, of the process's imposing, over millions of years, continual change in the forms of life *and in species themselves*—Darwin's title became for many readers a scandal.

Probably the most disturbing thing about Darwinism was not its biological information—that man was the product of an evolution that began eons ago in single-celled life—but its implication that the creation was not infused with or even molded by divinity and that things in this world therefore stood for themselves and not for something beyond nature. Things could, of course, be grouped and correlated for scientific and practical purposes. Analogies, though they "prove nothing," as Freud said, were useful in making "one

11. Francis Galton, *Memories of My Life* (London, 1908), 252.
12. Francis Galton, *Finger Prints* (1892; New York, 1965), 197.

feel more at home."[13] But all that is quite different from using things as evidence of Design and Designer; and it continued the process of taking the holiness out of certain human institutions and beliefs, especially those that emphasized caste and rank. When Galton found that the fingerprint, though identifying the individual, could not be correlated with any other anthropological data, he not only displayed an ultimate lesson in philosophical descendentalism but broadened the basis for questioning the validity of certain racial and social classifications as well.

If the Darwinian revolution robbed certain abstractions of their authority, it had the healthy effect, in Philip Appleman's words, of forcing people, "in art as in life, to mature to finiteness."[14] There is evidence that between writing *A Connecticut Yankee* and writing *Pudd'nhead Wilson*, Mark Twain matured to finiteness, and that behind the change was a new Darwinian vision of life.

*A Connecticut Yankee* is laden with theory. Besides Mark Twain's contesting theories of human nature, there are his theories of what the primitive mentality was like and what "Arthurian" society and politics were like. As a result, much of the novel is didactic or illustrative. Situations are contrived, characters are invented, dialogue is composed for the purpose of teaching theory. As a further result, the only developed character in the book is Hank Morgan, and he is a mess. *A Connecticut Yankee* is unrealistic not simply because it is a fantasy but because of its a priori assumptions. *Pudd'nhead Wilson*, in contrast, is full of down-to-earth details, strongly realized people, and dialogue that rings with the authenticity of time, place, and character. Its meanings are to be induced from the facts displayed in the novel.

*Pudd'nhead Wilson* is so thoroughly Darwinian that one is tempted to suggest that Mark Twain secretly saluted Darwin when he chose twenty-three as the number of years that David Wilson toiled in obscurity (that is, from 1830 to 1853) before his scientific study of fingerprints afforded him a "revelation" (104) that made him locally famous. Twenty-three is also the number of years that Darwin toiled in relative obscurity, from the time he debarked from the *Beagle* with his planetary data and specimens until those and other data were

13. Sigmund Freud, *New Introductory Lectures on Psychoanalysis*, trans. W. J. H. Sprott (New York, 1933), 103.

14. Philip Appleman, "Darwin: On Changing the Mind," in Appleman (ed.), *Darwin: A Norton Critical Edition* (New York, 1979), 550.

coalesced into his theory of natural selection and published in the *Origin of Species* (that is, from 1836 to 1859). No doubt the identical lengths of those gestational periods is a lucky accident, as probably is this further coincidence: Twenty-three years elapsed between the time Mark Twain first responded to Dr. Holmes's analytical philosophy in the *Autocrat* and the time Galton's book inspired him to introduce Pudd'nhead and Roxy into his Siamese twins story (that is, from 1869 to 1892).[15]

Coincidence or not, did Mark Twain know and respect Darwin well enough for us to infer an interest and influence beyond the ordinary? A reading of *The American Claimant's* Chapter 11 suggests that he did.

A main virtue of *The American Claimant* (1892) is that it further explores the problem of caste, this time in the form of a dramatic experiment. Young Lord Berkeley, possessed with the radical notion that hereditary lordships are a usurpation, migrates to America, where, divested of his rank and wealth, he intends to live as an equal in the land of equality. His adjustment is not easy, and helpful in explaining to him the difference between American and English society are Hattie, his landlady's daughter, and Barrow, a fellow boarder: In America "[e]verybody calls himself a lady or gentleman, and thinks he *is*," whereas in England a small minority are so designated and the rest of the population "accept that decree and swallow the affront which it puts upon them." Caste's "being bred" into the average Englishman condemns him to an artificial status of inferiority. In searching for an analogy that, by way of contrast, would show the value of a worthy individual when merit instead of rank is recognized, Barrow says:

"You couldn't conceive of the Matterhorn being flattered by the notice of one of your comely little English hills, could you?"

"Why, no."

"Well, then, let a man in his right mind try to conceive of Darwin being flattered by the notice of a princess. It's so grotesque that it—well, it paralyzes the imagination."[16]

15. That first response was apparently his writing "True, Livy" in the margin of the *Autocrat* where Holmes had written "education always begins through the senses, and works up to the absolute idea of right and wrong." Bradford A. Booth, "Mark Twain's Comments on Holmes's *Autocrat*," *American Literature*, XXI (1950), 459.

16. Samuel Clemens [Mark Twain], *The American Claimant and Other Stories and Sketches*, Author's National Edition: The Writings of Mark Twain (25 vols.; New York, 1907–18), 91–94.

Nearly a decade after Darwin's death, and with a world of nature's noblemen to choose from, Mark Twain appointed Darwin to stand as the Matterhorn of personal achievement.

On the basis of that salute, it may not be farfetched to infer parallels among Darwin, Wilson, and Mark Twain—each working for a long time in a lonely way toward revelation. For Mark Twain, the revelation was seeing plainly the causes and consequences of caste and slavery. So seeing, and relieved of his guilt, he could write plainly. Like David Wilson, he had been ironic most of his life; now he was free to write a story whose ironies, if it held any, would be those of matter, not manner.

*Pudd'nhead Wilson* is patently Darwinian in the way it presents certain of its characters as formed by the interaction between their native selves and their environment, and less obviously so in the way Roxana makes up her mind. Darwin saw the decision-making process as a transaction between past experience and current impulse: "[T]here would often be a struggle which impulse should be followed; and satisfaction or dissatisfaction would be felt, as past impressions were compared during their incessant passage through the mind."[17] The process is dynamic in that both experience and impulse would change with time, and it is uniquely personal in that no one's experience is identical with another's. To be Darwinian—one might say to be realistic—a writer would need to show a character as acting and reacting authentically within the unique web of his or her experience. The character should not be contrived for the purpose of standing for something.

I am by no means saying that the more "Darwinian" a work of fiction is, the better it is; nor am I ignoring the fact that some of Mark Twain's work before *Pudd'nhead Wilson* could be called Darwinian. The process of Huckleberry's making up his mind to go to hell for Jim—in which his resolve to turn Jim in founders under the flood of his memories of Jim's kindnesses—is a textbook illustration of Darwin's discussion of decision making. Nevertheless, Huck and Jim and Tom can be seen as standing for classes of people, and their characterizations tend to change with their author's changing attitudes toward his subject. They are not "realistic" entities allowed to live their own lives.

17. Charles Darwin, *The Descent of Man in Relation to Sex* (2 vols.; New York, 1871), I, 70.

Roxana is developed not only authentically but with an extraordinary combination of objectivity and understanding. As a slave woman she could not have been drawn from her author's life experience in the way Tom and Huck were. Nevertheless, Mark Twain dared not only to bring her to life but to make us intimate with her thought and feelings. His audacity and sympathy should not be obscured by the efficiency of his characterization.

Mark Twain's maturing to finiteness was at least partly a self-conscious process. It gave rise to a statement of novelistic theory that distilled what he had learned from the science of piloting, from Taine and Howells, from Darwin and Galton, from the weaknesses in those novels of his written about times and places he had not lived in and the strengths of those written about times and places he had lived in. It is a theory that covers creative method, the author's responsibility to reality, and the nature of that reality. Written some months after the publication of *Pudd'nhead Wilson*, it is expressed in "What Paul Bourget Thinks of Us" (1895).

Bourget, a French novelist and critic, had written *Outre-Mer*, an assessment of American life as seen by a foreign visitor; and Mark Twain was skeptical of the validity of that assessment. Bourget's method was all right as far as it went: "[H]e was an Observer, and had a System—that used by naturalists and other scientists." He observed Americans and was presently able to classify them and to label the groups. But naming—as the cub pilot had learned—is not the same thing as understanding: "The Observer of Peoples has to be a Classifier, A Grouper, a Deducer, a Generalizer, a Psychologizer; and, first and last, a Thinker. He has to be all these, and when he is at home, observing his own folk, he is often able to prove competency. But history has shown that when he is abroad observing unfamiliar peoples the chances are heavily against him. He is then a naturalist observing a bug, with no more than a naturalist's chance of being able to tell the bug anything new about itself." All that a foreigner can do, really, is "photograph the exteriors of a nation." He cannot "report its interior—its soul, its life, its speech, its thought."

Only the native novelist can know the soul of a people, and he learns it through "years and years of unconscious absorption; years and years of intercourse with the life concerned; of living it, indeed; sharing personally in its shames and prides; its joys and griefs, its loves and hates, its prosperities and reverses, its shows and shabbinesses." The native novelist does not, however, try to generalize the nation. "No, he lays plainly before you the ways and speech and life of a few people grouped in a certain place—his own place—and that is one book." Only "when a thousand able novels have been written [will] you have the soul of the people, the speech of the people. . . . And the shadings of character, manners, feelings, ambitions, will be infinite."[18]

"Soul of the people," a clear echo from Taine, means a total impression of life rather than essence. The vision of life here has nothing to do with ideals. The most thorough understanding of human affairs will reveal not a mystic unity but paradoxes and infinite variety. In the absence of that unity, it is the role of the novelist to participate and sympathize, to observe, absorb, and understand, and then to lay "plainly before you" his vision of the reality of the lives of a few people. As a statement of literary realism, it is thoughtful, modest, and penetrating; and more clean-cut than what most of his colleagues could manage.

One of Mark Twain's musings in later life concerned the way a person's native abilities could flower in a favorable environment or be stifled in an unfavorable one. Thomas Edison's "surroundings and atmosphere . . . [had] the largest share in discovering him to himself and to the world," and Mary Baker Eddy came into prominence only late in life because "[t]he qualities that were born in her had to wait for circumstances and opportunity." In heaven, Captain Stormfield discovered, there were geniuses who had been nobodies on earth because there they had had no opportunity to exercise their talents. Earth's greatest potential poet was a tailor from Tennessee, and her finest military mind was a bricklayer "from somewhere back of Boston."[19]

Roxana is Mark Twain's prime example of a superbly endowed individual crippled by her environment. Tall, beautiful, and vital, she is one of nature's royalty—a fact her author keeps reminding us of: "She was of majestic form and stature, her attitudes were imposing and statuesque, and her gestures and movements distinguished

18. Samuel Clemens [Mark Twain], *Literary Essays*, Author's National Edition: The Writings of Mark Twain (25 vols.; New York, 1907–18), XXII, 143–47.

19. Samuel Clemens [Mark Twain], "St. Joan of Arc," *The $30,000 Bequest and Other Stories*, Author's National Edition: The Writings of Mark Twain (25 vols.; New York, 1907–18), XXIV, 153; Clemens, *Christian Science*, Author's National Edition: The Writings of Mark Twain, XXV, 263; Clemens, "Extract from Captain Stormfield's Visit to Heaven," *The Mysterious Stranger and Other Stories* (New York, 1922), 263, 273–74.

by a noble and stately grace" (8). Such was her appearance at twenty, and even in middle age she can be "queenly" (43) and can assume "all the majesty and grace of her vanished youth" (38).

Queenly though her nature, she will rise to no high place; nor will she be allowed to develop a unitary sense of self. As "white as anybody" (8), she is nevertheless a slave. As a slave, she dwells in a community that denies her what its free members take for granted—a sense of belonging, of having a place among the generations with their cycle of parents, schooling, courtship, marriage, family. Since Roxy is one-sixteenth Negro, it is possible that each member of her maternal line, back to her great-great-grandmother, was the mistress of a white man. At any rate, Roxy never speaks of her parent or parents. Denied schooling, she cannot read or write. Her only family is her bastard son, and her only home is what her master provides. When her master dies and she is set free, she has "no home now" (22). There is little that she can be proud of or call her own. Her sense of identity is famished. With little knowledge of her ancestry, she invents or receives a legendary lineage that includes Pocahontas and Captain John Smith. She has no real roots in her African origins (she does not even have Jim's repertory of superstitions, though not many of those are African), and her church— Methodist, led by a minister no doubt unlettered himself—is an English import.

Lack of roots and room is one thing; at least as limiting is the servile attitude required of the slave. It overlies and muffles Roxy's queenliness. As a twenty-year-old, she has an easy, independent way among other slaves but she is "meek and humble enough where white people were" (8). In middle age she approaches her grown son (who knows himself as Tom Driscoll) "with all the wheedling and supplicating servilities that fear and interest can impart to the words and attitudes of the born slave" (37). In authority the master is absolute; in acquiescence the slave must be perfect. When Roxy's master threatens his four slaves with being sold down the river unless the thieving ones confess, and when after their confession he deigns to sell the three guilty ones locally instead, "[t]he culprits flung themselves prone, in an ecstasy of gratitude, and kissed his feet, declaring that they would never forget his goodness and never cease to pray for him as long as they lived. They were sincere, for like a god he had stretched forth his mighty hand and closed the gates of hell against them" (12). Roxy, the only guiltless one of the four, learns a terrible lesson from the episode: Her infant son "could grow up and be sold down the river!" Crazed with horror, she spends a sleepless night, during which countless thoughts and plans race through her head. Looking at her master's son, born the same day as hers and lying in his cradle nearby, she bursts out with: "Dey can't sell *you* down de river. I hates yo' pappy; he hain't got no heart—for niggers he haint, anyways. I hates him, en I could kill him!" (13). Her next impulse is to kill her own son in order to "save" him and to kill herself as well. Dressing him in Tom Driscoll's long white baby gown so that he will be fit to meet the angels, she is struck with how much he looks like the heir of the house—"Now who would b'lieve clo'es could do de like o' dat?" (14)—and decides to switch the two infants.

Once the switch is made, Roxy realizes that she has condemned her master's son to a life of slavery. Full of remorse, she flings herself on her bed "to think and toss, toss and think." Suddenly, "a comforting thought . . . [flows] through her worried mind—'Tain't no sin—*white* folks has done it!' " (15).

Her comforting thought is based on a vague memory that she has trouble recalling. When she brings it to light, it turns out *not* to support her statement that "*white* folks has done it"; but she blithely ignores that fact, even repeating the statement at the end of her musings, and arises from her bed "light-hearted and happy" (15).

Her memory is of a sermon by a visiting Negro preacher. A Calvinist, the preacher explained God's method of electing his saints. Her switching the babies would emulate that method: "He s'lect out anybody dat suit Him, en put another one in his place, en make de fust one happy forever en leave t'other one to burn wid Satan." Following the explanation, the preacher, as Roxy recalls, recited a parable illustrating God's method: Long ago, in England, the queen left her baby "layin' aroun' one day," and "one o' de niggers roun' 'bout de place dat was mos' white" (15) switched her baby with the queen's. The switch went undetected. The servant's child grew up to be king and eventually sold the queen's son down the river.

Mark Twain's depiction of Roxy's night of anguish and decision is a remarkable literary feat. Not only does he honor Darwin's analysis in detailing Roxy's conflicting impulses and the "incessant passage" of impressions through her mind, but he chooses such details as dramatize her suffering, her impossible situation, and her strength of mind. In spite of a problem that is nearly hopeless, she solves it by switching the babies; in spite of a moral question that is virtually unanswerable, she overrides it with a powerful (but baseless) rationalization ("*white* folks has done it") and with an obvious projection of her own act into "the dim particulars of some tale she had heard some time or other" about the queen's baby. She is not easily thwarted—"her nature needed something or somebody to rule over" (46)—and she is ready to employ audacious logistics and strenuous psychological gymnastics to win her way.

And not only does Mark Twain suggest a parallel between the Calvinist doctrine of election and damnation and the imposition of slavery, but in having Roxy play God—in having her imitate "de Lord," who can save "anybody He please,"—he has her commit a conspicuously prideful act. With that act, she joins the sisterhood of tragic figures, and her career will conform to the Aristotelian pattern of tragedy through the moment of Lawyer Wilson's revelation ("For a purpose unknown to us, but probably a selfish one, somebody changed those children in the cradle") and her own recognition ("De Lord have mercy on me, po' misable sinner dat I is!") (112, 113).

The Calvinist analogy is apt. Dawson's Landing is made up of the damned and the elect. About half the population are, for no good reason, condemned to be slaves; and the other half are exalted over them. Playing God is old stuff to the masters, and they apparently get by with it; but Roxy's exalting her son leads her into troubles she does not foresee. Her first task is to learn how to replace the mother-son relationship with that of slave-master. Mark Twain anatomizes the process in a brilliant paragraph that highlights the power of the *idea* of slavery on the enslaved:

With all her splendid common sense and practical every-day ability, Roxy was a doting fool of a mother. She was this toward her child—and she was also more than this: by the fiction created by herself, he was become her master; the necessity of recognizing this relation outwardly and of perfecting herself in the forms required to express the recognition, had moved her to such diligence and faithfulness in practicing these forms that this exercise soon concreted itself into habit; it became automatic and unconscious; then a natural result followed: deceptions intended solely for others gradually grew practically into self-deceptions as well; the mock reverence became real reverence, the mock obsequiousness real obsequiousness, the mock homage real homage, the little counterfeit rift of separation between imitation-slave and imitation-master widened and widened, and became an abyss, and a very real one—and on one side of it stood Roxy, the dupe of her own deceptions, and on the other stood her child, no longer a usurper to her, but her accepted and recognized master. (19)

By the time of Tom's adolescence (I will call Roxy's son by his stolen name), the "abyss of separation" is complete. Roxy is merely Tom's "chattel, now, his convenience, his dog, his cringing and helpless slave." Now and then, when Tom happens to be kind to her, Roxy can feel proud that her "nigger son" is "lording it among the whites"; but more often she boils with "impotent rage" under his beatings and insults and nurses a "vengeance-hungry heart" against his downfall (21–22).

What did she expect in Dawson's Landing? It is a two-caste town. Everyone growing up and living there is trained to think and behave as either a master or a slave. Roxy's self-imposed training in becoming a slave to her son and in making her son feel like a master is, though conscious at first, an epitome of the unconscious training the town's inhabitants are always undergoing. So rigorous is that training and so contrary the roles that anyone forced to shift from one to the other at maturity would suffer a profound psychic upheaval. When Tom discovers as a young man that he is a "nigger," Mark Twain, searching for an analogy to convey the extremity of his shock, finds it in one of the most violent geologic cataclysms of modern times: Tom's "moral landscape" is changed as drastically as was the geography of Krakatoa after the volcanic explosion (44). When Chambers (the true heir) at age twenty-three finds that he is rich and free, he is, in his illiteracy and with his slave ways, terrified at the prospect of living in "the white man's parlor" (114).

Roxy is a special case. She is fitted by nature to rule, though she is forced instead to be ruled. She has been the mistress of an aristocrat and is the mother of his child; and she is given her freedom when she is thirty-five. She consequently has a feeling for both roles; and within the limits imposed on her, she plays both of them. The limits are narrow. She is not, on gaining her freedom, faced, for example, with Chambers' problem of moving into the white world. Instead, she becomes for eight years a chambermaid on a riverboat, a life she mightily enjoys. Then, forced to retire because of rheumatism and impoverished because her savings are lost in a bank failure, she finds that she will have to play the most abject of roles. She has no alternative but to return to Dawson's Landing, where she will "roost" in an abandoned house and hope to live off the charity of the slaves she used to know, who will steal food from kitchens for her. As for Tom, "[s]he would go and fawn upon him, slave-like—for this would have to be her attitude, of course" (34).

Tom's insolence in their first interview sparks an amazing trans-

formation in Roxy and leads to one of the most electric confronta-
tions in literature. Roxy has just asked her wastrel son for a dollar; he
has refused it and any future help as well. "Now go away and don't
bother me any more," is his command. "Roxy's head was down, in
an attitude of humility. But now the fires of her old wrongs flamed
up in her breast and began to burn fiercely. She raised her head
slowly, till it was well up, and at the same time her great frame
unconsciously assumed an erect and masterful attitude" (38). From
this moment on, she dominates Tom, who is soon on his knees
begging to know the secret knowledge she has, which she claims
would ruin him:

The heir of two centuries of unatoned insult and outrage looked down on
him and seemed to drink in deep draughts of satisfaction. Then she said—
  "Fine nice young white gen'lman kneelin' down to a nigger wench! I's
wanted to see dat jes' once befo' I's called. Now Gabrel, blow de hawn, I's
ready.   .   .   .   .   .Git up!" (39)

She eventually tells him the secret of his birth; and although Tom
feels the "nigger" rise in him with the knowledge of his origin and
for a while shrinks from contact with his former friends, and although Roxy is now in charge, it is not quite accurate to say that their
roles are reversed. For one thing, their relationship is complex and
ambivalent. She is his bitter antagonist and also his accomplice
against their white lords. She can pity him when he is in debt and
sacrifice herself for him; she can also show him a knife and threaten
to stab him with it. For another thing, her secret is now their secret.
Within their relationship, she can act the proud mother of a white
aristocrat; and in doing so, she gives Tom better training than he has
gotten from either his "father" or his "uncle."

Mark Twain is careful to show how Tom's weak and selfish character
could be the result of training. From the time Tom usurped his
master's cradle, at the age of seven months, "[h]e was indulged in
all his caprices, howsoever troublesome and exasperating they
might be. . . . Tom got all the petting, Chambers got none. Tom got
all the delicacies, Chambers got mush and milk, and clabber without
sugar" (18). As boys, Chambers did Tom's fighting for him. He
pulled Tom's sled uphill, strapped ice skates on Tom's feet, and stole
fruit for Tom, getting as his share pits, cores, and rinds. There is no
record of Percy Driscoll's guiding or disciplining Tom, although he

did give Chambers three severe whippings for resisting Tom's tyrannies, after which Chambers "took Tom's cruelties in all humility"
(19). Percy Driscoll was preoccupied with land speculations and
apparently had little time or inclination to train his motherless son.
Percy died when Tom was in his sixteenth year. Tom was then
adopted by Judge Driscoll and his sister, who "petted and indulged
and spoiled" him until he was nineteen. As a young gentleman he
was then sent to Yale, where he learned to drink, gamble, and dress
fashionably; as for the academic struggle, he gave that up after two
years and returned home (23).

Tom's being so badly brought up should explain why, as a
young man, he was meanspirited and dissolute. With his slack
rearing, it does not surprise us that he turned to burglary to cover
his gambling debts or that, caught by his uncle in the act of stealing
his uncle's money, he stabbed him to death. Is training everything
in Tom's case? Roxy herself points to the other factor, to heredity:
Tom's refusal to fight a duel comes from the "nigger" in him. Full of
contempt at Tom's cowardice, Roxy rails at him, "Thirty-one parts
o'you is white, en on'y one part nigger, en dat po' little one part is
yo' *soul*" (70).

Her accusation is disturbing enough to require nearly every one
of the dozens of critics of *Pudd'nhead Wilson* to pay attention to it.
Most of them refuse to treat Roxy's accusation as Mark Twain's or to
be led into a serious discussion of Tom's heredity. One critic, however, finds that Mark Twain's "examination of whether heredity or
environment is responsible for character" is muddled by Roxy's
declaration. "Is Roxy mistaken, or is Twain setting forth a genetic
doctrine of racial inferiority? . . . On one hand, training is responsible for the character of Tom and Chambers; on the other hand, Tom
is a coward because he is part black."[20]

Without in the least agreeing with that critic, I would like to go
beyond where other critics have generally gone by asking if Mark
Twain does not, after all, attribute a part of Tom's character to heredity. Mark Twain's "Training is everything" rings so loudly in our ears
that, like the Young Man in *What Is Man?*, we may think that training
*is* everything. "You remember," the Old Man says, "you said that I
said training was *everything*. I corrected you, and said 'training and

---

20. Philip Cohen, "Aesthetic Anomalies in *Pudd'nhead Wilson*," *Studies in American Fiction*, X (1982), 67.

*another* thing.' That other thing is *temperament*—that is, the disposition you were born with."[21]

*Pudd'nhead Wilson* is an affirmation and a definitive exploration of Mark Twain's intuitive theory not only that each human being is genetically unique but that he or she does not discernibly inherit parental characteristics or share such characteristics with siblings. I doubt that the basis for the theory was scientific.[22] It may have come from observation, from an emotional complex having to do with parents and siblings, or from the dramatic possibilities in contrast. At any rate (as I have pointed out), his major characters are either without next of kin or quite unlike them.

The creative entrée to *Pudd'nhead Wilson*—*Those Extraordinary Twins*—provides the ultimate illustration of his theory. As Siamese twins, Luigi and Angelo Cappello were forced to share the same environment. If there were differences of character, they must have been genetic. And differences there were, even though the twins issued at once from the same womb. Dark-skinned Luigi was mischievous as a boy; blond Angelo was "good as gold." Luigi was rude and overbearing, Angelo sweet and considerate. Luigi was a smoker, drinker, and freethinker; Angelo was an abstemious Baptist. Consequently, there were implacable tensions between them, symbolized in their simultaneously singing (a cappella, as it were) discordant songs at the top of their voices, thus creating a "crazy uproar" (129). (Such symbolism was perhaps metamorphosed into a concept of Dawson's Landing as a Siamese twin of a town, whose two populations, profoundly at odds with each other, were shackled together by the laws of slavery.) In the Cappellos' reappearance in *Pudd'nhead Wilson*, they are normal twins, in looks almost exact duplicates; and although not as much is made of their differences in character, they do persist.

Just as the twins are in many ways opposite, Tom is hereditarily opposite from his mother. Where she is physically large and strong, he is small and weak; where she has a vigorous mind and personality, he is poorly endowed. It is evident in Tom's and Chamber's early boyhood that Chambers evinced over Tom "superiorities of

21. Samuel Clemens [Mark Twain], *What Is Man? and Other Philosophical Writings*, ed. Paul Baender (Berkeley, 1973), 168, Vol. XIX of the Works of Mark Twain.

22. Mark Twain would, however, find some corroboration for his theory in Galton, who observed that although in their "signs of heredity" twins are often similar, "[m]ore rarely, they are remarkably dissimilar." Galton, *Finger Prints*, 185.

physique and pluck, and . . . manifold clevernesses." Tom was not, like Chambers, good at games of skill; nor was he athletic. He shrank from fighting and gave up diving, for it gave him splitting headaches. If heredity has anything to do with ability to socialize, Tom was again skimped; he was thoroughly disliked by his play-mates, who called him "coward, liar, sneak, and other sorts of pet names." At any rate, Mark Twain wants us to know that Tom's mean streak (he once stabbed Chambers nearly to death with his pocketknife) owed something to heredity: Tom was cruel to Cham-bers "partly out of native viciousness" and to Roxy because of his "vicious nature" (19–21).

As a young man, Tom is remarkably ineffectual. His dropping out of college, his finding no useful employment back in Dawson's Landing, his continuing inability to socialize (with his sly insults and veiled jealousies, he is an agent of discord) may, of course, be attributed to his pampered upbringing; but they also indicate a lack of such native resources as could resist the effects of such upbring-ing. Certainly, nature was not generous to him in the matter of physical size and virility. He is not so tall or large as his mother. Disguised in a suit of Roxy's clothing, made to fit someone who marches as "erect as a grenadier" (40), Tom manages to look like "a stoop-shouldered old woman" (65). In another disguise, a smart pink and white summer frock, he makes a perfect girl. David Wilson sees Tom, through Tom's window, practicing his role. "The distance was not great, and Wilson was able to see the girl very well" (32). Tom's movements are so graceful that Wilson never doubts he has seen a young woman in Tom's room. The Cappello twins remark the undisguised Tom's effeminateness: He is "smooth and undulatory in his movements—graceful, in fact" (48). Roxy, in contrast, has a presence that could be called virile. Disguised as a man, she sur-prises Tom and frightens him badly until "he" (Roxy) says "in a low voice—'Keep still—I's yo' mother!' " (84–85).

In the matter of inherited characteristics, it pleased Mark Twain to make Roxy a masterful woman and her son a spineless man. The result is symmetrically to round out his heredity-environment ex-ploration: The twins (in both stories) are born with different disposi-tions but grow up in similar circumstances. Roxy and Tom are not only genetically opposite but are brought up in classically opposite environments. The result in the case of Roxy and Tom is to cripple them both. Roxy's queenly nature is deformed by the requirement that she be servile and illiterate; and where it has a chance to assert itself, it does so in a parody of the values of the ruling class. Tom is thrust into that ruling class not only ill equipped by nature to play the part but hopelessly mistrained for it. His life becomes another parody of the role of mastership, itself a sarcasm.

It is inconceivable to me that Mark Twain's genius constructed this elegant parable to prove that Tom is cowardly because of the "nigger" in him. He *is* genetically inferior to Roxy; but that fact botches the equation between black blood and cowardice, Roxy being infinitely braver than her son (infinitely because here one is dividing by zero). There is no point in examining the mother-son relationship for its genetic meaning; that relationship is simply the ligature that binds the two together in their oppositenesses. It is their slave-master relationship that points up the meanings of the book. It is a fundamentally perverted relationship which is pushed to the extremity of perversion by the fact that a strong slave is held in subjugation by a weak and cowardly master.

For nearly twenty years—since 1874, when he wrote his "True Story" about former slave Aunt Rachel—Mark Twain had been thinking and writing about the causes and consequences of caste and slavery. In *Pudd'nhead Wilson* he saw the problem with such singular clarity that he chose to separate it from the question of race. I had not been aware that he had done so until a few years ago, when a black student in one of my classes protested a trend in our discussion of the novel. "This book," he said, "is not about black folks. It's about the mean way some white people treat other white people."

Mark Twain has been more emphatic than we have perhaps noticed in asserting that Roxy and Tom are white: "From Roxy's manner of speech, a stranger would have expected her to be black, but she was not. . . . Her complexion was very fair, . . . her eyes were brown and liquid, and she had a heavy suit of fine soft hair which was also brown. . . . To all intents and purposes Roxy was as white as anybody." To *all* intents and purposes. Roxy's son is blue-eyed and flaxen-haired and only "by a *fiction* of law and custom a negro" (8–9, emphasis mine).

*Pudd'nhead Wilson* is about the *fiction* of race and bloodlines—about the poisonous way it classifies people as inferior or superior, about its enormous social authority and about its persistence in the face of contrary evidence. To observe that two of the novel's white people are born slaves, and to note as well the community's total complacency in the matter, should raise in the reader's mind fundamental questions about race—where it begins and ends and what it means anyway.

It is the fiction of race that condemns Roxy's son to slavery and that, when the infants are switched, claims Percy Driscoll's son as hostage, no matter that his veins flow with the best blood of Old Virginia. It is the fiction of race that changes Tom's personality when he finds out he is the son of a slave, that makes his arm hang limp when friends greet him, that makes him give way on the sidewalk to white rowdies, that makes him "ashamed to sit at the white folks' table" (44–45).

It is, on the other hand, the fiction of noble bloodlines that makes the townspeople worship the highborn Cappello twins and gives the town's aristocrats an exalted opinion of themselves. When the Florentine counts Angelo and Luigi Cappello announce that they will arrive in Dawson's Landing, the town is agog. People will get a "glimpse of Real Nobility" (74). The twins will stay in Patsy Cooper's house, and her nineteen-year-old daughter Rowena anticipates something like a religious experience with their coming: "[T]his was to be the greatest day, the most romantic episode in the colorless history of that dull country town, she was to be familiarly near the source of its glory and feel the full flood of it pour over her and about her" (28). When Luigi the next day duels with Judge Driscoll, the citizens are transported by the privilege of witnessing an affair of honor between the finest blood of Florence and of Dawson's Landing. "It was a glory to their town to have such a thing happen there. In their eyes the principals had reached the summit of human honor" (74).

It is to the twins' credit, and to the further discredit of the townspeople, that they do not claim distinction because of their titles. They carefully explain to Patsy and Rowena that their noble parents had been banished from Italy and forced to flee to Germany, where they became "strangers, friendless, and in fact paupers" (27). The twins, ten years old at the time and soon orphaned, had to learn to take care of themselves. Their titles, so dazzling to the minds of the citizens of Dawson's Landing, were worthless in Europe.

Judge Driscoll's being descended from the First Families of Virginia "exalted [him] to supremacy" (58) in the eyes of the townspeople; it also requires his obedience to certain rules of conduct and his consent to certain articles of faith. One of the tenets of his faith is the efficacy of blood—men born in his line will be paragons of courage, never mind their training. It is, of course, an absurd notion, and Mark Twain takes pains to demonstrate its absurdity; but in this matter, Judge Driscoll is a true believer. When the Judge hears the first rumors of Tom's having shrunk from an affair of honor, he blithely mistakes them; after all, Tom is of "the true old blood." When rumor becomes statement, the Judge turns to his friend, Pembroke Howard, another son of the FFV, pleading, "Say it ain't true"; and Howard, in "deep organ-tones," responds: "You know it's a lie as well I do, old friend. He is of the best blood of the Old Dominion" (59). It is Tom himself who blandly assures the Judge that he has indeed gone to court over an insult rather than to the field of honor and who then listens incredulously to his foster parent's outburst: "You cur! you scum! you vermin! Do you mean to tell me that blood of my race has suffered a blow and crawled to a court of law about it? Answer me!" (60).

Later, when Tom has fled to David Wilson for consolation and advice, Wilson asks him if his uncle "didn't find any fault with you for anything but those two things—carrying the case into court and refusing to fight?" Wilson is perhaps thinking of Tom's sprees in St. Louis and his profligate habits in general, but Tom assures him that "he didn't find any other fault with me" (63). Apparently, the one cardinal sin that a gentlemen of the true old blood can commit is to sully his honor.

In this matter, Roxy exactly echoes the Judge. As she sees it, the only one of Tom's vices that discredits his heritage is his unwillingness to defend his honor. His burglarizing does not bother her. She "approved of his conduct, and offered to help" (43), and later she matter-of-factly receives his stolen goods. (Their opposite natures' reacting to opposite circumstances have made them alike in some ways.) She accepts without moralizing the fact that her son would shoot her in the back if he got the chance; and when he does in fact sell her down the river, she denounces him for a "hound" and a "Judas" but makes no mention of his ancestry. It is only Tom's violating the southern gentlemen's code of honor that makes him a "nigger."

What ever has 'come o' yo' Essex blood? Dat's what I can't understan'. En it ain't only jist Essex blood dat's in you, not by a long sight—'deed it ain't!

My great-great-great-gran'father en yo' great-great-great-great-gran'father was ole Cap'n John Smith, de highes' blood dat Ole Virginny ever turned out; en *his* great-great-gran'mother or somers along back dah, was Pocahontas de Injun queen, en her husbun' was a nigger king outen Africa—en yit here you is, a slinkin' outen a duel en disgracin' our whole line like a ornery low-down hound! Yes, it's de nigger in you! (70)

Roxy's aristocratic indignation and her pride in her garbled genealogy are a parody of the Judge's faith in bloodlines. Roxy is at a disadvantage when it comes to assessing the effects of heredity, for being illiterate she has had to depend on local folklore. She does not, for example, see the illogic of Tom's having "nigger" in him when his black ancestor was African royalty. But her illogic is no worse than the Judge's. Their two speeches berating Tom for not living up to his blood are parodies of each other and mock each other out of countenance.

Lawyer Wilson's triumph in the climax of the novel is a limited one, and it is all that his author intended to grant him. Wilson's twenty-three years of collecting and studying fingerprints have enabled him to identify the prints on the murder knife as Tom's and to discover that Tom and Chambers had been switched in their cradles. They are revelations of some consequence, but he does not point out a further one—the utterly absurd position that the town's faith in the fiction of race and bloodlines has placed it in. For twenty-three years, the town has treated a slave as an aristocrat and an aristocrat as a slave. No one seems to feel sheepish about it. In fact, now that the young aristocrat's "race" has been identified, he is, as a matter of course, sold down the river to help satisfy the late Percy Driscoll's creditors.

For all the bitter irony of the ending, there are hopeful signs. The Pudd'nhead Wilson maxim in the epigraph of this chapter and the Darwinian observation that likely inspired it posit a progressive evolution directed by man's intelligent control of both heredity and environment. The Italian twins' making their own way in life once their titles have turned to ashes is possibly a sign of Europe's democratization. Roxy's overpowering her overseer on the Deep South plantation—"All de hell-fire dat 'uz ever in my heart flame' up, en I snatch de stick outen his han' en laid him flat" (86)—is in the heroic tradition of resistance of the young Frederick Douglass. By the end of the book the town's aristocrats have all but died out. Only the Judge's bachelor friend and lawyer, Pembroke Howard, and the

Judge's widowed sister are left. Both are in their sixties. Lawyer Howard, it seems likely, will be superseded by Lawyer Wilson, still in his forties. Wilson's careful way with facts and his being unimpressed with the fictions of race and bloodlines should have their influence on Dawson's Landing.

# PART IV

# The Inner Universe

# CHAPTER 12

# Man: Machine or Dreamer?

*You keep me confused and perplexed all the time by your elusive termi-
nology. Sometimes you divide a man up into two or three separate
personalities, each with authorities, jurisdictions and responsibilities
of its own, and when he is in that condition I can't grasp him.*
   —The Young Man chiding the Old Man, in *What Is Man?*

MARK TWAIN'S AUTHORIAL SERENITY was sorely tested by
the shocks he suffered in the three years following the writing of
*Pudd'nhead Wilson*—his bankruptcy in 1894, his exhausting round-
the-world lecture tour begun a year later, and especially the death of
Susy on August 18, 1896. The circumstances around Susy's death
could hardly be crueler. Samuel Clemens with Livy and their
daughter Clara debarked at Southampton on August 1, with the last
leg of the yearlong lecture tour behind them. They rented a house
near London with the intention of sending for Clara's sisters Susy
and Jean, still living in Elmira and Hartford. Before the sisters could
make the move to rejoin the family, however, Susy fell ill; Livy and
Clara sailed for America to nurse Susy, and upon landing were told
that Susy had died. Sam, alone in the rented house, had already
received the same message by cable. He would not be able to attend
Susy's funeral. When Livy and Clara arrived in Elmira, where Susy
was to be buried, it was, according to Sam's doleful transoceanic
calculations, one year, one month, and one week from the time that,
on leaving Elmira, they had waved goodbye to a Susy who was
"brimming with life & the joy of it."[1]

   Clemens took Susy's death as a cosmic insult aimed not only at
Susy but at Livy and himself. It was the deliberate act of an unpity-
ing providence: "What a ghastly tragedy it was; how exactly and
precisely it was planned; and how remorselessly every detail of the
dispensation was carried out," he wrote bitterly to Howells. "You
want me to believe it is a judicious, a charitable God that runs this

---

1. Henry Nash Smith and William M. Gibson (eds.), *Mark Twain–Howells Letters*
(2 vols.; Cambridge, Mass., 1960), II, 663.

world," he ranted to Livy and Clara after they were reunited. "Why, I could run it better myself."[2]

The insult failed to flatten him, a fact he found puzzling. In two months he was at work on *Following the Equator;* and in seven more he finished it, setting his speed record for composing a travel book, or any other full-length work. While still in the process of writing it, he explained to Howells that he supposed he had become two personalities—the one destroyed with grief, the other blithely determined to write. He and Livy, he said, "are dead people who go through the motions of life. Indeed I am a mud image; & it puzzles me to know what it is in me that writes, & that has comedy-fantasies & finds pleasure in phrasing them. It is a law of our nature, of course, or it wouldn't happen; the thing in me forgets the presence of the mud image & goes its own way wholly unconscious of it & apparently of no kinship with it."[3]

During the last thirteen years of his life, he continued to write as voluminously as before; but after Susy's death, his field changed. The bulk of his later writing was private, and the three ideas just expressed—the uncaringness of God, the law of one's nature, and the dual personality—appear in it many times. Neither there nor in his writing for publication does he wrestle with his subject again. "Does the Race of Man Love a Lord?" (1902)—to which question his answer is yes—is the faint coda of that major theme. Although his writing for publication includes significant and enduring pieces, such as "The Man That Corrupted Hadleyburg," it does not deal specifically with the philosophical and critical problems that his openness to science had engendered in him. For his final response to those problems, we must turn to his private writing.

Loosely classifiable under the rubrics of fantasy and philosophy, that writing (amounting to something like a million words) was at first a kind of therapy for his wounded spirit and then, as William R. Macnaughton puts it, became motivated by "a strong, persistent drive to answer large questions and to confront mammoth problems before his death."[4] It stretches from the early lost-at-sea fantasies such as "The Enchanted Sea Wilderness" (1896) to "Letters from the Earth" (1909), with its cranky impieties, and includes *What Is Man?,* "Three Thousand Years Among the Microbes," and the *Mysterious*

2. *Ibid.,* 663; Clara Clemens, *My Father, Mark Twain* (New York, 1931), 179.

3. Smith and Gibson (eds.), *Mark Twain–Howells Letters,* II, 664.

4. William R. Macnaughton, *Mark Twain's Last Years as a Writer* (Columbia, Mo., 1979), 203.

*Stranger Manuscripts*. Although it affords us a long look at the scintillations of an unguarded and extraordinary imagination, its value as literature has not been settled. Sholom J. Kahn feels that "by writing 'not for publication' [Mark Twain] seems to have released energies that enabled him to reach new profound, rich levels of literary achievement"[5]; but Twain's writing not for publication can also be blamed for the slack stretches and the bewildering twists and turns and breakings off in this later work.

The most telling criticism of Twain's private writing, and particularly of the *Mysterious Stranger Manuscripts*, has been made by John S. Tuckey: In his older age, Mark Twain found himself so separated from his Hannibal experiences and otherwise so rootless that he turned to making "something out of nothing." In concocting his fantasies, he in effect denied "that art must have access to nature, must nourish itself on reality, must have matter as well as form."[6] As a storyteller he exercised a genius divorced from everyday life.

As a thinker he unbraided and separated certain contradictory ideas that he had been struggling to integrate. He laid each out in its singular wholeness, causing the tensions among them to evaporate. For example, in "The Secret History of Eddypus," there are these two paragraphs following his synoptic history of the dying out of the geocentric point of view, when "the proud globe was shrunk to a potato lost in limitless vacancy, the sun was a colossus and millions of miles removed, the stars, now worlds of measureless size, were motes on the verge of shoreless space":

That is what had happened. The lid had been taken off the universe, so to speak, there was a vastness, emptiness, vacancy all around and everywhere, the snug cosiness was gone, the world was a homeless little vagrant, a bewildered little orphan left out in the cold, a long way from any place and nowhere to go.

A change? A surprise? It is next to unimaginable. What should you say would happen if prisoners born and reared in the stench and gloom of a dungeon suddenly found their den shaken down by an earthquake some day, and themselves spilt out into a far-stretching paradise of brilliant flowers, and limpid streams, and summer-clad forests, set in a frame of mountains steeped in a dreamy haze,—a paradise which is a wonder and a miracle to their eager and ignorant eyes, a paradise whose spiced airs bring refreshment and delight to their astounded nostrils, and whose prodigal

5. Sholom J. Kahn, *Mark Twain's Mysterious Stranger* (Columbia, Mo., 1978), 7.

6. John S. Tuckey, *Mark Twain and Little Satan* (West Lafayette, Ind., 1963), 78–81.

sunlight pours balm and healing upon their sick souls, so long shut up in a smother of darkness?[7]

The two paragraphs are absolutely incompatible; yet there they are, shoulder to shoulder—the one responding to the discoveries of astronomy by bewailing man's cosmic loneliness, the other responding to those same discoveries by celebrating man's escape from the dungeon of ignorance into the paradise of enlightenment.

The two responses are no doubt authentic as reflections of discrete aspects of Samuel Clemens' intellectual experience, but they are also rudimentary. There is no attempt to choose between them, to integrate them, or to bring to bear on them the later considerations of science.

Mark Twain wrote those paragraphs early in 1901 and shortly thereafter laid the manuscript aside. When he returned to "Eddypus," about a year later, it was for the purpose of constructing a unified vision of science. In preparation for that task, "he wrote to F. A. Duneka of Harper & Brothers asking for a copy of Andrew D. White's *A History of the Warfare of Science with Theology in Christendom* and also for 'any up-to-date books' he might have 'on the *half-dozen great sciences*, by experts' "(24–25).

His reading of White's book, which champions science and surveys its accomplishments, had its effect. Twain's own vision of science was put into some order. He quit burlesquing science. In previous chapters, Sir Izaac Walton is given as the discoverer of gravity, Martin Luther as "the Father of Geology," and so on; now his summary history of science in "Eddypus" (with one playful exception) is serious and sophisticated, as in this capacious sentence touching on geology, paleontology, and evolution:

It was found that the earth's crust consisted of distinct layers, one on top of another; that in the bottom layers were no fossils; that in the next layers above, were the fossils of primitive and poorly contrived and inconsequential animals and plants; that in the succeeding layers, these developed improvements; and so on, up and up, each layer improving the breeds, and now and then dropping one out of the scheme and leaving it extinct, like the dodo and the moa, the pterodactyl and the mastodon; until finally the

7. John S. Tuckey (ed.), *Mark Twain's Fables of Man* (Berkeley, 1972), 360. Further references to *Mark Twain's Fables of Man* are indicated by parenthetical page numbers in the text.

surface is reached and we have an immense and highly organized fauna and flora; and then, belated Man appears. (377)

Through Twain's masterly language, we have been deftly guided across a vast stretch of prehistory; but with the appearance of "belated Man," we are launched on an amazing verbal roller-coaster ride. Three times we are elevated by ecstatic rhetoric to where we can view the marvelous panorama of man's progress under universal law, and three times we are swooped back to earth by the curt reminder that evolution is automatic, mindless, and meaningless. The first climax comes at the end of this breathtakingly long sentence:

All this happened just in time to powerfully reinforce Herbert Spencer, who was introducing his wonderful all-clarifying law of Evolution, a law which he claimed was in force throughout the universe, and proved that the never-resting operation of its authority was exhibited in the history of the plants, the animals, the mountains, the seas, the constellations, the rise and development of systems of morals, religions, government, policies, principles, civilizations: the all-supreme and resistless law which decrees slow, sure, implacable, persistent, unresting change, change, change, in all things, mental, moral, physical, out of one form into another, out of one quality and condition into another, shade by shade, step by step, never halting, never tiring, all the universe ranked and battalioned in the march, and the march eternal! (378)

How dynamic and awesome is the march of universal evolution! But then, in a series of terse, matter-of-fact sentences, Mark Twain reminded himself of what he had momentarily forgotten—that there is no divine direction behind that evolution and hence no meaning in it. "Evolution is a blind giant who rolls a snowball down a hill. The ball is made of flakes—*circumstances*. They contribute to the mass without knowing it. They adhere without intention, and without foreseeing what is to result." In their folly, people marvel at evolutionary progress "and wonder how the contriving of it came to be originally thought out and planned. Whereas there was *no such planning*" (378).

The second peak comes at the end of a listing of the accomplishments of a dozen scientists, from Newton through Darwin, and closing again with Spencer's "climaxing mighty law of Evolution, binding all the universe's inertnesses and vitalities together under its sole sway and command—and the History of Things and the

Meanings of them stood revealed!" That last triumphant clause, as Twain's manuscript shows, survived a welter of indecisions and revisions,[8] only to be diminished by the reflection that it is simply *"circumstance"* that brings about the "unforeseen condition of things" (379).

The third climax is the most jubilant. Two hundred years of science had set men free:

> The vast discoveries which have been listed above created an intellectual upheaval in the world such as had never been experienced in it before from the beginning of time, nor indeed anything even remotely resembling it. The effects resulting were wholly new. Men's minds were free, now; the chains of thought lay broken; for the first time in the history of the race, men were free to think their own thoughts instead of other people's, and utter their conclusions without peril to body or estate. This marked an epoch and a revolution: a revolution which was the first of its kind, a revolution which emancipated the mind and the soul. (380)

The jubilation is soon canceled by the inevitable rebuttal that this apparent progress is simply the result of "forces inherent in massed circumstances." It may, indeed, have been the single word *automatic* that brought his soaring language down. First he wrote "forces inherent," then "automatic forces inherent"; next he canceled "automatic" and inserted "automatically," so that the final phrasing reads, "the natural law of Evolution, automatically directed and executed by the forces inherent in massed circumstances."[9]

Mark Twain's surges and subsidences are his troubled rehearsals of a historically developing syllogism. The major premise of that syllogism was established by deism. It was, as Thomas Paine put it, that the creation is obedient to "the system of laws established by the Creator that governs and regulates the whole." (Paine listed "the geometry of the universe," "the properties of inanimate matter," and "the systems of animal and vegetable life" as aspects of the creation subject to universal law—but not man. Men, he said, were "free agents," separated from the other creatures by the gift of reason.)[10]

8. See *ibid.*, 692, for Mark Twain's cancellations and interlineations.

9. *Ibid.*, 693.

10. Harry Hayden Clark (ed.), *Thomas Paine: Representative Selections* (New York, 1944), 332, 334, 329.

Darwinism supplied the minor premise, that (in Thomas Huxley's words) "man, physical, intellectual, and moral, is as much a part of nature, as purely a product of the cosmic process, as the humblest weed."[11]

Mark Twain and other thinkers of his time supplied the conclusion: Historically, socially, and individually, men are governed by the same system of laws as governs the universe.

In rehearsing the syllogism, Mark Twain thrice celebrated the Enlightenment's vision (corroborated, as he thought, by Spencer's "mighty law of Evolution") of the world of men set free by the dependability of universal law and thrice interrupted that celebration with the unmediated consideration (sponsored by the fact that the purview of science now included the study of social and individual behavior) that the world of men was so regulated by universal law as to make what they did automatic and meaningless.

The most amazing instance of Mark Twain's separating and sealing off conflicting ideas from each other is his developing, at the same time and during a period stretching to nearly a decade, both his *What Is Man?* (1898–1906) and his *Mysterious Stranger Manuscripts* (1897–1905).[12] The *Manuscripts* are as fantastic as *What Is Man?* is unrelentingly rational and logical. *What Is Man?* aims to prove that man is a machine, the *Manuscripts* that he is spirit.[13] The two works point exactly away from each other. If we try to contemplate them in duo, we end up not with a psychodrama of ideas in conflict but with a Beckettian play in which two self-absorbed, loquacious, and quite different personalities speak without listening.

The answer to the titular question, *What Is Man?*, is that he is "a machine, made up of many mechanisms; the moral and mental ones acting automatically in accordance with the impulses of an interior

11. Thomas Huxley, *Evolution and Ethics and Other Essays* (New York, 1903), 11. For Clemens' familiarity with these essays, see H. H. Waggoner, "Science in the Thought of Mark Twain," *American Literature*, VIII (1937), 357–70.

12. A single chapter, 33, of "No. 44, The Mysterious Stranger," was written in 1908.

13. John S. Tuckey discussed this dichotomy in "Mark Twain's Later Dialogue: The 'Me' and the Machine," *American Literature*, XLI (1970), 532–42. Stan Poole has discussed a similar kind of "divided sensibility" in Mark Twain's later writings, between his admission of a harsh form of social Darwinism and his "sense of compassion" ("In Search of the Missing Link: Mark Twain and Darwinism," *Studies in American Fiction*, XIII [1985], 201–15).

Master who is built out of born-temperament and an accumulation of multitudinous outside influences and trainings."[14] His one aim is self-gratification. The product of heredity and environment, and with no will of his own, he deserves neither praise nor blame for his acts. He is intellectually akin to the other animals. He differs from them in having a moral sense, a possession that degrades him, because it destroys innocence.

Scholars have not had much to say about *What Is Man?*. Besides overlooking the work, they have, as Paul Baender has shown, speculated on Mark Twain's personal reasons for writing it or pointed out that his deterministic ideas are not new (18–20). That humanist scholars have refused to take its ideas seriously is understandable. Mark Twain's philosophy here is nothing to live by. It is cursed with a built-in paradox: The more it is proved to be true, the less meaning it has.

Nevertheless, I would like to make four points that may serve to show that, in spite of the loneliness Mark Twain must have suffered in composing *What Is Man?* and in spite of its surface queerness, deriving from his being altogether too clear in explaining uncomfortable ideas, it deserves notice as a document in the history of behavioral thought.

My first point is simply that the problem of man's free will or lack thereof, a problem Twain worked at doggedly, is a venerable philosophical enigma that remains unsolved. My second point is that the idea of man as a machine is not altogether queer. At the folk level, people had been making analogies, conscious and unconscious, between humans and the machines that surrounded them for a century and more. Such analogies are even more deeply a part of our culture in the late twentieth century—with its chess-playing computers, automatic pilots, and assembly-line robots, and when we have largely adopted computer lingo to describe our mental functions.

My third point is that, without being directly familiar with most of the speculations about and experiments with human behavior during the preceding two and a half centuries, Mark Twain presents the salient ideas of the tradition in chronological order. The way the ontogeny of *What Is Man?* recapitulates the phylogeny of behaviorism is startling: Descartes's (1596–1650) contention that man's

---

14. Samuel Clemens [Mark Twain], *What Is Man? and Other Philosophical Writings*, ed. Paul Baender (Berkeley, 1973), 205, Vol. XIX of the Works of Mark Twain. Further references to *What Is Man?* are indicated by parenthetical page numbers in the text.

body was a machine is said to have been inspired by his witnessing actuated statues in the royal gardens; Mark Twain begins *What Is Man?* with analogies between man and mechanical processes he was familiar with—those in the mines, the metal refineries, and the machine shops. John Locke's (1632–1704) dictum that ideas are derived only from experience is exactly the Old Man's pronouncement in most of the first chapter. Julien Offray de La Mettrie (1709–1751) not only went beyond Descartes's hypothesis that the body was a mechanism to insist that the soul was material as well but added the doctrine that all human motivation was selfish; the second chapter of *What Is Man?* is devoted to the idea that self-gratification is man's only impulse. Although studies by James Mill (1773–1836) and John Stuart Mill (1806–1873) of the association of ideas were more sophisticated than Twain's meditations on the subject, Twain does give the kernel of their conclusions in "Men perceive, and their brain-machines automatically combine the things perceived" (182). In the Old Man's saying that thought is "the mechanical and automatic putting together of impressions received from outside, and drawing an inference from them" (190), he echoes Hermann von Helmholtz's (1821–1894) doctrine of unconscious inference. Herbert Spencer's (1820–1903) theory that instinct in animals is an inherited complex of activity that originates in viable associations often repeated is aptly paraphrased in Twain's definition of *instinct* as "an inherited habit which was originally thought—that is to say, observation of an exterior fact, and a valuable inference drawn from that observation and confirmed by experience" (190). And in a sense, Twain congratulates George Romanes (1848–1894) for his achievement in pioneering comparative psychology in his *Animal Intelligence* by devoting eleven pages (189–99) to the similarity of animal and human intellects.[15]

My fourth point is that the focus of *What Is Man?*—its determinism, its emphasis on environment and heredity, its clinical analysis of human behavior, and its equation of men with animals—is similar to that in literary naturalism, a new movement that Mark Twain apparently did not identify. For example, the theme of Stephen Crane's *The Red Badge of Courage* (1895), about the soldier boy who at first runs from battle and later returns to fight, partly because he fears the "shafts of derision" from his comrades and partly to live up

15. For this survey of behaviorism, I have drawn upon Edwin Boring, *A History of Experimental Psychology* (New York, 1950), and Erwin A. Esper, *A History of Psychology* (Philadelphia, 1964).

to his lie about the wound he received from a fellow deserter, is succinctly expressed in Mark Twain's "A brave man does not *create* his bravery. He is entitled to no personal credit for possessing it" (131). Something of Crane's mechanics of courage is repeated, too, in this longer passage from *What Is Man?*: "At the command—and trembling—he marched out into the field—with other soldiers and in the daytime, not alone and in the dark. He had the *influence of example*, he drew courage from his comrades' courage; he was afraid, and wanted to run, but he did not dare; he was *afraid* to run, with all those soldiers looking on. He was progressing, you see— the moral fear of shame had risen superior to the physical fear of harm" (132–33). For another example, Drouet, in Theodore Dreiser's *Sister Carrie* (1900), is described as having "his future fixed for him beyond peradventure. He could not help what he was going to do. He could not see clearly enough to wish to do differently. He was drawn by his innate desire to act the old pursuing part."[16] Drouet's impulse could be said to originate from what Mark Twain described as "The Master Passion"—"a *colorless* force seated in the man's moral constitution. Let us call it an instinct—a blind, unreasoning instinct, which cannot and does not distinguish between good morals and bad ones, and cares nothing for results to the man provided its own contentment be secured; and it will *always* secure that" (206).

Without connecting with the movement of naturalism, Mark Twain expressed naturalistic ideas and emphases. Without studying two centuries of behavioristic science, he apprehended its ideas in historical order. He did all that in spite of his friends' and family's disapproval of his notions. In the matter of *What Is Man?* he was a stubborn literary circle of one, depending on a few seminal books read years before, on private thoughts, and on an exquisite sensitiveness to ideas in the air.

The *Mysterious Stranger Manuscripts* consists of three texts: "The Chronicle of Young Satan," "Schoolhouse Hill," and "No. 44, The Mysterious Stranger." Each is a fantastic narrative about a human community visited by a stranger with supernatural powers. The first two narratives are unfinished; the third has a concluding chapter.

---

16. Theodore Dreiser, *Sister Carrie* (New York, 1957), 72.

In one detail the *Manuscripts* begin at the same philosophical level as *What Is Man?* before ranging to the opposite pole. "The Chronicle of Young Satan" posits a system of determinism that complements that in *What Is Man?*. In *What Is Man?* people's impulses and thoughts are given as automatic and their characters as inevitably formed by temperament and training. In the "Chronicle" their entire careers are determined by the inevitable chain of cause and effect. To the question, "Does God order [a person's] career?" Satan replies: "Foreordain it? No. The man's circumstances and environment order it. His first act determines the second and all that follow after."[17]

This "row of bricks" determinism probably has remote roots in Taine but more recent ones in Samuel Clemens' contemplation of the careers of his fellow Hannibalites. In July and August, 1897, after completing *Following the Equator*, and when his life was still in pieces, he wrote "Villagers of 1840–3," containing capsule biographies of more than a hundred people he knew as a boy.[18] Upon finishing "Villagers," he did his first writing on "The Chronicle of Young Satan" and began the long process of searching for meaning in his life and life in general. "Villagers" seems to have been Mark Twain's attempt to put his own calamities into perspective by making his life one of a community of lives.

What he remembered about his fellow townspeople was not likely to convince him that there had been a providential pattern to their careers. Some lived prosperous and respected lives. Some amounted to little. Some turned to vice and crime. Many endured tragic twists of fate. Charley Meredith "went to California and thence to hell." Mary Moss survived a sleighing accident "with a terrible limp, and forever after stayed in the house." Tom Nash "[w]ent deaf and dumb from breaking through ice." Old Kercheval's apprentice "saved Simon Carpenter's life—aged 9—from drowning, and was cursed for it by Simon for 50 years."[19] Such evidences,

---

17. William M. Gibson (ed.), *Mark Twain's Mysterious Stranger Manuscripts* (Berkeley, 1969), 115.

18. Walter Blair counted 168 villagers mentioned or referred to; and through a prodigy of research, he established "A Biographical Directory" for 120 of them. Blair found that "with remarkably few exceptions," Mark Twain's statements about the villagers "prove to be entirely correct" (Walter Blair [ed.], *Mark Twain's Hannibal, Huck and Tom* [Berkeley, 1969], 24).

19. *Ibid.*, 28, 29, 31, 36.

some of which reappear slightly changed in "The Chronicle of Young Satan," might well lead a skeptical mind to the conclusion that what orders a person's career is nothing more benevolent or purposeful than "circumstances and environment."

Nevertheless, an early impulse of Twain's seems to have been to worship God in spite of the calamities heaped on the human race. The second chapter of "The Chronicle of Young Satan" presents us with a religious statement of great purity and power. Satan creates for Theodor, Nikolaus, and Seppi a medieval community of tiny human figures. He lets the boys try their hands at creating. They make men and horses out of clay, but so badly that when Satan touches them and they come alive, "it was just ridiculous the way they acted, on account of their legs not being of uniform lengths. . . . It made us all laugh, though it was a shameful thing to see." With the boys' consent, Satan causes the tiny castle-town to be raked by storm and wrecked by earthquake so that of "all that innocent life, not one of the five hundred poor creatures" escapes. The boys are heartbroken; but to their protestations, Satan simply replies, "Oh, it is no matter, we can make more."

It was of no use to try to move him; evidently he was wholly without feeling, and could not understand. He was full of bubbling spirits, and as gay as if this were a wedding instead of a fiendish massacre. And he was bent on making us feel as he did, and of course his magic accomplished his desire. It was no trouble to him, he did whatever he pleased with us. In a little while we were dancing on that grave, and he was playing to us on a strange sweet instrument which he took out of his pocket; and the music—there is no music like that, unless perhaps in heaven, and that was where he brought it from, he said. It made one mad, for pleasure; and we could not take our eyes from him, and the looks that went out of our eyes came from our hearts, and their dumb speech was worship. He brought the dance from heaven, too, and the bliss of paradise was in it.[20]

The theology implied here is a complete one, explaining God's and man's relationships to each other and to the world; and although its elements are presented in a startling way, the elements themselves are traditional. Human life is given as brief, imperfect, and subject to undeserved calamities; Job and Ecclesiastes say as much. In agreeing, Mark Twain waived his faith in progress and reform. God is the Creator, the abundant fountain of life. He is also spirit; and although His feeling for mankind is not evidenced in a

20. Gibson (ed.), *Mark Twain's Mysterious Stranger Manuscripts*, 52.

worldly system of justice, He is the source of spiritual joy for those in tune to receive it. This last idea is, of course, an ancient one; and it was being expressed again and again in Mark Twain's time in the spirituals and gospel songs he loved to sing.[21] It is not unlikely that the aging Clemens was visited with moments of spiritual exaltation. At the very least, he respected those moments in others. There is nothing ironic in his narration of Theodor's rapture, perhaps because he was still under the spell of his *Joan of Arc* (1896), where he treated Joan's transfiguration when she was visited by her angel with utmost reverence. The sum of the theology is that in man's brief time on earth, where he walks on the graves of those who have gone before him, his duty is to praise life and love God.

But that noble theology soon crumbles. As the tale continues, man changes from a pitiable victim to a rather mean affair, cruel to the defenseless and sheeplike in following wrongheaded leaders. Satan's angelic presence, awesome and charismatic at first, is frittered away. Claiming to be quite indifferent to humans, Satan nevertheless becomes so meddlesome in the affairs of the villagers that even his author laments the mess he makes of people's lives with his "enthusiastic diligence and morbid passion for business" (111). He becomes capable of petty emotions and on two occasions uses his show-off magic to inflict spectacular and vindictive punishments on minor villains. The moments of rapture the boys feel in his presence dwindle away. By the end of "The Chronicle of Young Satan," Satan has fairly lost his connection with heaven. Mark Twain was turning from the subject of God's relationship to man to that of the godlike power of the creative artist.

He was also turning away from his determinism. A part of Mark Twain loathed his own "Gospel,"[22] as he called *What Is Man?*. It rebelled against being confined by circumstance and corporeality. In its grand design, the *Mysterious Stranger Manuscripts* shows its author's moving from the worship of a transcendent spirit to becoming

21. Alan Gribben's *Mark Twain's Library: A Reconstruction* (2 vols.; Boston, 1980) lists dozens of such songs that Clemens referred to and of hymnals and other song collections he owned. Theodor's expressions of love for Satan—for example, "so noble and beautiful and gracious" (49), "joy of being with him" (50), "the touch of his hand" (50), "no voice like that before" (93)—could have been inspired by current devotional hymnody.

22. Albert Bigelow Paine (ed.), *Mark Twain's Letters* (2 vols.; New York, 1917), II, 720.

one. He discovers on the way that his newfound magic—his power to transcend—is akin to the magic of authorship.

The supernatural figures in all three texts of the *Manuscripts* are ideal artists. Their knowledge and experience, their powers of imagination and expression, their mastery over time and space are, in their impossible perfection, such as a writer might crave. With powers like that, a writer would clearly be exempt from the tyranny of circumstance. In the last of the texts, those powers are, in a measure, given to the mortal narrator. Mark Twain's musings in "No. 44, The Mysterious Stranger" are of the miraculous element in his own life, of the genius to which he had been an amanuensis and that the law of circumstances could not account for. "My life," he wrote in 1907, "is hardly real: it must surely be a dream, a fairy tale."[23]

In his "Mysterious Stranger" musings he paid tribute to four people who helped him realize his genius. One is Rachel Cord, who appears as Katrina, again in the role of surrogate mother. The cook in Heinrich Stein's household, Katrina is "erect, straight, six feet high, and with the port and stride of a soldier" (233). It is she who protects No. 44 from the hostility of Stein's printshop crew. "Her hungry old heart was fed, she was a mother at last, with a child to love—a child who returned her love in full measure, and to whom she was the salt of the earth" (244). Another is Jervis Langdon, who as Stein says to No. 44: "You haven't [a friend] . . . except Katrina. It is not fair. I am going to be your friend myself" (251). Some thirty years before, Jervis Langdon had said to his daughter's suitor, who could find no one to vouch for his character: "I'll be your friend, myself. Take the girl."[24]

Marget Regen, Stein's niece, is the Livy whom Sam Clemens courted: "She was lithe and graceful and trim-built as a fish, and she was a blue-eyed blonde, and soft and sweet and innocent and shrinking and winning and gentle and beautiful" (232). Her presence is vividly and erotically felt in those chapters written during Livy's final illness, in the spring of 1904. Forbidden by Livy's doctor to see her except briefly and infrequently, Clemens gave August Feldner, the printshop apprentice who is in love with Marget, the

23. From a letter to William J. Bryan, quoted in William White, "Mark Twain to the President of Indiana University," *American Literature*, XXXII (1960), 32.

24. Dixon Wecter (ed.), *The Love Letters of Mark Twain* (New York, 1949), 62.

power to become invisible and walk through walls. Except for this poignant fantasy, the symbolism in the chapters is murky and troubled. Chapter 34, written while Livy was dying, contains the notorious solipsistic declaration: *"Nothing exists save empty space—and you! . . .* [and] you are but a *thought"* (404). The declaration may signify no more than the ultimate loneliness Samuel Clemens felt in anticipating his wife's death.

William Dean Howells' presence in the fantasy is, it seems to me, the most potent, and yet the least particular. At one moment, he is the same Heinrich Stein that represented Jervis Langdon. He makes No. 44 an apprentice in the printer's art, "the noblest and the most puissant of all the arts," to the indignation of the other printers that this "pauper and tramp without name or family" should be admitted "to the gate leading to the proud privileges and distinctions and immunities of their grand order" (251–52). "I owe as much to your training," Clemens had written Howells in 1878, "as the rude country job printer owes to the city boss who takes him in hand & teaches him the right way to handle his art."[25]

Later, Howells is No. 44 himself, bringing August Feldner into touch with his dream-self. Early in 1904, just before returning to the writing of "No. 44," Mark Twain wrote exultantly to Howells that he had found a new way of freeing his mind. If you dictate your thought, "you will be astonished (& charmed) to see how like *talk* it is, & how real it sounds, & how well & compactly & sequentially it constructs itself." Howells replied: "You do stir me mightily with the hope of dictating, and I will try it when I get the chance. But there is the temperamental difference. You are dramatic and unconscious; you count the thing more than yourself; I am cursed with consciousness to the core, and can't say myself out."[26] *You are dramatic and unconscious!* Howells' words may have forced a revelation. Only after Howells wrote them does No. 44 effect a separation between August's waking-self and his dream-self and, later still, a fruitful reunion. The dream-self's explanation of his and other dream-selves' activities is a hymn to the freedom of the imagination:

We have no character, no *one* character, we have *all* characters; we are honest in one dream, dishonest in the next. We wear no chains, we cannot abide them; we have no home, no prison, the universe is our province; we do not

---

25. Smith and Gibson (eds.), *Mark Twain–Howells Letters,* I, 226.
26. *Ibid.,* 778, 780.

know time, we do not know space—we live, and love, and labor, and enjoy, fifty years in an hour, while you are sleeping, snoring, repairing your crazy tissues; we circumnavigate your little globe while you wink; we are not tied within horizons, like a dog with cattle to mind, an emperor with human sheep to watch—we visit hell, we roam in heaven, our playgrounds are the constellations and the Milky Way. (370)

This peroration is a high point in an amazing fantasy. As a definition of the *creative* imagination it fails because it mentions neither the materials nor the *work* of creating; indeed, the fantasy itself would have been better if more of that work had gone into it. It does, however, prompt us to contemplate a curious paradox: If Mark Twain's calling *What Is Man?* his "Bible" means that its determinism was the religion of his old age, then August's dream-self, conceived and nurtured in that same old-age mind, is a flaming heretic.[27]

In his responsiveness to warring world views, Mark Twain could be divided but not defeated. He could see that under science the earth had become a homeless wanderer in empty space and a paradise of intellectual freedom; that men were machines in a mechanical universe, willing participants in a mighty progress, and even transcendent spirits. If among these views he declined to arbitrate, the fact of his responsiveness—and of his resilience—must not be slighted. Nurtured in an ancient creed, surprised in youth by a century-old philosophy, he spent his maturity adventuring, unarmored with academic devices, among the parlous ideas of modern science. Though often dismayed, he was never beyond regaining his zest in the adventuring.

"I believe in the new planet," he wrote in 1909, in response to Professor William Henry Pickering's claim that perturbations in Neptune's orbit were caused by an undiscovered planet. Mark Twain explained that he had himself perturbated during the two months before Neptune was discovered in 1846; now he was perturbating again, and "I don't perturbate for nothing." "I hope," he continued, that the planet "is going to be named after me; I should just love it if I can't have a constellation."[28]

When the trans-Neptunian planet was finally located in 1930, several names, not, unfortunately, including Mark Twain, were offered; and the one settled on was Pluto. Mark Twain was, however, eventually to be given a celestial memorial; and if it is not so grand as

27. *Ibid.*, 689.
28. Samuel Clemens [Mark Twain], "The New Planet," in *Europe and Elsewhere*, ed. Albert Bigelow Paine (New York, 1923), 355–57.

a planet, it attests to his having joined the constellation of world authors. Discovered in 1976, asteroid 2362 was named by its discoverer, Russian astronomer N. S. Chernykh, "for Mark Twain, pen name of Samuel Langhorne Clemens (1835–1910), world-famous American writer."[29]

29. *Minor Planet Circular 9214*, Smithsonian Astrophysical Observatory, November 8, 1984. I am indebted to Eleanor F. Helin of the Jet Propulsion Laboratory for information on asteroid Mark Twain.

# Index